Strategic Management

Regularly considered to be the capstone element on many a business or management degree course, strategy has developed into a wide-ranging and sometimes overwhelming field of study. However, in recent years the theory of strategy has come under increasing scrutiny for its perceived failures and detachment from real world practice.

With an engaging and conversational tone, this concise new textbook offers an accessible and timely review of the theory and practice of strategic management, explored from a more critical perspective. In a refreshing change from much of the literature, Richard Godfrey takes a wider view of strategy, incorporating insights from the worlds of sociology, psychology and history to highlight the complexity and plurality at the heart of the discipline. The book also incorporates a number of extensive case studies on contemporary business strategy from the likes of Apple, Nike, Zara and IKEA.

Written for both an undergraduate and a postgraduate audience, the book challenges a number of underlying assumptions and beliefs about strategy and seeks to add clarity and context to the field.

Richard Godfrey is Lecturer in Strategy at the University of Leicester, UK.

Strategic Management
A critical introduction

Richard Godfrey

LONDON AND NEW YORK

First published 2016
by Routledge
2 Park Square, Milton Park, Abingdon, Oxon OX14 4RN

and by Routledge
711 Third Avenue, New York, NY 10017

Routledge is an imprint of the Taylor & Francis Group, an informa business

© 2016 Richard Godfrey

The right of Richard Godfrey to be identified as author of this work has been asserted by him in accordance with sections 77 and 78 of the Copyright, Designs and Patents Act 1988.

All rights reserved. No part of this book may be reprinted or reproduced or utilised in any form or by any electronic, mechanical, or other means, now known or hereafter invented, including photocopying and recording, or in any information storage or retrieval system, without permission in writing from the publishers.

Trademark notice: Product or corporate names may be trademarks or registered trademarks, and are used only for identification and explanation without intent to infringe.

British Library Cataloguing in Publication Data
A catalogue record for this book is available from the British Library

Library of Congress Cataloging in Publication Data
Godfrey, Richard David.
Strategic management: a critical introduction / Richard Godfrey.
  pages cm
  Includes bibliographical references and index.
   1. Strategic planning. 2. Management. I. Title.
  HD30.28.G634 2016
  658.4'012--dc23
              2015018924

ISBN: 978-0-415-73875-0 (hbk)
ISBN: 978-0-415-73876-7 (pbk)
ISBN: 978-1-315-81713-2 (ebk)

Typeset in Bembo
by Taylor & Francis Books

Contents

List of illustrations	vi
1 What is strategy?	1
2 Strategy: a brief history	12
3 Strategy by design and an emergent critique (part 1)	27
4 Strategy by design and an emergent critique (part 2)	37
5 Strategy and the multi-business firm	53
6 Creating strategy from the outside-in	72
7 Creating strategy from the inside-out	100
8 Creating strategy through value innovation	120
Concluding discussion	144
Case 1: IKEA: daring to be different	147
Case 2: fast fashion at Zara	153
Case 3: innovation and change at Nike	157
Case 4: Apple Inc. in 2014	162
References	171
Index	182

List of illustrations

Figures

5.1 The experience curve	62
5.2 The growth share matrix	65
5.3 The growth share matrix	67
6.1 The five forces	76
6.2 The generic strategies	83
6.3 The value chain	88
8.1 The strategy canvas	131
8.2 The Four Actions framework	132
8.3 The strategy canvas	133
8.4 The disruptive innovation model	135

Tables

4.1 Building and dwelling worldviews	42
7.1 Xerox's path to achieving strategic intent	115
8.1 Competing logics on value creation	121
8.2 Assumption of experience-based value	142

1 What is strategy?

> Of the topic areas taught in business schools on a global scale, few can be seen as more significant than strategy in its various forms. Equally, of the various discourses and practices that are involved in managing a large organization whether a private or public corporation, none is treated with as much importance and secrecy as strategy.
>
> (Knights and Mueller 2004: 55)

Set against the importance of strategy as outlined in the quote above, we begin our study of the fascinating subject of strategy with something of a problematic: no one really knows what strategy actually is! As we will quickly discover, there is no single agreed-upon definition of the term either in the business field or in any wider context in which the term is used. For many, strategy simply means a plan, possibly with the instigation of a predetermined objective or goal. For others the word is synonymous with the military and the conduct of war and military campaigns. A cursory glance at the newspaper, our favourite blog site or any current affairs television programme and we find the word 'strategy' used with increasing frequency: businesses have strategies of growth and expansion, hospitals have strategies for improving healthcare, universities have strategies for recruiting more students, and individuals have strategies for managing their finances, improving their fitness or completing their work on time. As Clegg *et al.* (2010) observe, we increasingly live in a world constructed and shaped by strategies and yet we seldom know much about how these strategies come into creation, who has constructed them and what processes have been employed in their development. The outcome of strategy-making often simply appears to us in the form of a shiny company brochure, government policy document or dazzling PowerPoint presentation. However, such texts are simply the tip of the iceberg. What we need to do, as students of strategy, is delve beneath the surface into the murky waters where the jagged, impenetrable yet curiously beautiful iceberg reveals its full majesty. By exploring the processes and practices that constitute the doing of strategy we can better understand the strategies of companies and organizations and hopefully develop better strategies for ourselves.

In this chapter we begin by introducing a number of different ways of thinking about the question 'what is strategy?' We discuss the distinction between strategy as a management practice and strategy as a business subject. We look at different ways of framing strategy as an academic discipline and discuss some different definitions of (business) strategy. We conclude by outlining the structure of the book and a case is made for the value of a critical approach to studying strategy.

Strategy: the oldest and newest of management disciplines?

So where do we begin in seeking to tackle the question, 'what is strategy?' One useful starting point could be to draw from Alvesson and Willmott's (1996) keen observation that strategy is both one of the oldest management disciplines and also one of the newest. It is old in the sense that 'managers' and 'organizers' have always had to deal with issues that we would today define as 'strategic'. From the running of a humble market stall in ancient Rome to the building of the pyramids, the Great Wall of China and Mayan temples, from the management of the fourteenth-century Italian city states to the birth of the industrial revolution, issues such as how to allocate scarce resources, concerns about competition and other external forces, and the need to identify some sort of *advantage* have always been of key concern. And yet the academic discipline of (business) strategy really only emerged in the 1950s and 1960s (see Chapter 2 for a detailed history of the strategy field). As such, we can suggest that the *practice* of strategy has always been of importance even if, for much of its history, there was no common language for describing strategic phenomena. In this regard strategy shares a similar history to its sister discipline of marketing, where the practices of advertising, product placement, premium pricing and market segmentation have existed since the earliest forms of market exchange and yet only developed into a coherent business discipline in the 1950 and 1960s.

Is strategy a science, an art or a humanity?

We might also seek to locate strategy within a wider paradigm of knowledge. As a business discipline, it might reasonably be suggested that strategy is best conceived of as a science. In its most familiar form, what we might call the *orthodox version of strategy*, it bears all the hallmarks of management science, drawing as it does on positivist methodologies and quantitative methods of enquiry. To this day, the mainstream literature, as indexed in the best-selling textbooks and most cited journal articles, still reflects this position, with many of the most famous strategy models and tools, from Porter's five forces, to SWOT, to the Boston Box, all reflecting a set of underlying assumptions that speak to a science of strategy. So, with some confidence we might say that strategy is, or has been, conceived of as a science.

However, we can also think of strategy as an art. Here we borrow from the military antecedents of business strategy and conceive of the charismatic (entrepreneurial) leader who can *envision* certain futures and certain scenarios that do not come from rational, quantitative scientific planning but from intuition, perception and self-belief. There is a strand of the literature that sees strategy very much as an art form to be crafted and mastered by those few true visionaries and geniuses that, like their counterparts in other artistic pursuits, are capable of things that we mere mortals cannot possible comprehend (note, for example, the number of times the words 'visionary' and 'genius' were used in the obituaries of Apple co-founder and CEO, Steve Jobs, when he passed away in 2011).

Finally, Leavy and McKiernan (2009) also encourage us to think of strategy as a humanity. That is to say, strategy is also concerned with, and shaped by, the emotional, the spiritual, the historical, the cultural and the linguistic dimensions of organizational life. For example, the language of strategy is neither neutral nor objective but is infused with a grammar of power and control; with a vocabulary that is deeply gendered and which renders that which is knowable and speakable on matters of strategy. Equally, strategies can be seen as historical artifacts: shaped by the social, cultural and economic forces directing organizational activity – in this regard they act as windows on the past. In sum then, and reflecting the vagueness surrounding the term, strategy can be equally conceived of as science, art and humanity.

For some, this disciplinary vagueness is a source of concern. Gavetti and Levinthal (2004: 1309) for example worry that such 'intellectual diversity … may perhaps relegate strategy to a low-paradigm status.' Elsewhere, Meyer (1991: 821) expresses concern that such diversity of interest makes it difficult to 'determine unequivocally whether a given contribution is unique to the strategy area'. This seems like a strange and perhaps overly protective view. Surely any contribution that enhances our understanding, appreciation and ability to 'do' strategy is a welcome one? That Michael Porter is an economist, that Alfred Chandler was a historian and that Peter Selznick was a sociologist surely adds to rather than detracts from their credentials as commentators on strategy as they bring to bear on the subject a range of academic knowledge, complementary and oftentimes competing perspectives, and a tool box of methods, models and interpretive lenses that can only enrich our understanding. In the post-disciplinary world of organization theory it seems strange that this should still be deemed problematic. Does it make the question 'what is strategy?' harder to answer? Yes, but its value and contribution far exceed such challenges. The desire for unequivocal boxing off of knowledge is something we should resist.

Strategy or strategizing?

One of the more recent contributions to the strategy field and one that helps us better articulate an answer to the 'what is strategy' question is to distinguish between strategy as a *product*, typically in the form of a document, policy or presentation, and the *process* of strategizing itself – the doing of strategy, or what goes into making the strategy product. Historically, these have been referred to as *strategy content* and *strategy process*, respectively.

The distinction between content and process is well summed up by Chia and MacKay (2007: 219), who report that: 'strategy content research focuses on the question of *what* strategic decisions are taken, strategy process research examines *how* a particular organizational strategy emerges'. They go on to distinguish underlying practices between the two approaches, where strategy content research typically takes place 'from afar', studying strategy documents and other texts to understand what the strategy contains, relying primarily on secondary data sources to decode the strategy and predicated on a 'variance model of explanation that uses contingency thinking and the language of states and positions to conceptualize the "fit" between the resource base of an organization and its strategic location within a competitive environment' (Chia and MacKay 2007: 220).

In contrast, strategy process research seeks to capture the actual organizational doing of strategy-making, in practice. Relying more on primary research methods of observation, interviews and ethnography, process researchers are interested in the who, how, where and why of strategy: 'In seeking to capture the dynamic and evolving qualities of human conduct in organized settings the process perspective is underpinned by the premise that it is the basic strengths of everyday operations that drive strategy process and emergence' (Chia and MacKay 2007: 220–1). Today, the growing strategy-as-practice field is leading the way in developing new insights into strategy process (see, for example, Jarzabkowski 2004; Whittington 1996, 2006).

4 *What is strategy?*

So let us sum up the discussion so far – strategy is both old and new; it is a science, an art and a humanity; and it is both a process of doing (a verb) and a thing, a product (a noun). While embracing such diversity we are still left with the difficulty of making strategy a manageable feast. How are we to make sense of it and work with this rich, diverse literature? How are we to create working parameters around the discipline? How are we to distinguish the strategic from the non-strategic in organizational life? Perhaps one way of narrowing down our answer is to consider some of the ways in which strategy has been more explicitly defined within the discipline of business and management studies.

Defining strategy

Before delving into specific definitions drawn from the management field it is perhaps worth thinking briefly about wider definitions of strategy and how the word itself came about. The origins of the word strategy can be traced back to Greek the word *strategos* – itself a compound; of *stratos*, which means army – 'or more properly an encamped army spread out over ground' (Cummings 1993: 133) – and *agein*: to lead. Thus, in its earliest form strategy was used to describe a military leadership role; we shall revisit this theme in the next chapter.

The Anglo word *strategy*, according to Freedman (2013), only came into widespread use in the western world in the late eighteenth century with the emergence of the state-controlled military apparatus. In was in the relationship between the state and the military that many of the common features of contemporary strategy first emerged – for example, distinguishing the separation of formulation and implementation, or in other words, those who craft the strategy (generals, politicians) from those that implement it (the soldiers on the ground). The rational logic of the Enlightenment also informed the structure and management of the military in which rationality, accounting and logistics drove military practice (of which more in the next chapter also).

In the world of business, it was only in the post-World War II era that strategy really began to appear in common usage; prior to this time issues of a strategic nature were referred to as *policy*. One of the first definitions of business strategy as we understand it today was provided by Alfred Chandler, the business historian and, according to some, one of the founding fathers of the strategy discipline. In his seminal work of 1962, *Strategy and Structure: Chapters in the History of the Industrial Enterprise*, he defined strategy as: 'the determination of the basic, long-term goals and objectives of an enterprise, and the adoption of courses of action and the allocation of resources necessary for those goals' (p. 13).

From Chandler's early definition we can identify a number of important terms and concepts. First, strategy is about the *long term*. It is not something that reflects the here-and-now but is somehow connected to the distant future of the organization. Second, strategy reflects organization-level *goals* and *objectives*. This suggests that it has a high level of importance. Third, the definition sees strategy as being about not just the setting of long-term goals but also concerned with the *processes* of getting there. So, strategy is both *product* – the articulation of a desired goal or outcome, and *process* – the more practical concern of how to achieve the goal or outcome. Fourth, it introduces the term *resources*, and the recognition that that which the organization possesses, its resources and assets, is of strategic value. In sum, for Chandler strategy is about setting direction at the highest level combined with the more nitty-gritty business of how to get there.

As both testament to the early work of this strategy pioneer and perhaps a reflection on how little we have travelled since, a contemporary definition of strategy from a leading textbook offers what is in essence a minor revision or update to Chandler. According to one of the best-selling contemporary strategy textbooks, Johnson, Scholes and Whittington's *Exploring Corporate Strategy* (2009: 21), 'Strategy is the direction and scope of an organization over the long term, which achieves advantage in a changing environment through its configuration of resources and competences with the aim of fulfilling stakeholder expectations.'

In many ways this might be seen as an updated version of Chandler's definition, adding a number of terms that have become more important in the intervening years. It still considers strategy to be about organizational direction over the long term and about allocating resources, but it introduces a more explicit end: that of achieving '*advantage*'. We will explore the notion of competitive advantage in more detail elsewhere, but suffice to say for now that this is a recurring term in the strategy field and one that has vague connotations. This definition also brings in another dimension: that of the *external environment*. Thus, it makes us aware that strategy is not just about what goes on inside the organization but must also reflect, engage with or at least consider issues outside the organization's area of influence or control, as indexed by the mention of this environment being a '*changing*' one. Finally, we can identify a very explicit element to this definition, which sees the ultimate goal, or outcome of achieving this advantage, as being one that fulfils the expectations (however defined) of those with an interest or '*stake-hold*' in the organization. So strategy carries with it the burden of being accountable to numerous groups, parties and individuals.

Let us take just one more. This time we turn to Richard Rumelt, a long-time writer and student of strategy who seeks to bring the worlds of business strategy and military strategy closer together. He defines strategy as: 'a cohesive response to an important challenge. Unlike a stand-alone decision or goal, a strategy is a coherent set of analyses, concepts, policies, arguments, and actions that respond to a high-stake challenge' (Rumelt 2011: 6).

Rumelt's definition is interesting for a number of reasons. First, he draws attention to the relative importance of a strategy versus a more routine or everyday decision. A critic of the excessive use of the word strategy to define any and all activity, Rumelt wants to reaffirm the elevated status of strategy. Second, Rumelt draws attention to the art and humanities aspects of strategy-making when he observes that it is more than just plans and goals. It is about courses of action and arguments. This draws our attention to the contested nature of strategy and offers a glimmer of the politics and power inherent in strategy. Recognizing the action dynamic in strategy-making also draws our attention to not only the way strategies are written, or formulated, but also how they come to be enacted or implemented. Thus, for Rumelt, strategy is both a verb and a noun: it is a doing word as well as a describing word.

In sum, what these three definitions show us is that while there is a set of recurring themes that might in and of themselves be considered 'strategic', the possibility of a universally agreed-upon definition is unlikely to materialize, partly for the reasons captured in Rumelt's definition. Indeed, so numerous and varied are definitions of strategy that Markides has even suggested that 'nobody really knows what strategy is' (1999: 6).

With this in mind, perhaps the best way to progress with our investigation is to recognize the multiplicity of meanings that strategy possesses and not to rest comfortably on any one clear, clever or simple definition. Indeed, this is something that Henry

Mintzberg, who we shall be hearing a lot more from as we travel the strategy path, has sought to do when offering his own definition(s) of strategy.

Mintzberg's 5Ps

Henry Mintzberg (1987a), who has been studying strategy, management and organizations for more than four decades, rejects any simple or singular definition of strategy and instead provides us with five separate but interrelated ways of answering our question, 'what is strategy?' In a trademark act of academic branding he refers to these as the 5Ps.

Strategy as plan

For Mintzberg, strategy is first and foremost a plan. At least in the sense that this is how most people think of strategy, and with good reason. Type the word strategy into any online dictionary or even leaf through a paper edition and you will see that in common parlance strategy is frequently conceived of as a plan, or as Mintzberg describes it, 'some sort of consciously intended course of action'. This, of course, is very much the orthodox definition of strategy, as provided by Chandler and by Johnson *et al.* earlier. It is also, as we shall see, the dominant notion of strategy within the literature. Fundamental to this definition, Mintzberg tells us, is that plans are 'made in advance' and are 'consciously intended'. In other words, strategies, in a scientific vein, are deductive in nature and rest on an ability to forecast the future with some certainty. Strategies become an organizational formula for both predicting that future and achieving some kind of advantage within it, through conscious, rational, systematic thinking and courses of action. But, of course, few managers believe that the future can be predicted with complete certainty or that plans do not have to change with the ebb and flow of time. Thus, to accommodate this, Mintzberg adds a complementary definition to plan: that of strategy as ploy.

Strategy as ploy

Ploy is to plan as tactics are to strategy. Drawing from the military analogy, strategy is often conceived of as the long-term vision or goal (grand strategy) which is then achieved through short-term ploys, the tactical plays, reactionary responses, flanking, defensive and offensive manoeuvres that take place in the short term. As Mintzberg notes, conceiving of strategy as ploy 'takes us into the realm of direct competition' (1987a: 20). Levy *et al.* (2003) go even further and suggest that conceiving of strategy as ploy 'implies a certain deviousness' and allows for the possibility of 'effective challenges', which will become a key theme in Chapter 8 on value innovation.

Strategy as pattern

However, strategy is not just about plans and ploys. As Mintzberg notes, for some, strategy is more about *patterns*; patterns of behaviour in a stream of actions, that develop through the everyday routines and practices of organizational life. Under this definition we can see how organizational forces such as culture, leadership, and power and politics, and practices of control, surveillance and resistance shape the patterns of behaviour enacted by organizational members. These behaviours, which can be considered strategic, may, or may not, accord with the long-term plans described previously. What Mintzberg is hinting at here is the idea that there is an organic element to strategy, that sometimes strategies *emerge* without conscious deliberation or rational planning – they may develop out of the idiosyncratic behaviour of the organization combined with the serendipity of everyday life; sometimes they even develop in an opposite direction to the plan. In Chapters 3 and 4 we shall see how strategy as plan and strategy as pattern have formed one of the great and enduring debates within the field of strategic management.

Strategy as position

The idea of pattern and interaction leads us to Mintzberg's fourth 'P' and the idea of strategy as position. Strategy as position is really the first in our list that seeks to consider the organization within a wider context, referred to as the 'environment'. This approach is perhaps best exemplified in the work of Michael Porter (1980), who sees strategy as being about the 'fit' between an organization and its external environment. Here, and in recognition that each organization has scarce resources and is positioned within a distinct environment full of competing forces that can either hinder or help, strategies are required that allow the organization to successfully utilize its scarce resources within the confines of environmental forces, for best effect. In short, strategy is the mediating force between the internal and external environments; it is the bind, or glue, that links them together. We will explore this approach in much more detail in Chapter 6.

Strategy as perspective

Finally, strategy can also be about perspective. Here Mintzberg alludes to our notion of strategy as a humanity; that is, strategy as a reflection of the culture, beliefs, attitudes and personality of the organization and its members: a reflection of its unique ways of thinking about and seeing the world. It is, if you will, the heart, soul or spirit of the organization. What does this have to do with strategy? Well, so the argument goes, the perspective of the organization will both consciously and unconsciously shape the way that organizational members behave, the way they think about the organization and its resources and capabilities, how they 'read' the external environment, and so on. It is, as Prahalad (2004) calls it, the 'dominant logic' of the organization.

By way of a simple example, in the 1970s, three organizations saw the future of home computing through three very different perspectives (reflecting their organizational culture, position, leadership, etc.). IBM, at the time one of the world's biggest organizations, saw a future in which the hardware (i.e. the computer components) would be the most important feature, and adjusted their strategy accordingly by outsourcing all its software development – and got it wrong! An emerging new company, Microsoft, thought software would be the most important aspect of this blossoming marketplace, and acted accordingly by striking a deal with IBM to write the software for its hardware – an agreement that would lead to the dominance of the Windows operating system on a global scale – they were seemingly right. Finally, another start-up, Apple, saw the future as being about the integration of hardware and software, and pursued a strategy based on that perspective – while it took a long time to materialize, Apple is currently enjoying unprecedented success in the now stagnating PC market, due in no small part to this integration strategy. In each instance the 'perspective' of the organization led these three companies to think very differently about the same phenomena and resulted in very different strategies and very different futures.

Of course, Mintzberg does not want us to simply pick the 'P' we prefer but to recognize that they are interrelated. For example, *plans* often lead to certain, consciously sought *positions* which require certain *patterns* of behaviour. Equally, a particular *perspective* might lead to a certain *pattern* of behaviour from which might emerge a formal *plan* and *position*. The important point is that the way an individual organization interrelates the five Ps and the way it preferences some over others (not always consciously, of course) may, to a greater or lesser extent, inform their strategic approach, and thus the content and processes of their strategy-making activity. We might suggest that this is why companies making similar products, or offering similar services, to the same customers in the same industry can have such staggeringly different levels of success or failure. It is, Mintzberg would say, the interrelation of the 5Ps and where the organization lays greatest emphasis, be it on formal planning, or positioning, or emergent patterns of behaviours, or historic-cultural perspectives, that determines the uniqueness of its strategy and thus the potential of the organization to achieve competitive *advantage*.

Situating the field of strategic management

Finally, we might also look to understand the strategy problem by locating the academic discipline within the specific socio-economic context in which it has developed. To put it simply, the mainstream (orthodox) literature on strategic management has been produced either in, or as a reflection of, a North American business and research environment. Practically all of the ideas we shall review in this book have developed out of the work of American business schools and US-based academics, researchers, consultants and practitioners. Thus strategy, as a body of knowledge, bears all the hallmarks of American political and economic ideology and is underpinned by an Anglo-western cultural perspective. This is not necessarily to dismiss its worth; rather, we need to be aware of this situatedness when reading the literature and recognize that there are other ways of thinking and doing strategy – it is just that few of these have achieved mainstream status.

Thus, while observing that the strong leaning toward 'rationality', 'logic' 'short-termism' 'individualism' and 'top-down control' in the strategy literature reflects a certain western viewpoint, we should equally acknowledge that in other parts of the world greater emphasis might be placed on 'luck', 'fate', 'God's will' and 'intuition'. The Chinese, for example, often explain events in terms of '*Joss*', a combination of luck and fate. Such alternative ways of thinking and doing manifest themselves in the everyday practices of a particular society and culture, including the way in which it does business. Pascale (1996), for example, reports that the Japanese do not even have a phrase for 'corporate strategy'. Thus, as Whittington observes: 'Strategy reflects the particular social systems in which strategies participate, defining for them the interests in which they act and the rules by which they can survive. Class and country make a difference to strategy' (2001: 4). This in turn leads to different economic systems and different forms of relationship between the organization, state and society. So whereas the dominate business structure in the US is the publically owned large diversified corporation, in South Korea the local interplay of the state, family business and market structure have led to the rise of the large and powerful *chaebol* conglomerates. In China, a preference for family-run business led historically to a much larger preponderance of small and medium enterprises connected through family networks (Whitley 1990). The rise in economic power of Brazil, Russia, India and China (known as the BRIC countries) and, more recently, Mexico, Indonesia,

Nigeria and Turkey (the MINT countries) will likely reveal even wider variation in business models and market systems in the future.

So while there may appear to be a preference for a US-centric reading of strategy in this book, this is more a reflection of how the literature has developed over its lifetime. It also allows us to explore in more detail the failures of western approaches to strategy once the forces of globalization and international competition emerged as a key theme in the strategy literature from the 1980s onwards. Indeed, it might be suggested that one of the reasons that the US lost much of its economic power and competitive edge was precisely because of the limitations of western management theory and practice.

So what is strategy?

Thinking about these varied understandings allows us to draw a number of conclusions that bring us closer to answering the question 'what is strategy?' First, we can now say with some confidence that there is no one best way of defining or thinking about strategy. It is a science, an art and a humanity and is both a process and a product. It informs, and is informed by, the planning activities of organizations, by the patterns of behaviour that are enacted within the organization, and by the perspective held by the organization. It is also a culturally specific practice that reflects wider social and economic structures. All of this points us toward an understanding of strategy that is deeply context-dependent. That is, strategy means different things to different people at different times and in different spaces. Thus, to answer our overarching question, what is strategy, we have to be sensitive to context and exercise caution in accepting any grand, universalizing or singular explanations of its meaning. This is an important lesson to remember as you work through the book: many of the strategy theories we shall explore are extremely persuasive in the way in which they convey (or sell) their advice but as yet none have provided a universal solution to the problem of achieving sustainable competitive advantage. Therefore we must exercise caution and a critical distance when evaluating their worth.

In this light we might think of strategy less as a fixed or concrete term and more as a floating signifier or an empty vessel. Something that can be defined as whatever we deem important, necessary or relevant. This presents both a challenge and an opportunity. That we cannot agree on what strategy is makes it a challenging subject to study for, as we have seen, pretty much any activity undertaken with an organization can, from a certain point of view, be considered strategic. Therefore, creating parameters around the object of study is very difficult indeed. This challenge also presents an opportunity for us to flex our powers of critical thinking, for in its vagueness comes the opportunity to explore the strategy beast in many different ways and from many different perspectives; we are not restricted to a particular interpretation, viewpoint or logic. This is a deeply satisfying and liberating experience when so much of the academic theory we are presented with appears so dogmatically set in stone.

Of course, this is not to deny that strategy does not have its fair share of dominant (or domineering) themes, theorists and formulas. Indeed, despite this vagueness of definition, the academic study of strategy seems to have been governed by a very narrow set of theoretical and practical concerns indeed. Pick up any textbook on strategy and you will see the same topics, often covered in exactly the same way, drawing on the same case studies and making the same arguments. However, and this is the important point, it does not have to be this way. We can bring to bear on the strategy field not just the economic theory that has driven the orthodox literature but also the sociology, psychology, cultural anthropology, philosophy, and all of the other influences that now inform our understanding of work, management and organization. That is the aim of this book. While it is written primarily as a teaching text and thus conforms to certain standard conventions that hopefully make it accessible and 'user-friendly', it is also written from a very distinctive viewpoint, one that we might refer to as a critical stance.

What does this mean exactly? To talk of criticality in management studies has been given new meaning since the 1990s with the rise of *Critical Management Studies*: a loose but growing group of scholars who have sought to bring to bear on the world of work, management and organization the moral, social, political and philosophical questions that are more frequently posed in the disciplines of the humanities and social sciences.

By subjecting the mainstream literature to a more critical lens of analysis we will be able to discuss not only the contributions that have been made but to locate them in their context of emergence to give consideration to the environmental conditions that allowed certain ideas to rise to prominence at certain times. We will give consideration to the underlying political dimensions of strategy-making both internal and external to the firm, and to the politics of strategy as an academic field. We shall also consider the internal and external impact of the changing discourse of strategy on both organizations and wider social structures to see how they have come to shape one another.

So how might this critical lens be put to use in addressing the question of 'what is strategy'? In a sense, for the critical scholar, that question matters less than the next question, 'what are the (power) effects of defining strategy in any particular way?' As Mats Alvesson and Hugh Willmott (1996) warn us, language use has 'colonizing tendencies'. Thus, by framing certain issues as 'strategic' we frame both the presentation of the issue and its reception. As the authors observe: 'Strategy talk frames issues in a way that privileges instrumental reason; it tends to give the initiative with those who successfully claim to be 'strategists'; it also has clear masculine connotations that reproduce and reinforce gender biases' (Alvesson and Willmott 1996: 133).

So how do such colonizing tendency manifest themselves in the realm of business and management? One curious and seemingly endemic effect of the increasing language of strategy is a shift in the way organizational activity is presented and considered. Thus, marketers now present marketing strategies, personnel management has been rebranded as strategic human resource management, accountants prepare financial strategies and manufacturing has become an issue of operations strategy. This language also feeds into the personal narratives that organizational actors employ when outlining their career strategies, strategies to secure promotion, strategies to complete a task or project.

To date there have been few strategy books that have taken an explicitly critical stance (for a notable exception see Clegg *et al*. 2010) but it is hoped that the book you are currently reading will help to fill this gap. The potential contribution of critical management studies is that it provides a particular lens on the field of strategy that challenges many of the received wisdoms, dominant perspectives and accepted norms. By both reviewing and then challenging the field the current text is designed to provide a solid grounding in the basics of strategy but presented from a critical standpoint with a view to developing a more critical appreciation of the role and influence of strategy, of the power of dominant discourses in shaping the organization, and of the influence of history, language and practice as important forces in the shaping, construction and dissemination of strategy as an academic discipline and management practice.

In order to present both a comprehensive overview of the field while also operating through a critical lens of analysis, the book has been structured as a chronology, or more correctly a genealogy: a genealogy that traces the historical development of strategy as an age-old practice and more recent academic management subject. The value of such an approach is that it allows the reader to locate the ideas in the specific context in which they emerged. Thus, we come to understand why planning was seen as such a useful strategic tool in the 1960s but not so much by the 1980s. We understand why Michael Porter's work on industry analysis became so popular in the 1980s and yet would be superseded in the 1990s. This approach stands in contrast to many strategy textbooks, where the contributions of key authors or of particular time periods are broken up to suit a prevailing structure that is more focused on the practical application of strategy rather than considering it also as an intellectual and historically constituted record of the development of business practice and thinking. By piecing the ideas back together we come to a deeper appreciation of the what, how and who of strategy and, most importantly, the why.

The book is structured as follows. In Chapter 2 we present an historical account of the development of strategy as both practice and academic discipline. We note strategy's military origins and the interconnectedness of military and business strategy up until the mid-twentieth century. We also provide an account of the more recent development of the academic field of strategic management from the 1960s to the present time. The remaining six chapters then elaborate on each of the main periods in the recent development of strategy by identifying the main theorists, frameworks and ideas that shaped strategy at that time. So, in Chapters 3 and 4 we consider issues around strategic planning that dominated the literature in the 1960s. In Chapter 5 we look at corporate-level strategy and the idea of portfolio management that widely informed the strategy agenda in the 1970s. In Chapter 6 we look at strategy-making as it developed in the 1980s, with emphasis on the contribution of Michael Porter. In Chapter 7 we look at how, in the 1990s, the strategy field concerned itself with issues of resources and competences. And finally, in Chapter 8, we look at contemporary debates in strategy around the notion of value innovation. We conclude with some broad observations on the field of strategy and some final reflections on the question: what is strategy?

2 Strategy
A brief history

Introduction

Whenever we undertake the study of a new area of inquiry there is a temptation to jump straight in with both feet; to explore the latest research, ideas and debates; to identify the currently fashionable figures, and begin to adopt the language and jargon of the day. However, the more conscientious student will resist such an approach. Far better to spend some time exploring the history of the subject matter in order to appreciate where the ideas have come from, how they have developed, and why. By exploring the past we come to a more detailed and more sophisticated appreciation of the present. As such, do not be tempted to skip this chapter nor see it as simple filler before we get on to the juicier parts. Spend some time exploring the history of strategy and you will be rewarded with a deeper understanding of the subject matter. You will come to understand why strategists talk in such a 'macho' aggressive, even militaristic, language. You will better understand why certain dominant ideas within the strategy field rose to prominence while others fell by the wayside, and importantly, you will know why and how they developed and therefore will be able to consider their contemporary relevance within a contextual frame of time and space. Surprisingly, few strategy texts spend much time thinking about the history of their subject matter nor of locating particular tools, frameworks and concepts within the economic, political and social context in which they originally emerged. Strategy suffers from what Kornberger (2013: 1059) calls a 'historical amnesia resulting in a shared ahistoricism.' We hope to address those shortcomings in this chapter.

In this chapter, we will do the following. First, we will take a short trip back into ancient history in an attempt to come to terms with the 'origins' of strategy and to mark out some of its earliest characteristics, many of which, you will soon discover, still inform the subject today despite being hundreds, if not thousands, of years old. This will lead us into a discussion of the connections between military strategy and business strategy, for the two have a curious and intertwined history that laid the foundation for many of the main concerns in the field today. We will then offer a review, albeit brief, of the recent history of strategy in the business and management literature. This history, beginning in the 1960s, is marked by a continual shift in interests, priorities and concerns in response to the wider social, political and economic concerns of the day. We will arrive at our final destination – strategic management today, much the wiser and ready to locate our contemporary study of the subject within the historical context of its emergence and development.

Military antecedents of (business) strategy

As noted in the previous chapter, the word strategy can be traced back to the Greek word 'strategos', meaning 'to lead an army' or 'the art of generalship'. Therefore, it is unsurprising to learn that strategy has its origins in the military. Indeed, the earliest permanent, large-scale organizations were military forces, such as the armies of ancient Greece, Rome and China. As Davies (2003) has noted: 'More than 2000 years before Ford and General Motors, these armies practised division of labour, routines, span of command and planning' (p. 156).

Perhaps the earliest western text on strategy is *How to Survive under Siege*, written by Aineias the Tactician (*c*.550 BC), in which he details many issues of contemporary relevance to strategic management, such as the deployment of resources, flexibility in planning, the value of 'learning', and the importance of gaining 'advantage'. Elsewhere, Xenophon outlined the desirable attributes and characteristics of a (military) leader thus: '[He] must be ingenious, energetic, careful, full of stamina and presence of mind, loving and tough, straightforward and crafty, alert and deceptive, ready to gamble everything and wishing to have everything, generous and greedy, trusting and suspicious' (cited in Cummings 1993: 134). Such traits strike a chord with much of the contemporary leadership literature, particularly that which leans toward the charismatic and transformational agenda.

Digging deeper into the annals of Ancient Greece and the emergence of strategy, Cummings (1995) details the rise of a particular group within Athenian society, known as the strategoi. These were the district leaders who made up the Athenian War Council and who governed Athens following the political reforms instituted by Kleisthemes in 503 BC. Perhaps the most famous straetgos was Thucydides, whose works, including *History of the Peloponnesian War*, are still seen as seminal texts in political science and international relations to this day. Also important to note about the position of the strategos was that it was both a military and a political appointment, thus requiring many of the organizational skills of modern leaders. Many strategoi, like Thucydides, were also scholars, philosophers and writers and therefore balanced martial skills with academic learning. Moreover, the position of strategos was one that was not inherited but earned: the individual working their way up to the role through proven skill, charisma and leadership.

While Ancient Greece was developing a distinctive notion of strategy suitable to the conditions of the time, elsewhere military leaders and thinkers were producing alternative treaties on strategy, based on the specific idiosyncrasies of their own societies and cultures. In the East, the most famous of these was possibly the military general, Sun Tzu, who, around the same time, produced what is still to this day a highly influential text on military strategy called *The Art of War*, a text that has been appropriated by fields including politics, sports and, of course, business – it even gets a mention in the classic 1980s movie *Wall Street*, being referred to as the 'corporate raider's bible'. Written as a series of aphorisms, *The Art of War* has made numerous lasting contributions that include the distinction between 'strategy' and 'tactics', the importance of planning, and the avoidance, where possible, of direct confrontation in the pursuit of achieving one's goals. Sun Tzu also focused attention on the importance of morale, good and responsible leadership and the welfare of military forces; this some 2,500 years before the emergence of 'strategic' Human Resource Management.

There was also a marked difference in the approaches to strategy based on wider sociocultural influences. In Rome and Greece, greater emphasis was placed on rational planning, on structure and hierarchy – think, for example, of the precision and operational effectiveness of the Roman legionary structure. In contrast, in the East, far greater attention was placed on the spiritual, on the individual and on self-awareness (Cummings 2007).

From these early beginnings the importance of strategy has remained a prominent feature of military and political thinking and numerous other weighty tomes would be added throughout the years, including: Myamoto Musashi's *Book of Five Rings*, written in seventeenth-century Japan; Niccolò Machiavelli's *The Prince*, written in sixteenth-century Florence; and Carl von Claustewitz's *On War*, written in nineteenth-century Prussia. All would bring their own understanding of military strategy and all would come to enrich and inform the study of strategy across disciplinary boundaries.

We can still see the influence, both direct and indirect, of this military lineage in business strategy today. There is much anecdotal evidence of organizational rituals in which, on reaching a certain 'executive' level, employees are expected to familiarize themselves with key strategy texts. In Honda it is rumoured that Sun Tzu is the thinker of choice, while at Sony it is Myamoto Musashi's writings that are preferred. Rosalie Tung (1994) notes that at Sanyo Electric Corporation of Japan, when an employee is promoted to a senior management position they are ceremoniously handed a 'lined notepad and a copy of *The Three Kingdoms*' (p. 58).

Whether these stories are true or not, it is certainly the case that airport book shelves are crammed with titles such as Krause's (1996) *Sun Tzu: The Art of War for Executives*, and Bose's (2004) *Alexander the Great's Art of Strategy* – testament surely to an enduring market for these ideas. In the academic literature we find articles such as Ho and Choi's (1997) 'Achieving marketing success through Sun Tze's Art of Warfare'; Pheng and Sirpal's (1995) 'Western generic business and corporate strategies: lessons from the thirty-six Chinese classical strategies of war'; and Ma's (2003) 'To win without fighting: an integrative framework' as attempts to capture and translate these military texts into models and methods for organizational application. Even in seminal works, such as that of Igor Ansoff (1965), we see direct reference to the influence of military practice on his notion of strategy. Likewise, James Brain Quinn (1980) draws on the military campaigns of Alexander the Great to convey a number of lessons for the business strategist. Chief amongst them the notion that 'effective strategy develops around a few key concepts and thrusts, which give them cohesion, balance, and focus', and also a 'sense of positioning against an intelligent opponent' (cited in Mintzberg et al. 2009: 96).

All are testament to a certain audience's desire to unlock the secrets of military strategy for the modern commercial world – and it seems to have worked, too. Indeed, Jack Welch cited von Clausewitz as his inspiration when outlining his views on strategy when taking up the position of CEO at General Electric. Another fan of von Clausewitz, Fred Smith, founder of Federal Express, was also not averse to citing a little '*On War*' in interviews and speeches (Mintzberg et al. 2009). To this day, many large organizations regularly employ military strategists to assist in developing their business plans – companies such as McDonald's, Motorola and Electronic Arts, to name but a few (Pech and Durden 2003).

Inevitably perhaps, the legacy of the military origins of strategy and its frequent referral in both the popular and academic literature, have resulted in various lasting vestiges of influence, what Winsor (1996) calls 'organizational militarism'. For example, the language of strategy is riddled with military metaphors: we hear competitors referred to as the 'enemy' who occupy 'positions' on the 'battlefields' (marketplace). These competitor/enemies are then regularly 'engaged' by our own (labour) 'forces' and 'fought' with in the marketplace/battlefield, often with the goal of 'beating', 'destroying', and 'outmanoeuvring' them. As Carter *et al.* observe: 'The macho talk also suited the identities of many strategists in large corporations, who were happy to imagine themselves as warriors or field marshals directing a war' (2008: 3). A similar viewpoint is shared by Winsor who suggests that the industry for military informed management offers executives the opportunity to 'self-metamorphose into leaders of potential heroic status' (1996: 35) through reading and enacting the lessons distilled in these manuals.

Much depends, of course, on one's perception of the military and of military strategy. As Cummings (2007) has argued, for many, their perception of the military as an organization is one governed by a rigid, hierarchical bureaucratic structure in which strategies are formulated by staff officers and then implemented through strict systems of top-down communication. While not denying that an element of this still exists, what is frequently presented in much of the extant literature is very much a rendering of a nineteenth and early twentieth-century military model (as we shall see below). However, in the late twentieth and early twenty-first century, following a 'Revolution in Military Affairs' and the advent of technological and network warfare, the military constitutes a very different institution than that depicted in many of the debates in the (business) strategy field.

For example, Mutch (2006) discusses the flexibility in contemporary military organizations through the use of a wide range of organizational structures, dependent on need and circumstance. Most notably he distinguishes between what he calls 'heavy' and 'light' military forces, with the former being exemplified by the familiar 'tight discipline and strict hierarchies, with officers drawn from particular social groups and a considerable gulf between them and the ranks' (p. 761). Against this, though, he situates the light forces that tend to be characterized by 'a considerable degree of responsible autonomy being granted to the rank and file, especially in battlefield situations' (p. 762). As we shall see later, similar kinds of flexible and adaptive structures have proven crucial to the business success of many firms. Even within the 'heavy forces', if one studies military command structures, one sees empowerment right down to the eight-person section level (the smallest organized unit within the military). When situated against the structures of many large-scale commercial organizations, the military can be seen, at times, as more flexible and more empowering than one might imagine. As Peter McKiernan has observed, it is not just in battlefield tactics and strategy that business can learn from the military but 'in certain areas of the subject e.g. procurement, empowerment, intelligence, control and communications, the military are decades ahead of the academics. Hence, this pathway cannot be denied easily' (1997: 791).

Not all agree of course and there are numerous authors who challenge the relevance of these military origins (see, for example, Mintzberg 1987b; Stacey 1990). To chart a direct line from Ancient Greece to the present day is too simplistic, they suggest. Even the very idea that there is any relevance of military strategy to the 'peaceful' world of business is, for some, untenable. Indeed, one of the strongest advocates of this rejectionist view was Alfred Chandler, the great historian of business strategy, who as we shall see below, was pivotal in writing the recent history of strategy and in so doing helped minimize, if not remove, any linkage to the military, at least within the mainstream literature. We could argue the relevance of the military to business strategy all day but perhaps Richard Rumelt says it best when he remarks 'if you are careful about the level of abstraction, you can take certain fundamental lessons from military history and be the wiser for doing so' (Rumelt 2011: 124).

Strategy, the rise of 'big business' and the West Point connection

Hoskin *et al.* (1997) dismiss the notion of an unbroken line of thinking from the distant past to the present, offering instead a history on the relationship between military and business strategy that considers more explicitly their 'mutually reaffirming' influence. Specifically, Hoskin and his colleagues argue that the antecedents of contemporary military and business strategy can be found, not in Ancient Greece, but in nineteenth-century America, specifically at the juncture of West Point Military Academy (the US Army's officer training centre), the American Civil War (which, they argue, was the first 'industrial' war – by which they mean that logistics and production were as important as operational issues), and the building of the American railroads. It was, they argue, a small group of individuals who feature in all three of these arenas that did most to shape both military and business practice in America and subsequently, as America developed into a global economic power, helped spread these management practices and business theories throughout much of the rest of the industrialized world.

Let us start at West Point. So the story goes, under the superintendence of Sylvanus Thayer (between 1817 and 1833), West Point Military Academy was significantly remodelled and reorganized, based on Thayer's experiences in Paris at the *École Polytechnique*. He instituted a series of reforms in which written communication, grading and examining became the means by which the academy operated (in other words, it was bureaucratized). Thayer himself would seldom leave his offices, instead practising delegation and the division of labour by issuing *written* orders and commands and expecting, in return, *written* reports. These reforms, in many ways, marked the emergence of a science of (military) management and a new kind of 'human engineering' (Hoskin *et al.* 2006: 168) in which bodies were made manageable and productive: a form of control vividly described in Adam Smith's *Wealth of Nations* in his example of the pin factory.

It was from this reformed academy that individuals such as Daniel Tyler and George W. Whistler (later to become directors of two of the most influential and innovative organizations in American history, namely Springfield Armoury and the Western Railroad respectively), would graduate. It was at West Point, Hoskin *et al.* (1997) argue, that these men would learn about M-form organizational structures, (military) reporting and grading structures, and the division of command and labour that they would later employ in their civilian, commercial enterprises.

Alfred Mahan, whose father was one-time superintendent of the academy, would also employ the lessons learnt at West Point – first in business and later during the Civil War when he established the first military staff office, employing the detached command-and-control structures studied at West Point. He introduced a focus, not just on short-term operational issues, but also on longer-term strategic horizons, and looked beyond issues of battlefield tactics to consider the wider environment in which military action took place. In this regard he was concerned with logistics, with access to key resources, raw materials and labour – not just on the field of battle but in the production of war and the support industries necessary for extended military campaigns. To this end, Hoskin *et al.* state: 'the first theorist of modern strategy, we suggest, is not Clausewitz, but Alfred Mahan' (1997: 4).

The industrial North's victory in the Civil War (1861–65), led by its West Point graduates, enabled the subsequent completion of the transcontinental railway. Even in their construction, and that of the vast canal systems that preceded it, we see the vestiges of military methods of management and organizing inform these projects. As Chandler (1962) describes it, each project was managed through the hierarchical divisional structure of the military model, with a central headquarters from which direction was given to a series of field officers responsible for particular 'divisions' of the laying of the railroads.

Once completed, military methods also informed the running of these vast transport networks. Herman Haupt, another West Point graduate, who became superintendent of the Pennsylvania Rail Road (PRR), implemented a 'structural and strategic reorganization' of American management grounded in his West Point learning. It consisted of:

> the collection and analysis of operating statistics, costs and revenues, including comparison with other railroads, and leading to strategic analyses of the advantages and costs of organic growth, of potential alliances and/or takeovers, and of what should be the State of Pennsylvania's tax policy on rail freight, given the competition with New York and the Erie Canal.
>
> (Hoskin *et al*. 2006: 171)

An underlying military model was further reflected in the operational running of the railroads with the use of fixed timetables, uniforms for staff, division of labour and a hierarchy based on rank (Clegg *et al.* 2010). It was also at the PRR that one of America's most famous industrialists, Andrew Carnegie, received his business education, under the tutelage of Thomas C. Scott, Haupt's subordinate.

What began with the railroads was soon writ large across a whole range of industries including oil, steel and manufacturing, with the railroads serving to connect the entire continent of North America while also serving as a model of organizational structure and managerial practice. By connecting industries and geographical markets with fast railroads, so competition increased. As competition increased, new technologies were developed to outperform rivals. As new technologies were developed, productivity increased. As productivity increased, prices went down. As prices went down, demand went up. As demand went up, new competitors emerged, and so on and so on. Thus was ushered in America's industrial revolution.

To cope with the growth in the size and spread of markets, the increase in competition, and an emerging consumer class, more and more family businesses were handed over to professional managers who were better equipped and trained, often via West Point, to manage these sprawling industrial empires. Waves of diversification, acquisitions and mergers followed and the contemporary corporation was born, and with it a new educational institution, the business school.

The emergence of the first business schools

The late nineteenth century saw the emergence of the first business schools, located in American universities. The very first to teach business *policy*, the preferred name for business strategy right up until the late 1970s and sometimes still used to this day, was the Wharton School at the University of Pennsylvania. Founded in 1881 and named after its first dean, Joseph Wharton, the school predominantly taught economics, accounting and business law (Schachter 2010), as well as focusing on practical management, primarily of unruly workforces:

> The 'labor issue' was a major preoccupation. Joseph Wharton wished the school to teach 'the nature and prevention of strikes' as well as 'the necessity for modern

industry of organizing under single leaders or employers great amounts of capital and great numbers of labourers, and of maintaining discipline among the latter'.

(Freedman 2013: 461–2)

In 1908, Harvard Business School was founded with a mandate to teach an 'applied science' of management. In order to do this, Edwin Gay, the first dean of the school invited Fredrick Winslow Taylor to deliver a series of classes based on his principles of scientific management. At first Taylor resisted, suggesting that management was something that could not be taught but only experienced, but later he capitulated and offered the course (Schachter 2010).

The pursuit of this 'scientific' approach to management at Harvard, and other newly emerging business schools, of which there were over 30 by 1917, was partly a response to a number of private endowments and donations from wealthy early industrialists who established both schools and funds for programmes that adhered to certain principles of business teaching and research. Examples include Vanderbilt University, named after Cornelius Vanderbilt, the shipping and rail tycoon who provided a $1 million endowment in 1873 to establish the university. Elsewhere, Andrew Carengie established Carnegie Technical School, later to become Carnegie Mellon University, in 1900. Foundations such as the Ford Foundation and Carnegie Foundation reinforced a view of business schools as having a practical leaning toward the development of a science of management. Scientific 'credentials' were also actively pursued by many business school deans, who faced much criticism from more established academic disciplines that refused to take management and business seriously as scholarly pursuits, instead seeing them as 'the handmaidens of industry'. By the 1940s and America's entry into World War II, strategy (or policy) had established itself as a 'capstone' course in management education, designed to integrate the knowledge acquired in all other management disciplines into a strategic perspective on the organization. During World War II the role and importance of strategy, both military and industrial, would be a defining factor in the outcome of that total war.

World War II: the widening exchange of ideas, methods and practices

Perhaps the final great influence of the military over the development of business strategy came during the Second World War. Whole nations mobilized in the war effort saw industry and manufacturing turned over to supplying the tools and resources necessary to sustain the war effort. Under such conditions, large organizations were assigned military attachés – senior military officers – who would help coordinate and instruct on effective and efficient forms of managing (Knights and Morgan 1991). What we therefore see at this time is the wholesale exportation of military management into the commercial field on an unprecedented scale. And again, of course, with this came the military way of doing things – specific management practices, forms of language and communication, methods of command and control, a division of labour, and the disciplining of staff.

Not only were military methods integrated into business practice but the scarcity of resources and raw materials resulting from the war forced a number of innovations that would influence both realms. As Ghemawat (2002) observes, the war encouraged a mind-set of frugality and lean practice that led to numerous developments in manufacturing and operations research of the kind that would later be credited as a key aspect of Japan's rise to economic dominance and technological innovation in the 1970s and

1980s. Indeed many historians of World War II credit the allied victory as more to their war production and resource management than to their military strategy and strength (Knights and Morgan 1991). At the end of the war, remnants of this military infusion would continue to resonate within management practices, if not in management theory. As Whittington *et al.* (2011) note, many senior managers of large organizations in the post-war era had learnt their craft while serving in the military. Examples of this military generation include the ten 'whizz kids' (ibid. p. 537) joining Ford after the war, the most famous of whom was Robert McNamara.

Elsewhere, Talbot (2003) argues that the contemporary notion of the N-form (network) organization structure was actually first developed in the practices of the German military in the closing stages of World War II. As the Allied powers and the Soviet Union began to encircle Germany, the armies of the Third Reich (significantly depleted of men and resources) needed to develop flexible and responsive forces on an ad hoc and short-term basis in order to fight on a number of different fronts simultaneously. The result, Talbot points out, was the 'Kampfgruppes', or 'battle groups' comprising mixed units put together to complete an objective and then dismissed and reformed based on the next priority. Talbot goes on to argue that the main reason why this flexible organizational structure did not appear in commercial organizations until much later was due to the Allies' victory in World War Two:

> It must be remembered that the victors write history and that despite the tactical successes of the kampfgruppe ultimately traditional M-form military forces defeated the forces of the Third Reich ... [As such] the transfer of this N-form model to the civilian environment did not occur [until much later].
>
> (Talbot 2003: 337 and 338)

The recent history of business strategy

While the legacy of the military's influence on management and strategy can still be seen in the day-to-day practices of organizational life, the academic field of strategic management, after World War II, sought to carve out for itself a whole new history: one undiluted by military influence and the product, instead, of conscious, rational and sophisticated management science, driven by an elite cadre of corporate leaders and business academics and a burgeoning strategy industry. Below, we shall recount the recent history of policy/strategy by reflecting on the major concerns, characters and contexts through which it rapidly developed into the form that we know it as today.

The 1960s: growth, planning and stability

The emergence of a coherent and distinctly managerial discipline of business strategy occurred in the 1960s through the influence, in particular, of three men: Alfred Chandler, Alfred Sloan and Igor Ansoff. This combination of historian, practitioner and management academic respectively, laid the foundations for a particular notion of strategy that still informs the mainstream literature.

Chandler's *Strategy and Structure* (1962), Sloan's *My Years with General Motors* (1963), and Ansoff's *Corporate Strategy* (1965) all published in close proximity to each other, were mutually reinforcing texts that produced the foundations of strategy, with General

Motors serving as the benchmark case study for strategy execution. For example, General Motors was one of the four 'exemplar' case study companies used by Chandler in his text (although cynics might note that Chandler's research was funded by the Sloan Foundation and that Alfred *Du Pont* Chandler's family owned a quarter of General Motors). Ansoff also regularly drew on Sloan's management of GM in his text. As Schendel (cited in McKiernan 1997: 792) observes: 'there is little written today that cannot be traced back to their work'. In particular, they advocated the importance of strategic planning, in which logical, rational and sequential decision-making processes would culminate in an executable strategy. The foundations laid down by these men included:

1 A belief in rational analysis.
2 The separation of formulation from implementation.
3 The goal of profit maximization.
4 Return on investment as a key indicator of strategic performance.
5 The decentralized divisional form.
6 The separation of 'policy' (strategy) from 'operations' (tactics).

(Whittington 2001)

A particular emphasis in this and other works of the time was a (continued) attempt to produce a managerial practice of strategy that was heavily influenced by decision theory and systems analysis, or what Gavetti and Levinthal (2004: 1310–1) refer to as an 'engineering' approach, in which rational analysis, forecasting and the management of processes become key strategic issues. As a practical example of this approach, *Sloan* stated in his biography, *My Years with General Motors* (1963) that: 'The strategic aim of business is to earn a return on capital, and if in any particular case the return in the long run is not satisfactory, the deficiency should be corrected or the activity abandoned' (p. 49).

It is worth noting that these ideas came about at a time of relative stability in the US economy. The country had emerged from World War II as an economic powerhouse with interests across the globe. America was still largely an industrial nation with agriculture and manufacturing primary exports and forms of rational planning, systems management and forecasting lent themselves well to these kinds of business. Out of this context came wider acceptance of Chandler's famous axiom, 'structure follows strategy' – due to the relatively stable market environment, strategy was seen as the primary driver of competitiveness, profitability and growth while issues of an organizational kind were seen as being of secondary concern, hence structure follows strategy. It was this statement (more on which later) that encouraged a second key concern with strategy at the time, namely that formulation of strategy should be separated from implementation. Formulation was seen to be an activity reserved for senior managers while implementation was an administrative and operational task undertaken by all others.

Interestingly, and perhaps reflecting Chandler's background as an historian, the methodological approach advocated for studying business policy at the time was broadly qualitative, with research focused on individual company case studies in pursuit of understanding 'best practice'. As Hoskisson *et al.* (1999) note, there was little attempt to try and generalize the findings from one case company to another. Instead, it was recognized that each organization was the product of its own idiosyncratic behaviour and therefore generalization would be rendered meaningless. Not only was there a focus on individual firms but there was also a disinterest in the potential contribution to knowledge that could be made by other disciplines, such as engineering, psychology and economics: 'Knowledge generated for one set of ends is not readily applicable to another' was a claim made by Learned *et al.* (1965: 6) in their seminal strategy textbook of the time.

1970s: crisis and change

By the early 1970s, (strategic) planning, utilizing more and more sophisticated and complicated models and frameworks, had been widely adopted. Indeed, as Mintzberg *et al.* (2009) note, the formalization of strategy sat neatly with the wider trend in management education and practice at the time: formal procedure, formal training, formal control, and formal analysis. Through the separation of formulation from implementation, policy should be managed by a 'cadre of highly educated planners, a part of a specialized strategic planning department with direct access to the chief executive' (Mintzberg 2009: 50).

However, the relative stability and growth of the 1960s and early 1970s would not last long and was quickly replaced by a period of uncertainty and change as the decade wore on. The escalating costs (both political and economic) of the Vietnam War put increasing strain on the American economy while the oil embargo initiated by the OPEC oil-producing countries in 1973 was felt across the globe. These events, combined with repeated cycles of inflation and recession, had a profound impact on American business and challenged many of the assumptions of business policy that had been laid down in the previous decade. Suddenly, the external environment seemed less predictable; the value of planning became increasingly questioned (few companies, for example, had planned for the oil crisis, one notable exception being Shell, whom we shall hear more about in Chapter 4). In response, a new dominant logic emerged, one of diversification and growth, often undertaken in order to spread risk. The result was the rise of the corporation and, in particular, the conglomerate. Pivotal to this development was the rapidly growing strategy industry, made up of consultancies such as the highly influential McKinsey & Company with its PIMS database and GE/McKinsey matrix, and Boston Consulting Group with its experience curve model and Growth-Share matrix; of business schools with their flagship MBA programmes; and of practitioner-gurus selling the latest secrets to success. All were looking to carve out their own unique selling point by offering some variation or twist on the route to achieving sustainable competitive advantage. The result was an opening up of business policy to a wide range of actors and organizations. No longer was strategy something that was done internally by senior managers but was increasingly positioned as something that required strategy experts, whether in the form of consultants, graduates of prestigious MBA programmes, or strategy commentators.

One of the unique contributions that outside consultants brought with them was a new methodology that sought to produce industry-level analyses, such as the famous PIMS database. Through hard quantitative data, they argued, they could forecast industry change and growth and therefore help align businesses with their environments. While the individual case study method remained, especially in the teaching of MBAs, the growth in the processing power of computer technologies allowed for more and more sophisticated financial reporting, and strategy increasingly became a numbers game in this period and the business-as-portfolio logic began to take hold.

Against this growing commercialization of strategy knowledge, many academics became frustrated with the way in which the complex and rich topic of strategy was increasingly being reduced to boxes, bubbles and matrices. In 1976 and 1977 two academic conferences were convened to discuss the future of business strategy. The first of these conferences is seldom remembered today and infrequently cited in the literature. It was organized by Henry Mintzberg who initiated a call for a conference entitled 'Strategy Formulation: Different Perspectives' at l'Ancien Couvent Royal in St Maximin, France. It drew together a number of primarily European scholars including John Child, Andrew Pettigrew and Yves Doz, who were each invited to present a paper entitled 'Strategy formulation as an X process', with X standing for a range of different themes including 'historical' 'political', 'cultural', etc. The aim of the conference was to broaden the discipline of strategy by thinking beyond the limitations of financial measures, quantitative methods and rational analysis to think about the range of everyday organizational practices that influence and shape the processes of strategy-making. Key papers from the conference were subsequently published as a special issue of *International Studies of Organization and Management* in 1977. The conference and papers have been largely forgotten but on contemporary re-reading one is struck by the quality and depth of perception they offer, with many of them pre-empting by some 30 to 40 years many 'new' issues in the field of strategic management.

Far more influential was the second conference, entitled 'Business Policy and Planning Research: The State of the Art', convened by two American business academics, Dan Schendel and Charles Hofer, and held at Pittsburgh University. Ninety-three leading (predominantly American) strategy academics, consultants and practitioners attended for the purposes of considering and outlining the future scope and direction of business policy, with particular emphasis on the content, rather than the process, of strategy-making. Indeed, Schendel and Hofer argued explicitly against a pluralist approach in favour of a single guiding paradigm (Lampel and Baum 2010). Hambrick and Chen note that

> the Pittsburgh conference had a distinct undercurrent – as conveyed by the list of invitees, the organization of the sessions, and even the formal objectives – that this was to be an occasion to consider the virtues of normal science, theory, generalizability, and research methodologies other than case studies.
>
> (Hambrick and Chen 2008: 44)

In other words, the conference sought to establish a new research and teaching agenda for the field of business policy through rather strategic means. The conference was extremely successful in achieving this aim. The outcomes of the conference were threefold:

- the field of business policy was rebranded 'strategy';
- the conference confirmed the superiority of a 'science of strategy' reflecting the wider 'scientific turn' in management thinking and education;
- the conference ushered in a more practice-orientated approach to strategy research.

These outcomes were cemented in 1980 when the *Strategic Management Journal* was launched with Schendel as editor. According to Hambrick and Chen nearly one third of the Pittsburgh delegates served as the journal's editorial board. Furthermore, of the 25 articles in the inaugural issue, 11 were dedicated to scientific hypothesis testing and eight employed a quantitative method. Quickly rising to prominence as the preeminent journal in the strategy field, this ensured that the outcomes of the conference spread quickly through the academic community. This in turn led to a self-perpetuating cycle in which research that spoke to the conference themes were received more favourably in the embryonic strategic management literature and journals. A year later, the newly formed Strategic Management Society held its first meeting, thus 'completing the transformation of strategy into a full-fledged field of study' (Lampel and Baum 2010: xx–xxi).

Thus, by the end of the 1970s, the field of *strategy* had begun to develop into the form we recognize today. A discipline driven by a quantitative, positivist methodology employed for functionalist purposes, and underpinned by a managerialist agenda. Waiting in the wings with an approach to strategy that could capitalize on this shift was a young economist who would soon become synonymous with the field. The 1980s *was* the decade of Michael Porter.

1980s: competition and entrepreneurship

In the developed West, the 1980s were dominated by a political ideology of free market economics, known as neo-liberalism. Thatcherite economic policy, quickly adopted in Reagan's America, ushered in an era of free enterprise, deregulation, competition and support for big business. At the same time, American business was facing an increasing threat of competition from Europe and the Far East. Under these conditions, strategic attention shifted away from the internal environment of the firm, with its focus on SWOT analysis, portfolio management, product life cycles, detailed planning, and 'best practice', towards a focus on the external environment in order to better understand and explain the rise of unexpected competitors such as Germany and Japan, while at the same time developing frameworks for competing more effectively in an increasingly open, free but unstable environment.

Enter Michael Porter, a young economist who had recently completed his doctoral thesis in the Department of Economics at Harvard University. Porter, in a strategic move that even Sun Tzu would have been proud of, took his fairly orthodox industrial organization economics modelling from the economics department across the river to Harvard Business School, where his ideas were seen, after some initial resistance, as revolutionary, inspired, and the 'answer' to America's current competitive position. In part, the seeming novelty of Porter's ideas were perhaps a result of strategy's own inward looking past – recall the earlier dismissal of outside influence when constructing theories of strategy. Indeed, Porter's initial reception in the Harvard Business School was a frosty one and it took some time for him to persuade colleagues of the value of his economics-derived approach.

Porter's ideas on industry structure, grounded in 'scientific' economics, struck a chord and were quickly disseminated through the publication of his seminal text, *Competitive Strategy* in 1980, which was quickly followed up (at least in academic terms) by *Competitive Advantage* in 1985. Porter rapidly became established as *the* key thinker in strategic management, shaping both the academic and practice agenda. He also had the ear of the president, his 1990 book, *The Competitive Advantage of Nations*, being based on a project commissioned by Ronald Reagan. Porter's ideas were also in accord with the manifesto for strategy laid down by Schendler, Hofer and colleagues at the Pittsburgh Conference. It extolled the virtues of scientific modelling, quantification and generalization (we will explore the contribution of Michael Porter in much more detail in Chapter 6).

At the same time another, in some ways distinct but not uncomplimentary, view of strategy was emerging that again reflected a key theme in 1980s America – that of the can-do American spirit and the American dream of opportunity for anyone with a great idea and the will to see it through. In short, the 1980s saw a fascination with entrepreneurship: a theme that sat very comfortably with the neoliberal agenda. As such, a stream of literature emerged that sought to extol both the values of visionary 'transformational' leadership (Bass 1990) and the importance of strong corporate culture, as advocated by the likes of Peters and Waterman (1982) and Deal and Kennedy (1982). At the time it was believed that 'strong culture' was the source of Japanese competitiveness, and could therefore be a basis on which to reignite US competitiveness. This led to a wave of consultancy initiatives seeking to offer culture-transforming tools and processes.

Critics suggest that during the 1980s strategy became much more focused and narrowly defined and, in the process, lost some of its rich, deep and complex nuances. Bartlett and Ghoshal (1991), for example, note how the complex and multifaceted nature of the 'environment' increasingly became regulated, through the influence of Porter, to a focus only on industry and on specific and narrowly defined forces, with strategy reduced to a decision about picking 'positions' of 'fit'. Thus, 'as a result a field once distinguished by its breadth, scope and managerial relevance became academically elegant, but increasingly fragmented and compartmentalized' (Bartlett and Ghoshal 1991: 8).

Mintzberg et al. (2009) also note that the widespread popularity of Porter and others working to make strategy still more accessible, resulted in an explosion in the burgeoning strategy industry, with more and more boutique consultancies opening up and the rise of the professional guru and academic consultant. MBAs established themselves as cash cow products for business schools, with many charging substantial sums of money to equip future captains of industry with the toolkit necessary to successfully manage major corporations. However, by the end of the 1980s, the love affair with both Porter and the entrepreneurial approach had begun to wane as these strategic panaceas were proven (as if it could ever be otherwise) to be wanting in addressing the growing complexity and diversity of managing large organizations in an environment becoming increasing turbulent and chaotic. The answer to this failing, it was soon argued, could be found by looking back inside the organization at the resources and capabilities found there. Could this be the root to that elusive thing called competitive advantage?

1990s: renewed growth and the global economy

The 1990s was a decade dominated by a growing concern with all things 'global': global competition, global markets, global brands, global consumers, global culture, and more. The stable and predictable (home) market conditions upon which much of the strategy field had developed were increasingly a thing of the past. Competition was becoming more dynamic, fluid and unpredictable. The focus on the external environment had proven to offer only temporary gains for only some organizations, and yet there was now emerging a new wave of competitors that appeared to be in what Porter would term 'unattractive' industries performing beyond expectation while pursuing strategies that refused to fit neatly into the paradigms, matrices and frameworks of the MBA teaching curriculum. Out of these changing market conditions, a view of strategy began to gather traction that argued for greater consideration of the internal environment as the basis of competitive advantage. Building on the work of Edith Penrose in the 1950s, writers such as Birger Wernerfelt (1984), Jay Barney (1991) and Prahalad and Hamel (1990, 1994) argued that by harnessing the idiosyncratic bundle of resources, capabilities and competencies possessed by the organization, innovation, competitiveness and advantage could be achieved. This resource-based view (RBV), as it came to be known, proved to be highly influential in the academic field throughout the 1990s. However, due to its complexity of theory, vagueness of methodology and difficulty of implementation it attracted less attention in the practice field. That is until Prahalad and Hamel produced a more managerially friendly variation with their 'core competence' approach (we shall discuss both the RBV and the contribution of Prahalad and Hamel in Chapter 7).

However, by the end of the 1990s the terrain had begun to shift once again. Emerging competitors such as the BRIC nations of Brazil, Russia, India and China bought with them new forms of organizing, managing and strategizing. The increasing speed of technological change, the internet, globalization, ecological concerns, and more, all undermined the received wisdom of western (US-centric) strategy theory, and gave way to the rise of the 'start-up', small agile companies disrupting whole industries. In the first years of the twenty-first century, 'innovation', 'value' and 'networks' became the buzzwords of the strategy field.

2000s: innovation, value and networks

Drawing on the economics of Joseph Schumpeter, and reflecting wider moves in the management and organization literature, the early years of the twenty-first century were marked by a much more fluid and dynamic approach to strategy. While mainstream textbooks continued to regurgitate decades-old theory, devoid of the context and climate in which they were developed, at the spearhead of contemporary academic research during this time was an increasing focus on notions of value and innovation as the core of strategic success. Whether value and innovation emerges from the internal or external environments mattered less than the imperative to find it somewhere. One of the main arguments of this particular group of authors, who count amongst their number W. Chan Kim and Renee Mauborgne (2004), C. K. Prahalad (2004), and Clayton Christensen (2000), was that innovation and value can be found anywhere, and it is how the organization structures and orientates itself to foster and capitalize on potential routes to innovation and value creation that is, or should be, at the heart of good strategy.

Research in this area is still very much a work-in-progress (as we shall see in Chapter 8) but suffice to say that the combination of academic research, practitioner interest and a cadre of very capable 'gurus' able to communicate their ideas in easily packaged and digestible formats suggests that this particular approach to strategy has some way to go before it too runs its course, and we all start the hunt for the next big thing.

Summary

Offered above is a necessarily brief overview of the history of (business) strategy. We have charted its ancient, early and more recent military antecedents and also offered a more detailed review of the development of business strategy as an academic discipline. What is perhaps most obvious from this short narrative is that strategy is both a very old and in many ways a relatively new (business) discipline and yet, in its short recent history it has travelled quite some distance. What we can take from this is recognition that strategy does not lend itself to long-lasting theories, methods, tools or frameworks. Rather it has, quite rightly, shifted focus as the wider context in which it is situated has also moved. Rather than displacing what has come before, successive theories, models and frameworks have been added to the strategist's toolkit, producing a bewildering range of solutions to the problems of managing organizations. In the remainder of this book we will navigate this veritable minefield of competing ideas and claims, with their seemingly distinct and often conflicting theoretical foundations.

A word of caution though: having spent the time and trouble to get to know a little better the history of our subject, do not now forget what you have read above. When reading about, thinking about and applying the many tools and techniques of strategic management that we will consider in the remainder of this book, remember that each is a product of a distinctive socio-temporal space; developed and refined to address the needs of *that* day. While each may have become more, or less, popular with the passage of time, all still have something meaningful to say to the student of strategy, and in appreciating their context of emergence we may know better their value and limitations.

3 Strategy by design and an emergent critique (part 1)

Introduction

A view of strategy conceived of as a deliberate, rational, sequential planning process strikes a clear resonance with the way in which both the mainstream literature, and the organizational practice of strategy itself, have been thought about and discussed. If you recall from our history lesson, strategy as plan was a dominant theme amongst the early pioneers of the discipline, who subscribed to a belief that strategy could and should result from deliberate and calculated decision-making. In this chapter we will look at the development of rational planning as a particular approach to strategy. We locate the main theoretical underpinnings on which this approach is based and then explore just one incarnation of the many hundreds of planning models that can be found in the literature. Having done this we consider some of the perceived benefits of a planned approach to strategy.

As indicated in the title, the present discussion constitutes the first of two parts and in the next chapter we will develop a sustained critique of strategic planning by introducing another school of thought that presents an alternative reading of strategy – that of strategy as an emergent process of learning and crafting. This 'emergent' approach, most frequently associated with the writings of Henry Mintzberg, offers a useful foil against which to think about the value of strategic planning. We will conclude the 'planned vs. emergent' debate by introducing scenario planning as something of a midway point between these two approaches – a bridge, if you will, that draws on the best of both and has found increased popularity in recent years.

Strategic planning: underlying assumptions

Reviewing many of the earliest and most influential texts on business strategy, Mintzberg (1990) identifies what he sees as three underlying assumptions of strategic planning: strategy as a rational process; the CEO as strategy architect; and the separation of implementation from formulation. Let us take each in turn.

Strategy as a rational process

Underpinning the strategic planning approach is the belief that managers can and do operate in a logical, rational manner when making organizational decisions and when constructing strategies. This acceptance of rationality is underpinned by a number of further assumptions. First, that the external environment is sufficiently knowable and controllable to be able to predict, with confidence, future developments and thus forecast changes and plan accordingly. Second, that organizational decision-making takes place in an ordered, logical, sequential way, utilizing a range of technologies and tools that assist in each stage of the process. Third, that the organization itself is sufficiently malleable to be modified, adapted and reorganized to suit the needs of the future-directed plan – so that, in Chandler's (1962) famous phrase, 'structure follows strategy'.

Of course, none of this is to assume that the process of planning is not difficult or without challenge and obstacle, but the belief is that if sufficient data is collected and sufficient time is spent analyzing and exhausting all possibilities, then the linear process of strategic planning is possible.

For Mintzberg *et al.* (2009), this attention to, and belief in, rationality was very much a product of the times, in which bureaucracy was developing as a guiding paradigm for managing large-scale organizations. Hierarchy and formal structures and systems were deemed the most appropriate and desirable means of managing the emerging corporation. The success of any such approach necessitated a division of labour that, as we shall see below, required the decoupling of formulation from implementation, with the responsibility for developing strategy resting squarely with those at the very top of the hierarchy.

The CEO as strategy architect

Given the importance afforded to the strategy plan it is also argued that responsibility for constructing strategy should reside at the most senior levels of the organization, namely with the chief executive (CEO) and his or her advisers. Of course, this does not necessarily mean that they are the ones who undertake the research on which the strategy is based. Indeed, in the early 1970s General Electric, for example, had a planning department consisting of over 200 strategic planners for this labour. Rather, what is being argued is that the final decision on which strategy to follow rests with the CEO. Only the CEO, it is argued, has sufficient oversight, knowledge and experience to make those kinds of decisions. There are simply no other actors in the organization with the necessary abilities to undertake this role. Indeed, this is one of the justifications put forward for why we pay CEOs such large salaries – only they can make the big decisions. This emphasis on the CEO also reflects in some ways the historical antecedents of the field: the CEO, a *captain* of industry, likened to the military commander – the lone heroic warrior having to make decisions that will shape the (economic) lives of those under them.

We might go even further back in time and suggest that the 'strategy architect' is a contemporary embodiment of Adam Smith's 'rational economic man'. Hollander (1987 cited in Whittington 2001) argues that the basic principles of strategy, outlined above, are clearly present in Smith's writings in *The Wealth of Nations* (1776/1976). Hollander thus likens the purpose and process of planning to Smith's notion of *prudence*. An idea that captures both 'reason' – or the ability to foresee (forecast) the potential outcomes of decisions made – and 'self-command' – the ability to forgo immediate gratification in return for the promise of greater benefit in the longer term. Thus prudence, enacted by rational economic man, resonates most strongly with our understanding of long-term, rational strategic planning. It is also from Smith that we get that ubiquitous organizational objective 'profit maximization' (Jordi 2010). Maximization becomes a natural progression of the logic of rational man – rationality leads to maximizing efficiency, combined with prudence this allows for the achievement of maximum results, which, in the case of a profit-making enterprise, is witnessed on the bottom line. In this situation, rational economic man maximizes his personal utility (reward) while the firm maximizes its profit. The two are symbiotic.

As Alvesson and Willmott (1996) observe, such positioning of the CEO ascribes to them greater powers to direct the organization and to reap great rewards for doing so. By extension it also stands to reason that if only the few can create the strategy then it falls to the many to enact or implement it, and here we have the third feature underpinning the strategic planning approach.

Separation of implementation from formulation

The third component of the rational planning approach insists that the act of constructing, or *formulating* strategies, needs to be kept separate from the enacting, or *implementation*, of strategy. Thus, it is suggested, there are those in the organization with the necessary skills and abilities to make the plans, and there are others who are better placed to carry them out. In this sense we can draw a direct line from early classical management theory to the main tenets of contemporary strategic management.

For example, we can see a corresponding logic in Fredrick Winslow Taylor's notion of scientific management. For Taylor (1916), humanity could be systematically divided into two classes. A small number were seen to have the capacity to act as minds, 'scientifically' conceiving of production processes, strategic plans, and so on, while the majority would merely play out, as 'hands'; the roles written for them by the minds. The CEO and senior managers as minds is a pervasive aspect of the rational planning approach. Clegg *et al.* (2004) observe that such a distinction maintains the 'Cartesian split between the intelligible mind and the dumb body that has to be (in)formed' (p. 24).

Equally, Henri Fayol (1949) advocated that forecasting and planning were essential management functions in ensuring that an organization attained its objectives. Fayol (1841–1925), who rose through the ranks to become managing director of the French steel company, Commentry, Fourchambault and Decazeville, advocated 14 principles of management, later recorded in the English translation of his 1916 article 'Administration industrielle et générale' as the book *General and Industrial Administration*. These principles were: 'division of work; authority; discipline; unity of command; unity of direction; subordination of individual interests to the general interests; remuneration; centralization; scalar chain; order; equity; stability of tenure of personnel; initiative; and esprit de corps' (Pryor and Taneja 2010: 490). In addition, he identified five functions of management – functions that underpin the strategic planning approach. These were: planning, organizing, coordination, command and control.

What is persuasive about the contribution of Fayol in particular is that his ideas were not a result of academic study or analysis but of actual managerial experience. For example, the importance of the need for ever-present authority or 'command' was perhaps informed by experiences such as when he was working in the Commentary mine and observed that all work had to stop when a horse working in a pit broke its leg. The absence of a replacement horse came about because no one present felt they had the authority to act, even though all knew the simple solution to the halt in productivity (Wren 2001).

Unlike Taylor, Fayol also appeared to have more appreciation for the quality of employees and saw them as more than mere factors of production responding to monetary gain. He noted that 'of two organizations similar in appearance, one may be excellent, the other bad, depending on the personal qualities of those who compose them'

(Fayol 1949: 57). These underlying assumptions have resulted in the construction of a plethora of different processes, models and frameworks for devising strategic plans, as we shall go on to see.

Strategic planning: tools and techniques

There are literally hundreds of different strategic planning models, frameworks and processes. While each reflects the context for which it was written: for a particular firm; by a particular firm; for an academic textbook; by a consultancy; etc., most still resonate with the three basic principles outlined above. In addition, it is also important to recognize that there are multiple levels of planning that can take place in any one organization, and that these exist in a hierarchical structure.

Hierarchy of plans

Hofer and Schendel (1978) identified three levels of strategic planning that still constitute the core of the strategy hierarchy to this day. These levels are:

- corporate-level strategy;
- business-level strategy;
- functional-level strategy.

Corporate-level strategy is concerned primarily with how to manage a multi-business firm and thus addresses issues such as resource allocation and investment decisions. It also addresses the more fundamental question of 'what set of businesses should we be in?' (ibid.: 27). This guiding question will then drive growth, acquisition and resource allocation decisions (we will discuss this level of strategy in more detail in Chapter 5). Business-level strategy, sometimes referred to as competitive strategy, is that which occurs at the business unit level and addresses issues of competition and how to compete in a certain market or industry (we will discuss this level of strategy in more detail in Chapter 6 and 7). Functional-level strategy reflects the activities of each group, division or area of specialism within the business unit. Thus, there will be financial strategies, marketing strategies, product strategies, and so on. In a sense, this level constitutes the strategies of each department, or function, in the business unit. These strategies exist in a hierarchy, with each constrained by the one above resulting in a pyramid-type structure in which business-level strategies are informed by corporate-level strategy and functional strategies are informed by business-level strategy. Of course, this is not to suggest there are not times when strategy is driven from the bottom up, but as a theoretical construct, the relationship is assumed to be top down. Having distinguished these levels, let us now consider the main components of an ideal-type strategic plan.

A strategic planning model

Broadly speaking, the typical strategic planning process consists of five key stages:

1   Defining the organizational goals or objectives (often referred to in contemporary language as a mission or vision);

2   Situational analysis – an audit of the internal and external environments in order to achieve some variation of a SWOT analysis;
3   Identification and analysis of alternative courses of actions – achieved through a strategic decision-making process;
4   Formulating the strategy in the form of a plan or policy document;
5   Implementation.

In this model of strategy formulation, 'vision' and 'mission' are positioned as super-ordinate to the definition of more specific goals and objectives. Such objectives inform, and are informed by, a type of situation analysis in which the external and internal environment are made knowable and manageable – perhaps the best-known example of this is the SWOT model. Once the audit has been undertaken, alternative courses of action can then be weighed against one another and the best chosen, via a process of rational decision-making. This is the standard 'textbook' model of strategic planning. Let us look at each stage in turn.

Vision and mission

A typical strategy plan frequently begins with the articulation, revision, or refinement of an overall goal or objective for the organization, commonly referred to today as a mission statement or vision. Below are a few examples of missions and visions (although most will have likely changed by the time you read this – itself an indication of their transient nature):

- Starbucks: To inspire and nurture the human spirit – one person, one cup and one neighbourhood at a time.
- Microsoft: To enable people and businesses throughout the world to realize their full potential.
- Shell: To continuously deliver shareholder value by manufacturing and supplying oil products and services that satisfy the needs of our customers; constantly achieving operational excellence; conducting our business in a safe, environmentally sustainable and economically optimum manner; employing a diverse, innovative and results-orientated team motivated to deliver excellence.

In trying to distinguish mission from vision (although the terms are frequently used interchangeably) we might note the way in which *vision* (Starbucks and Microsoft) attempts to capture a romantic, inspirational, even fantastical expression of the organization's desired purpose, whereas a *mission*, or *mission statement* (Shell) is far more rational, detailed, conservative even.

However, there are important distinctions to be made between visions and missions and it is helpful to understand how they can operate in mutually reinforcing ways. For Cummings and Davies (1994), mission and vision serve complementary roles, with a mission statement articulating current behaviours and vision providing a future-looking aspiration:

> A mission empowers through a force which casts or steers the individual or group into the future in a particular direction. A vision empowers through the provision of knowledge or expectation about the future which can be aimed for, a future state

which becomes more known, and more 'real' in the present, and hence more likely to be achieved in the future, because it has been envisaged.

(Cummings and Davies 1994: 147–8)

Collins and Porras (1991) share a belief in the complimentary nature of vision and mission. However, they warn against some of the hyperbole around the language through which they are frequently conveyed. After all, how do you know if you are truly nurturing the human spirit or allowing people to realize their full potential?

For Collins and Porras, a vision should be more than just a clever use of words or an empty promise. For a vision to truly reflect the organization's intent it should explain *why* the organization exists and what *purpose* it serves. In doing so, the goal of the vision, as a form of strategy, is to provide something of a *guiding philosophy* that directs the organization's activities: something to inspire and channel commitment. Research seems to suggest that visions are most frequently realized when they have grown up with the organization and are a reflection of the founder's initial purpose or intent. As an example, we might claim that the business model that governs the activities of Virgin can be directly linked to the belief, vision and mission of its founder, Richard Branson. Mission, they go on to suggest, constitutes an articulation of the *tangible goals* for the organization: the mission must constitute a 'vivid description' that brings the vision to life through the articulation of achievements that can be measured, quantified and achieved.

While such a notion has some validity, Campbell and Nash (1992) warn that where there is little correlation between the mission of the organization and the actual attitudes, behaviours and beliefs of those that inhabit it, the stated mission is likely to fail in its intent. Or, perhaps more seriously, act as a demotivating force in the organization – especially when it is felt not to accord with the experiences of those who give their labour for the organization. Such practices then come to be seen as yet one more example of how 'out of touch' management really are.

Unfortunately, it is all too easy for such statements of intent to degenerate into the empty rhetoric and hubris of self-justification. This, of course, is strategy at its worst. However, at its best it provides something of a soul for the corporation and a set of ideals and a lens through which all decisions should be taken.

Once the overall goals have been articulated, the next stage in the sequential process of strategic planning is to undertake an audit of the external and internal environment: the outcome of which will serve as the basis for the development of potential future strategic options. In this regard, SWOT is perhaps the most familiar tool of choice.

Situation analysis (SWOT)

Before Porter came along with his five forces framework of industry analysis, the most commonly employed tool for analysing the environment was the SWOT model: a situational analysis tool that seeks to capture the internal environment by assessing the organization's strengths and weaknesses and the external environment by surveying possible opportunities and threats. While the origins of the SWOT idea appear shrouded in mystery, it came to prominence in the 1960s when its underlying message formed part of the central theme in one of the earliest strategy textbooks, Learned *et al.*'s *Business Policy: Text and Cases* (1965).

At its core is a very straightforward and rational proposition, namely that each organization has certain *strengths* on which to build a potential competitive advantage: this advantage can be pursued by identifying those *opportunities* in the marketplace through which its strengths can be exploited. Equally, every organization has certain *weaknesses*, vulnerabilities that it needs to strengthen or defend. These weaknesses can be exploited by *threats* in the marketplace, if not addressed. Thus, strategy should develop by pursuing those opportunities in the external environment that are uniquely exploitable by its internal strengths while simultaneously guarding against those external threats that are likely to impinge upon its internal weaknesses.

On the surface, SWOT analysis seems to provide an entirely sensible approach to strategy formulation and its apparent simplicity and rationality explains much of its immense appeal and popularity. In practice, however, the approach is far from simple and clear cut. As Lilley (2009) notes, questions such as 'Which strength is strongest?' and 'Which opportunity is most inviting?' are far from easy to answer, with attempts to quantify elements often degenerating more into arguments about technique than insights into competitive advantage. Moreover, much of the research on the process of conducting SWOT analysis tends to reveal that the audit itself is typically skewed to over-estimating the organization's strengths and downplaying its weaknesses. Indeed, the strategy workshops and away days in which this kind of activity is often undertaken can become rather heated, as competing departmental heads are quick to identify the weaknesses of others (Magretta 2012).

Hill and Westbrook (1997) suggest that despite inherent limitations and the subsequent introduction of more sophisticated and complex tools of situational analysis, the continuing popularity of SWOT may rest on its ease of use and straightforward format and as such, commonly features as an icebreaker exercise at the beginning of consultancy interventions.

The rational decision model

Once a situation analysis has been undertaken it is then necessary to begin to consider possible future directions for the organization. The dominant model of decision-making advocated in this regard is the rational model. The rational model of decision-making, developed independently of the strategy literature, is nonetheless based on a number of similar assumptions. First, it assumes a clearly defined goal or objective has been articulated, and thus the decision-making process serves to consider a number of alternative means of realizing that goal. Second, decisions are based on quantifiable data that has been collected and deemed accurate and reliable (as opposed to relying on intuition, feeling, hearsay or emotion). Third, each alternative solution can be considered for its merits (outwith the politics of organizational life) and an optimal course of action taken.

Much of the perceived value of the rational decision-making model may stem from the way in which it draws from the same theoretical underpinnings as the planning processes outlined above. Namely, from classical management and economic theory, especially in terms of the notion of a world populated by individuals 'rationally' seeking maximum rewards, using the best methods to achieve them: that is, profit or 'utility' maximization through choice optimization, as per 'economic man'. It also treats rationality as a property of the organization, as something it has 'rather than an outcome of a purposive work undertaken by actors inside the organization' (Cabantous *et al.* 2010: 1532).

Thus, the process of decision-making appears as follows:

- problem recognition;
- identification of alternative choice options;

- evaluation of alternative choice options (applying rational choice criteria);
- selection of optimal choice option;

Again, while based on rational and seemingly straightforward assumptions, Lilley (2009) draws attention to the absence of politics and tactics in the process of rational decision-making. Specifically, he draws attention to the context of the decision episode, asking questions such as how was the organizational agenda set that allowed these specific choice options to emerge? What other options were discounted in advance and left off the agenda, and why? Who stands to gain and lose from the optimal choice option and what are the implications of this? Who supplied the information on which the choice options were constructed and on which they will be evaluated? In this regard, 'strategic decision making is "channeled and restricted by the process of non-decision making"' (Crenson, 1971: 178, cited in Carter *et al.* 2010: 585)

However, putting this aside for a moment as rationalists are wont to do, if we assume the optimal decision can be arrived at, or at least played out to seem that way, the final stage in the strategy process sees the preferred strategic option written up as an executable plan on which the future of the organization rests. That is, until the next planning cycle.

What value strategic planning?

So does strategic planning actually work? In the sense that it is an approach that dominates the mainstream literature and indeed the talk of practising managers then we might be inclined to say yes. Of course, that something is widely used does not necessarily mean that it works. Indeed, the popularity of strategic planning might partially be accounted for by its overt simplicity and intuitive appeal – for practising managers calculated rational planning promises a systematic, comprehensive and ostensibly practical approach to formulating strategy. So what are the benefits of such an approach?

The benefits of planning

De Wit and Meyer (2010) identify six benefits of strategic planning. They suggest that planning can provide:

1. direction;
2. programming;
3. optimization;
4. coordination;
5. formalization and differentiation;
6. long-term thinking and commitment.

First, planning can provide the organization with a clearly articulated *direction*, a compass and detailed instructions that allow for the successful navigation from A to B. Without direction, supporters of the approach suggest, the organization may drift (Johnson 1992) off course, sailing into uncharted waters for which it has neither compass nor navigational chart. Setting a clear direction focuses the organization on a narrowly defined path, which, in turn, creates a second benefit of planning: it allows for *programming*. That is, the organization itself can be configured in order to implement the plan: a structure can be chosen, tasks assigned, roles defined, budgets allocated, objectives set, and so on. It is also assumed that the programming will be optimized toward realizing the tangible objectives of the plan. As we know, organizations operate in a condition of resource scarcity and there is an opportunity cost in every decision made. Thus, by focusing all organizational effort in one direction, for which the organization has been suitably programmed, there is (in theory) an *optimization* of that effort.

Planning also assists with the complex task of coordinating the activities of the organization: the larger the organization or the more complex its activities, the greater the need for some kind of *coordination* of effort. A carefully crafted plan can serve as a central point in the coordination of all other organizational activity. Such coordination is also frequently *formalized* through the planning process with those tasked with implementing the plan formally identified. Such formalization also permits *differentiation* – tasks can be defined and allocated and, importantly, accountability can be assigned to those whose position is formally articulated in the plan (department heads, for example, whose budgets are dependent on meeting their objectives, or the sales force who must meet their targets, and so on). Finally, planning, by its very nature, necessitates *long-term commitment*; the cost and resource implications of detailed planning mean that such an exercise cannot be undertaken frequently. As such, many organizations will adopt a planning cycle of perhaps 12 months, 24 months, or even five or ten years. Indeed, we might suggest that the length of the planning cycle is one of its most striking features.

Such perceived tangible benefits make a persuasive case for the value and importance of the plan. There is also, as noted earlier, a simplicity to planning – it is easy to comprehend and while the actual plan may seldom reflect the theoretical constructs on which it is based, the inherent value of having a plan cannot be denied. Moreover, aside from the tangible benefits of the plan (as a product), we might also identify softer benefits derived from the processes of planning. By way of analogy, Pierre Wack (1985a) recounts the fable of the Hungarian army detachment, during World War II, lost somewhere in the Alps, out of food, out of ammunition and near to death in the freezing and inhospitable landscape. Resigned to their fate, they sit down and prepare to die. As they do so, one of the soldiers suddenly discovers a map in his pocket and they use this to successfully navigate their way out of the mountains and back to their base. It is only once they are safe that they realize that the map they had used was of the Pyrenees, not the Alps!

The moral of the story is that even if the map (plan) is not right it can still lead us out of trouble. How? For Wack, the benefits of planning are not (just) in the production of a story (a plan) but in the processes of planning itself – the benefits of organizational members coming together to discuss important issues, taking stock of where the organization currently is and where it wants to be, providing confidence to the organization and its stakeholders that there is a positive future and a consciously considered notion of how to get there.

Whittington (2001) also argues that planning provides a kind of security blanket to the strategist – operating in an environment that is ultimately unknowable, turbulent and chaotic, the plan provides some attempt at establishing order, clarity and structure. Even if it is not seen through to its eventual goal – how many plans really are? – the process of formulating it offers benefit nonetheless. In this regard, Clegg *et al.* (2010) prefer to think of strategies as symbolic devices that are effective precisely because they constitute forms of shared sense-making. The plans foster commitment and support and a sense of shared responsibility. For Carter and colleagues, citing Ambrose Bierce, to plan is to 'bother about the best method of accomplishing an accidental result' (Carter *et al.* 2008: 89). This best method they argue is one that brings people together to think about where the organization is, where it has been and where it wants to go. In this regard 'strategy motivates and animates an organization' (ibid.).

Summary

In this chapter we have outlined the dominant approach to strategy-making. As a plan, strategy is most readily conceived of as a deliberate, conscious, intentional, sequential process out of which emerge detailed and articulate roadmaps that direct the future development of the organization. Such plans should be constructed by those at the very top of the organization (the minds) and implemented by the rest (the bodies). This is not to deny that planning, as an activity, does not take place at all levels, but rather that it exists in a hierarchy in which all plans feed into, and become subordinate to those constructed by the strategy architect, the CEO. While there are numerous examples, the proto-typical planning model consists of a sequential process, typically consisting of goal-setting, followed by some kind of situational analysis, and formal rational decision-making processes. There are numerous benefits in adopting such an approach to strategy both in terms of what the plan can produce but also in the form of softer benefits derived from the process of planning and the coming together of organizational members to discuss issues of importance. However, when conceived of as a process, we might argue that the outcome (the plan) becomes less important than the process of getting there. This will be the topic of our next chapter

When evaluating the contribution and importance of strategic planning, it is also important to remember the context in which strategic planning developed. The 1950s and early 1960s was a period of stability and growth in the US with demand outstripping supply in many industries. Thus it was possible to undertake, with some confidence, long-range planning. Moreover, as Fuller (1996) rightly notes, this was also a period before the large-scale diversification wave that occurred in the late 1960s and 1970s and as such many firms were still single structures and, consequently, most transactions were internal, thus providing a degree of knowability and predictability. However, against this, a view of strategy as an emergent process of adaptive responsiveness was gaining more popularity.

4 Strategy by design and an emergent critique (part 2)

Introduction

In the previous chapter we outlined the dominant perspective in the strategy literature – strategy as a deliberate, rational planning process. We identified the main components of the planning process and acknowledged its tangible and softer benefits. Despite its ubiquity however we should not assume that planning is the only, or even the best, way of *doing strategy*. Henry Mintzberg (1994), a prominent critic of strategic planning, suggests that not only is planning not the best way to *do* strategy but that it rests on a number of underlying assumptions that do not stand up to closer scrutiny. Moreover, he argues that the theory and rhetoric of planning does not accord with the lived experience of organizational life.

In this chapter we begin by briefly outlining Mintzberg's critique of strategic planning before moving on to look at an alternative reading of strategy – strategy as an emergent process of learning and crafting. As in the previous chapter we consider the underlying assumptions on which this approach is based and then go on to outline some of the main methods it advocates. We finish by introducing scenario planning as something of a midway point between planned and emergent strategy – a bridge, if you will, that draws on the best of both and has found increased popularity in recent years.

Henry Mintzberg and the three fallacies of strategic planning

Henry Mintzberg, a professor of Management Studies at McGraw University in Montreal, Quebec, has written extensively on issues of management, strategy and leadership. Among his many contributions to the field of strategic management, Mintzberg has been one of the most vocal critics of the planning approach. He has challenged not only the preferred methods of the approach but also the underlying assumptions on which they are based. In his book, *The Fall and Rise of Strategic Planning* (1994), Mintzberg identifies what he sees as the three great fallacies of strategic planning:

- the fallacy of predetermination;
- the fallacy of detachment of formulation from implementation;
- the fallacy of formalization.

In brief, Mintzberg first suggests that there is a *fallacy of predetermination* in strategic planning. He argues that while certain repetitive patterns may be reasonably anticipated and planned for – seasons, cycles and fixed events; for example, think of the way western confectionery manufacturers plan to scale up production in the lead-up to Easter and Christmas – the wider environment itself cannot easily be forecasted and predicted in the way suggested by the planning approach. Mintzberg suggests that this was likely always the case but, under the conditions of contemporary global capitalism, marked by 'liberalized markets, increasingly demanding customers, expanding sources of knowledge, revolutionary advances in information technology, drastically shortened time lines, and the empowerment of individual decision-makers' (Fuller 1996: 22), such attempts at prediction become even more redundant, the external environment is just too dynamic, turbulent and chaotic to anticipate with accuracy.

Therefore, to adopt an approach to strategy that is predicated precisely on the notion that the future is knowable makes the product of the strategic planning process redundant – it will not survive the first encounter with the marketplace. In short, Mintzberg argues that there is neither the stability nor predictability inherent in the external environment to enable precise and deliberate planning. For Mintzberg, strategy is a much more dynamic process, one associated with change, uncertainty and pragmatic adaptation to environmental factors: 'Strategies are not developed on schedule, immaculately conceived. They can appear at any time and at any place in the organization, typically through processes of informal learning more than ones of formal planning' (Mintzberg 1994: 16).

Second, due to the dynamic nature of both the external environment and the strategy process itself, the *detachment of formulation from implementation* is planning's second great fallacy. That strategy needs to be a responsive process and practice means that it needs to take place at all levels in the organization. From the rarefied and detached position of the CEO, strategy is little more than a series of numerical reports, targets and forecasts, or what McKinlay *et al.* (2010) refer to as 'management at a distance' but lower down the organization, at the 'coalface', strategy is about interaction with customers, buyers and competitors on a daily basis. It is about adapting and modifying *ploys* in order to address yet another unforeseen circumstance or opportunity. Thus, strategy is more inductive than deductive. For this reason, Mintzberg argues, it is crucial that those lower down the organization be involved in the strategy process as they are best placed to respond to the dynamic and uncertain environment – implementation and formulation need to be intertwined in processes of strategic interaction.

Not only that, but the unidirectional flow of strategic planning ignores the reality of organizational life. Not only does such an assumption fail to take into account the complex feedback processes through which implementation feeds back into later rounds of formulation (Clegg *et al.* 2004) but it also fails to consider the means by which implementation is enacted and the extent to which those tasked with implementing a strategy that they have been handed, often without their input, will respond to that strategy. This, Clegg *et al.* (2004) maintain, remains one of the key failings in both the theory and practice of much strategic management – the Cartesian split of mind and body – interpreted as managers and workers, or formulators and implementers respectively.

Third, in order to enable a bold reimagining of strategy-making, organizations need to relinquish the pursuit of *formalization*. Mintzberg argues that strategic planning's obsession with formalization means that little time or effort is given to the creation of strategies themselves: 'none of those fancy planning charts ever contained a single box that explained how strategy is actually to be created' (1994: 18). In other words, by seeking to formalize what are inherently dynamic, creative and emergent processes, you undermine the very basis on which strategy can achieve real organizational success. Innovation, Mintzberg says, cannot be institutionalized.

This failure of strategic planning was most explicitly felt at the great General Electric, which had been the pioneer of strategic planning in the 1960s and 1970s and makes for a perfect case study in the excesses of formalization and hard data. As retold by Whittington (2001), GE was especially hard hit by the recession of the 1980s and was experiencing a period of slow growth. In order to turn the company around, a new CEO, Jack Welch, was appointed. What Welch found at GE horrified him. The strategic planning department had grown so large and become so dependent on quantifying hard data that it was regularly pushing out daily reports on individual businesses 12 feet high. Welch, who came to be known by the nickname Neutron Jack, undertook a company-wide rationalizing programme in order to reduce the dependence on strategic planning and instead introduced a simple and powerful policy that required each GE business to be number 1 or number 2 in its industry or else withdraw. This simple policy instituted a powerful new strategic direction at GE and, in the process saw it shed over 25 per cent of the workforce, some 100,000 staff in total (Kaplan 2013b).

These three fallacies led Mintzberg to proclaim the great fallacy of strategic planning itself. In its place, Mintzberg favours an approach to strategy based more on learning and emergent patterns of organizational activity. Thus, we can read Mintzberg's critique as a primer for his own preferred approach to strategy. In this respect, Mintzberg (1994: 18–9) makes the following observations about the strategy process:

- Strategy formation must draw on all kinds of informational inputs, many of them non-quantifiable and accessible only to strategists who are connected rather than detached.
- The dynamics of the context have consistently blocked any efforts to force the process into a predetermined schedule, or onto a predetermined track.
- Strategies inevitably exhibit some emergent qualities, and even when largely deliberate, they often appear less formally planned than informally visionary. And learning, in the form of fits and starts, discoveries based on serendipitous events, and the recognition of unexpected patterns, inevitably plays a key role, if not the key role, in the development of strategies that are novel.
- As such, the strategy process requires insight, creativity, and synthesis, all the things that formalization discourages.

In place of detailed rational planning, Mintzberg advocates what he terms an 'emergent' strategy approach, also sometimes known as the learning approach. Let us look at this in more detail.

The emergence of the learning approach

In the same way that the planning perspective is informed by a set of underlying assumptions drawn from a broader disciplinary heritage, much the same can be said of the emergent/learning approach. Below we shall briefly outline some of the key contributions that underpin the idea of strategy as an emergent process of learning and adaptation.

Bounded rationality

Whereas the planning perspective drew its influence primarily through research from Harvard Business School, the learning perspective takes many of its key contributions from the Carnegie School, in particular from the works of Herbert Simon, Richard Cyert and James March (Whittington 2001). From this tradition, the first underlying assumption of the learning approach is one that challenges planning's belief in rational economic man. From the learning perspective, rational economic man is a fiction, as is the notion of perfect rationality on which strategic planning is based. Instead, according to Cyert and March (1956), we are always *boundedly* rational. In other words, we do not have (or we lack the ability to tap into) the cognitive capacity to absorb and process a perfect amount of information. Instead, we can only ever consider a relatively small number of pieces of information at any one time. Moreover, we will interpret this information in very different ways, depending on our subjective bias and the position from which we read the information: thus, our decision-making is constrained by the amount of information we can absorb and through the bias in our interpretation of that information. Such inherent limitations will therefore always restrict and influence decision-making processes in a way that move us away from the ideal of the rational model.

'Satisficing' behaviour

Relatedly, Simon (1960) challenges the perceived notion of prudence that underpins strategic planning. In Simon's terms we seldom if ever pursue or enact maximizing behaviours. Indeed, the idea of maximizing may itself be a misnomer – after all what, in real terms constitute the maximum? Is it really a finite quantity? Instead Simon coins the term 'satisficing' to reflect what he sees as the more common form of human decision-making. Satisficing is a behaviour that seeks both to *satisfy* and to *suffice*. To put it more simply, most of the time we compromise – we are constrained by factors such as time, money and our own bounded rationality and thus, more often than not, we will pursue an outcome, a decision, a goal that satisfices, within the limitations of the context in which the behaviour is enacted.

The idea that we satisfice, within the confines of bounded rationality, paints a portrait of organizational life that is far less structured, coherent and ordered than the planning approach would have us believe. Indeed, we might better conceive of strategy-making as a process of muddling through.

Disjointed incrementalism: 'muddling through'

A third key influence on the learning approach has been the work of Charles Lindblom, a political science professor at Yale University. In 1959, Lindblom wrote a seminal article on policy- (strategy-) making in government. Entitled 'The Science of Muddling Through' (1959/1990), Lindblom challenged the rational, ordered view of decision making that we outlined in the previous chapter. In observing the ways in which laws get made, Lindblom witnessed organizational decision-making marked by messy processes of negotiation, bargaining, satisficing and lobbying, of power games and political wrangling. Absent were the ordered sequential processes proposed by the rationalists, and in their place were substituted organizational actors with bounded rationality, working to tight deadlines in environments of confusion, conflict and complexity. Thus, policy-makers seek to muddle through and produce satisficing results.

In directly challenging the basic assumptions of rational decision-making, Lindblom's ideas found a great deal of support among managers and decision-makers in a wide range of organizational contexts, many of whom could readily identify with the practices he described. Moreover, the work of Lindblom and other political scientists at this time also began to draw attention to the political nature of organizations themselves (Eisenhardt and Zbarack 1992: 22–3). From such a perspective organizations do not display the unitarist characteristics so frequently suggested in the mainstream literature, nor the calculating, maximizing characteristics of the rationalists. Rather, organizations are seen as loose assemblages of groups with different interest and demands, competing with each other for resources, influence and attention, and in which conflict is a regular feature of everyday life. From this perspective strategies emerge not through rational processes but 'as an outcome of transactions of power and influence' (Narayanan and Fahey 1982: 27) in which the most powerful, which do not always equate with the most senior, frequently see their wishes, decisions or preferences win out against any pretence at the pursuit of an 'optimal' decision. In this regard, tactical behaviours, coalition-forming, bargaining and lobbying and the full array of political manoeuvering become key practices through which decision-making takes place (Eisenhardt and Zbarack 1992). While the political nature of organizations has seldom featured in the mainstream strategy literature, Lindblom's notion of incrementalism was subsequently developed by James Brian Quinn, who contributes the notion of logical incrementalism.

Logical incrementalsim

For Quinn (1980) Lindlom's idea of incrementalism in decision-making and policy development resonated with his understanding of the processes of formulating business strategy. However, he was less inclined to accept the more disjointed aspect of Lindblom's thesis. He resisted the belief that organizational decision-making was as chaotic and fragmented as Lindblom suggests. Instead, Quinn sees the process of strategy-making as one underpinned by a certain logic while retaining an incremental nature. To elaborate this claim he introduced the notion of strategy *subsystems*. A strategy subsystem is an activity set tasked with dealing with a particular strategic problem – an acquisition, a restructuring programme, new product development, or such like. Each subsystem, he suggests, works in an orderly and disciplined way toward reaching its goal. However, as each subsystem is somewhat independent of the others, it is the task of senior management not to control these activities but to link them together in some kind of coherent manner. It is out of this, sometimes opportunistic, and certainly incremental attempt to link organizational activities together, Quinn suggests, that strategies emerge:

> The real strategy tends to evolve as internal decisions and external events flow together to create a new, widely shared consensus for action among key members of the top management team. In well-run organizations, managers pro-actively guide these streams of actions and events incrementally toward conscious strategies.
>
> (Quinn 1980: 15)

Drawing on this rich and detailed literature from economics, psychology and political science, Mintzberg proposes an alternative view of strategy. In opposition to strategy as plan he advocates strategy as emergent pattern of behaviour. Mintzberg, with Waters (1985), distinguishes the two approaches by arguing that strategy as plan focuses on control whereas strategy as pattern focuses on learning:

> Emergent strategy does not mean management is out of control, only – in some cases at least – that it is open, flexible and responsive, in other words, willing to learn. Such behaviour is especially important when an environment is too unstable or complex to comprehend, or too imposing to defy. Openness to such emergent strategy enables management to act before everything is fully understood – to respond to an evolving reality rather than having to focus on a stable fantasy.
> (Mintzberg and Waters 1985: 127)

Referring to it as a *dwelling* mode of strategy-making, Chia and Rasche see the key characteristics of the emergent perspective as pertaining to a view of the organization in which the complexity of organizational life is acknowledged and in which strategic decision-making is seen as a process of 'wayfinding' in which individuals 'create action pathways that radiate outwards from their concrete existential situations' (Chia and Rasche 2010: 38). There is no 'bird's-eye' view or ivory tower from which a situation can be witnessed and rationally described and resolved. Organizations are complex systems that intersect in numerous and overlapping ways such that competing understandings of what the organization is and what its purpose should be develop in different contexts, situations and time frames.

Chia and Rasche (2010: 39) contrast the dwelling approach with the planned approach, which they term the *building* mode, in the following ways:

Table 4.1 Building and dwelling worldviews

Building worldview	Dwelling worldview
Actors are self-conscious, intentional and self-motivated	Actors are a non-deliberate, relationally constituted nexus of social activities
Actions are guided by predefined goals directing efforts towards outcomes – purposeful action	Actions are directed towards overcoming immediate impediment – purposive practical coping
Consistency of action assumed to be ordered by deliberate intent	Consistency of action assumed to be ordered by a modus operandi – an internalized disposition

If we subscribe to the views outlined above – that decision-makers are boundedly rational and have limited mental capacity to absorb information – then it is little more than common sense to suggest that their strategic decision-making will be increasingly restricted the further removed they are from the front line of the business. Indeed, in the large multinational conglomerate organization, strategies may appear as little more than a series of numerical reports by the time they reach the CEO's office. Thus, it is not unreasonable to suggest, so say proponents of the emergent perspective, that those lower down the organization, closer to the marketplace, may have deeper and more nuanced understandings of competitive-level strategy. As Andersen and Nielsen (2009: 97) rightly observe: 'lower-level responsive initiatives and middle management participation in important decisions, can generate and mobilize an abundance of relevant insights. The embedded emergent activities can generate ideas and experimentation with new approaches that may turn into viable alternative business opportunities.'

What therefore emerges is the need to both recognize and act on the tacit knowledge found in every organization. Knowledge that is 'acquired through living within and becoming intimately acquainted with local conditions "on the ground", and not from some detached observer's point of view' (Chia and Rasche 2010: 39).

When conceived of in this way, strategies can emerge from the most mundane and insignificant occurrences. For example, let us consider one of the most ubiquitous of office stationery items: the Post-it note. It is such a simple concept it is hardly worthy of mention until we consider the millions of dollars in revenue it has earned its parent, 3M, and the serendipitous sequence of events that led to its coming into being. As retold by Tsoukas (2010), a 3M research scientist by the name of Spencer Silver was working on a new form of adhesive gel for use on sticky tape. However, he consistently found the gel to be too weak to bind. Over the next five years he discussed the gel's qualities with colleagues but none could think up a use for it. Meanwhile, another 3M researcher, Art Fry, was having problems of his own. A member of his local church choir, Fry was continually frustrated that the paper bookmarks he inserted into his hymnal kept falling out every time he opened the book. A happen-by-chance meeting between the two employees, at which Fry mentioned his problem, led Silver to make the link and develop an adhesive-based bookmark for Fry: today we call it the Post-it note. No rational brainstorming session could provide a use for the gel. Rather, a solution emerged independently of any formal process.

So we are presented above with a seemingly accurate portrayal of organizational life, not one characterized by the ordered rationality that the strategic planning approach would have us believe but one in which we seek to muddle through, constrained by our bounded rationality, in pursuit of satisficing solutions. The question then presents itself: how do you formulate a strategy based on such ideas?

Formulating an emergent strategy

Given the very premise on which the emergent perspective rests, it is stating little more than the obvious to say that there are limited 'tools and techniques' with which to enact this kind of approach to strategy – it is very difficult to anticipate the unknowable – and to think otherwise implies a preference for the logic of the planning approach. Instead, the emergent approach advocates a series of practices, structures and principles that can help *facilitate* learning and enable the organization to capitalize on emergent opportunities for strategy development. Let us look at some of these in more detail.

The crafting metaphor

Mintzberg employs the notion of crafting (strategy as an art) to elaborate his view of strategy as an emergent pattern. He evokes the image of the potter sitting at the wheel sculpting, moulding and shaping clay into a particular form. Repeatedly producing what appear to be the same object – a cup, a bowl, a jar – but each is unique, a subtle difference informed by the combination of clay, potter and wheel at any one moment in time. For Mintzberg the process of strategy creation follows a similar logic. It is the outcome of the idiosyncratic forces at play within and outwith the organization at any one point in its history:

At work, the potter sits before a lump of clay on the wheel. Her mind is on the clay, but she is also aware of sitting between her past experiences and her future prospects. She knows exactly what has and has not worked for her in the past. She has an intimate knowledge of her work, her capabilities, and her markets. As a craftsman, she senses rather than analyzes these things; her knowledge is 'tacit!' All these things are working in her mind as her hands are working the clay. The product that emerges on the wheel is likely to be in the tradition of her past work, but she may break away and embark on a new direction. Even so, the past is no less present, projecting itself into the future.

(Mintzberg 1987c: 66)

Putting this metaphor into the language and practice of business strategy, Whittington (2001) suggests that what is required is a view of strategy as a 'continuous and adaptive process, with formation and implementation inextricably entangled' (Whittington 2001: 23). Let us take for example the case of the development of the collection of production systems such as just-in-time production, lean production, batch production and short cycle runs that constitute what is sometimes referred to as the Toyota Production System (van Driel and Dolfsma 2009). There are many myths surrounding the development of these production methods but in an attempt to put the pieces of the puzzle together van Driel and Dolfsma (2009) chart a historical course through the sequence of events that led to the gradual adoption of these practices and processes by Toyota from the 1950s. What they uncover is that it was not a rational, detailed and well-thought out in advance road map focused on efficiency and best practice but rather an adaptive response to external forces that drove Toyota to adopt such methods, not for competitive advantage but primarily for survival. As they retell it, van Driel and Dolfsma suggest that by the late 1940s, despite experiments in lean production techniques Toyota found itself approaching bankruptcy. Anti-inflation measures introduced by the Japanese government led to a downturn in the economy and the purchase of cars dropped dramatically. Toyota found itself with large quantities of unsold stock and a shortage of capital. By 1950 it had dropped production to just 300 cars per annum, down from 3,900 in 1947. Having already undertaken significant redundancies and now facing possible bankruptcy, Toyota was saved by the most unlikely of events, the Korean War. The US military placed orders for large quantities of military trucks and other vehicles from the nearby Japanese car manufacturers to reduce shipping costs. Toyota won a contract but now had the problem of how to meet this order with a significantly reduced workforce; the answer was to be found in lean batch production systems. It was this unanticipated emergent event that both saved Toyota and led it towards its place in history for the development of the Toyota Production System: a system that would, throughout the 1970s and 1980s, influence manufacturing practices across industries and across the globe and would be seen as a root cause of Japanese economic ascendency. Toyota had learnt about the failures of overstocking and had been able to adapt and respond to an emergent business opportunity.

The organization as garbage can

Against the rational model of decision-making outlined in the previous chapter, proponents of the emergent perspective also draw our attention to an alternative model of how decision-making often takes place in organizational settings. Indeed, Whittington (2001) notes that decisions often just 'happen' rather than being consciously 'taken'. To expand this view, the garbage-can model of decision-making is a useful conceptual frame. First introduced by Cohen et al. in 1972, the garbage-can model suggests that decisions occur when four variable, or independent streams, come into contact. These four streams are:

- problems – issues that need attention;
- solutions – answers looking for problems;
- choice opportunities – occasions that call for a decision;
- participants – organizational actors who may possess problems or solutions.

Put crudely, the organization is like a garbage can because each of the four streams above are thrown into the mix, shaken around and what falls out are decisions. Let us revisit the invention of the Post-it note as an example of a garbage-can decision:

- Participants: our two participants are Steven Silver and Art Fry whose connection is that they both worked for 3M.
- Problem: Art Fry had a problem in that he couldn't get his paper bookmarks to 'stick' in his hymnal.
- Solution: Silver had a solution – a mild adhesive gel – but no problem to solve.
- Choice opportunities: the chance meeting between the two allowed for a decision to be made using an existing solution for a current problem.

Of course, this kind of post hoc explanation suffers the same sort of failings as more 'rational' explanations of how the Post-it note came about, but perhaps most relevant to take away from this example is the element of chance and ambiguity around decision-making. It was certainly the case that Silver had been playing around with his adhesive gel for several years, unable to come up with a rationally informed use for it. His boundedly rational mind was unable to connect the gel to the type of problem Fry was having. It was only in that chance encounter, as the final stage in a 'confluence of events' (Eisenhardt and Zbaracki 1992: 27) that a use was found, a decision made and a new product introduced. Of course, leaving everything to chance would be a high-risk strategy indeed. Nor would we assume that all decision-making occurs in this unstructured way, but the garbage-can model does at least move us a step closer to recognizing the human aspect of organizational life and a step further away from the overly formulaic beliefs of the planning perspective with its 'cold "economic man" who acts as a robot' (Cabantous and Gond 2011: 575). Of course, there is still a need to manage the garbage can. The umbrella strategy offers one approach to doing so.

Umbrella strategies

Mintzberg and other proponents of the emergent view do not advocate an 'anything goes' approach to strategy – pushed to its extreme a purely emergent approach to strategy is no more useful or feasible that one than is pursued on the basis of perfectly rational decision-making. As Mintzberg says,

> In practice, of course, all strategy making walks on two feet, one deliberate, the other emergent ... there is no such thing as a purely deliberate strategy or a purely emergent one. ... Thus deliberate and emergent strategy form the end points of a

continuum along which the strategies that are crafted in the real world may be found.

(Mintzberg 1987c: 69)

Mintzberg (1987c) thus advocates, as a guiding principle, the notion of *umbrella strategies*. Within such an approach senior management would be responsible for setting overarching goals and tangible objectives – to manufacture only high-quality products at the cutting edge of technology, for example – whereas the specifics – which products, which markets, how to maintain an edge in technological R&D, etc. – would be left to other organizational members to decide. In this way, the implementers of strategy also become the formulators, given the freedom to experiment and learn. Hatchuel *et al.* (2010) refer to this as a form of 'distributed responsibility' in which strategic decision-making takes places at all levels of the organization.

The value of umbrella strategies, Mintzberg argues, stems from their built-in flexibility that allow the organization to react to unanticipated events and opportunities, while also allowing for some sense of general direction to be maintained, as per Quinn's argument about logical incrementalism. In this regard, the focus of the strategist is on managing the difference between emergent and planned strategy.

Moreover, as Andersen and Nielsen (2009) have observed more recently, the hyper-competitive market conditions of the twenty-first-century business environment lend further weight to support such a distributed approach to strategy-making. Building on Mintzberg's notion of umbrella strategy they see the value of strategic planning as providing for a focus on efficiencies, coordination of activity and integration of business units. Existing within a less hierarchical structure, these systems then allow for the benefits derived from adaptive and responsive behaviours lower down to be identified and shared across functions and business unit; thus learning becomes institutionalized.

In such circumstances, when formulation and implementation are intertwined and strategy takes place at all levels of the organization, the role of leadership necessarily changes. Instead of acting as the architects of strategy plans, the leadership becomes a *facilitator of learning* – a role more concerned with creating the structure, communications channels, mind-set and activities that encourage a more integrated approach to strategy and catering to their constituents. Many so-called 'Japanese' management practices, such as quality circles and employee empowerment schemes, can be seen as examples of a learning approach. Such an approach, in which decision-making is taken further down the organization, without the constraints of senior management intervention, allows for more immediate responses to the dynamic and turbulent environment in which the business finds itself: 'If the managers that oversee the actual business transactions are able to engage in responsive initiatives as they observe important changes in the environment, the organization can react faster and more effectively to dynamic conditions' (Andersen and Nielsen 2009: 96).

Moreover, recognizing that organizations are also inherently political institutions consisting of competing interest groups with different, often conflicting, agendas, the role of the leadership also becomes an increasingly tactical one. Thus the image of the CEO as strategy architect or field general is replaced by the image of the CEO as politician, seeking to manage coalitions of interests, engaged in processes of bargaining, negotiation and conflict resolution (Cummings and Daellenbach 2009).

Of course, to subscribe to such a view also requires a rethinking of the role and value of organizational employees. We have noted in the previous chapter the Taylorist perspective on the employee in the planning model in which it is assumed that only those at the top have the capacity for strategic thinking. However, in the emergent model there is recognition not only of the value of the tacit knowledge possessed by employees but also of the outright necessity to incorporate them into the decision-making processes. To return briefly to the example of Toyota, with its significantly reduced workforce by 1950 it simply would not have been possible to succeed had it not had the commitment and input of its workers. As Takeuchi, Osono and Shimizu (2008: 98) note: 'Toyota views employees not just as pairs of hands but as knowledge workers who accumulate *chie* – the wisdom of experience – on the company's front lines.' Without that commitment and involvement, Toyota may very well have succumbed to bankruptcy in the early 1950s, even with the US military contract.

Facilitating employee engagement in turn demands new decentralized organizational structures through which learning and emergent strategy initiatives can be identified and shared. As observed by Gary Hamel (2007), the traditional bureaucratic organizational structure that typifies the rational planning approach to strategy is one based on a 'small nucleus of core principles': standardization, specialization, hierarchy, goal alignment, planning and control, and the use of extrinsic rewards to shape human behaviour.

In contrast, McKiernan (1997) advocates the need for new organizational structures necessary to capitalize on the kinds of umbrella strategy described above: structures that seek to move away from the 'learned ABC of traditional hierarchy' (Pina e Cunha *et al.* 2011: 494) towards a more flexible and adaptable approach. Thus, whereas the hierarchical model was developed at a time of stability and its purpose was to maximize efficiency, today's organizational structures need to be built to prioritize adaptability and innovation. Where the traditional model emphasized formal planning techniques, organizations now need to 'embed' the entrepreneurial function at all levels of the organization. Third, where the traditional model emphasizes hierarchical and central coordination, horizontal coordination and adaptability are the buzzwords of the contemporary organization. Finally, where the traditional organizational structure emphasizes the responsiveness of individual business units through a logic of portfolio management, today's firms need to build synergy across activities so that innovation and learning can be shared (McKiernan 1997).

In summary then, proponents of the emergent perspective present a view of strategy that rejects the basic premise of rational planning and, instead, advocates an approach to strategy that emphasizes learning, creativity, flexibility and pragmatic adaptability. As the external environment becomes more and more complex and more and more turbulent (Mason 2007), the need for this kind of flexible approach to strategy-making has gathered momentum. However, this is not to deny the possible benefits of planning but rather reflects a desire to reduce the emphasis placed on rational control at the expense of learning. As an approach that combines the benefits of a planned approach to strategy with some of the more creative aspects of an emergent approach, *scenario planning* has increased in popularity in recent years as a tool for strategic learning.

Scenario planning

> Scenario planning is an approach that attempts to harness uncertainty, accept it, and build it into the planning process. Scenario planning involves intuition, creativity, the ability to wonder about the environment and its possibilities, as well as a deep understanding of industry trends, competitor actions and global forces that drive economic, social, and

political systems. Most of all, scenario planning allows organizations to balance deliberate and emergent approaches to strategy.

(Bodwell and Chermack 2010: 198)

Scenario planning dates back to World War II, although as a military activity its origins go back much further with the 'exercise' or war game a kind of early forerunner. Specifically in the context of business strategy, scenario planning developed out of Herman Kahn's work on 'thinking the unthinkable' while working at the RAND Corporation in the 1950s (Bodwell and Chermack 2010). However, it was not until the 1970s that scenario planning first demonstrated its potential value as a strategy tool, when employed by Shell in response to the oil crisis (more on which later). Today, many companies employ a form of scenario planning or at least hire consultants to undertake scenario planning exercises with them. As long-range forecasting has proved increasingly less valuable in the late twentieth and early twenty-first century, scenario planning offers a tool that seeks to draw together both planned and emergent strategy in a way that is managerially accessible and meaningful. In its simplest form it constitutes imagining various futures and then constructing strategies for how the firm might respond to each of those futures. In other words, it differs from rational planning by thinking about what *might* happen rather tying to determine what *will* happen. In this regard, scenario planning is both a tool of strategy development and also a vehicle for thinking strategically. Let us briefly consider how scenario planning developed and then outline a typical scenario planning process.

The emergence of scenario planning

As Carter *et al.* (2008) observe, scenario planning, as a tool of strategy emerged out of war, specifically the second Arab-Israeli War of 1973. In response to Israel's attempt to destroy the combined Arab forces, the latter responded with economic strength by establishing the Organization of Petroleum Exporting Countries (OPEC) cartel. One of its first actions was to increase the price of crude oil, thus restricting Israel's movements while also economically damaging its partners and supporters, such as the USA. As prices continued to rise, by the late 1970s demand collapsed and an oil crisis had developed with particularly adverse effects for the large oil companies. Historically, oil prices had remained constant and it was possible to predict with some certainty what future prices would be. Thus, none of the oil companies had ever really planned for such inflation in prices and restriction in output – except for one.

Royal Dutch Shell, as it was known then, was the only major oil company to emerge from the oil crisis stronger than when it had begun and through its response emerged as a powerful player in the global oil industry. But how did it manage to do this when all around had failed? The answer, it is suggested, comes from Shell's early adoption of scenario planning. Pierre Wack, Shell's head of long-range planning had been experimenting with scenario planning throughout the 1970s and so, when the oil crisis hit, he had a ready-prepared strategic response. As Wack commented, 'The better approach, I believe, is to accept uncertainty, try to understand it, and make it part of our reasoning' (Wack 1985a: 73).

As Mintzberg notes, the 'scenario is predicted on the assumption that if you cannot predict the future, then by speculating upon a variety of them, you might open up your mind and even, perhaps, hit upon the right one' (Mintzberg *et al.* 2009: 61), and this is precisely what Wack achieved at Shell, by constructing a range of scenarios that 'think the unthinkable'. And it was not just the 1973 oil crisis that Shell was able to imagine: the immediate response of many oil companies to the outbreak of the Iran–Iraq War in 1981, based on their experience in the 1970s, was to stockpile reserves of oil to avoid the potential for inflation. Shell, having undertaken a more through scenario analysis of this event, correctly recognized that in this instance there would be a collapse in the oil market and proceeded to sell off its reserves at a high price. Again it was proved correct.

In Wack's view, the scenario deals with two worlds – the world of facts and the world of perceptions (Wack 1985b). The goal of the scenario planning exercise is to bring these two worlds together in order to develop a number of meaningful and credible scenarios that the organization may want to develop strategic responses to. Thus the process combines the preferred methods of strategic planning by way of gathering data, often quantitative data on market trends and other environment forces, and combining it with the more creative aspects of strategy-making advocated by proponents of the emergent perspective. Porter (1985) advocates developing three types of scenario:

- Positive scenarios – in which the organization can capitalize on its strengths to exploit possible future opportunities.
- Negative scenarios – in which the organization will need to identify potential threats that it may need to respond to.
- Status quo scenarios – assuming business as usual. Wack also advocates the need to consider this third type of scenario:

> The surprise-free scenario is one that rarely comes to pass but, in my experience, is essential in the package. It builds on the implicit views of the future shared by most managers, making it possible for them to recognize their outlook in the scenario package. If the package only contains possibilities that appear alien to the participants, they will likely find the scenario process threatening and reject it out of hand'.
> (Wack 1985a: 77)

A typical scenario planning process

There are many different variations of the scenario planning model. Wack himself left Shell to set up Global Business Networks, one of the premier suppliers of scenario planning consulting packages; another is SRI Limited, established in the 1970s and having worked with large companies such as IBM and Du Pont. In the more practitioner-orientated literature, Wilson and Ralston (2006) provide an 18-step scenario planning process and Shoemaker (1995) offers a ten-stage model. While each is unique in some ways all draw on a number of key stages that make up the scenario planning process, we shall consider these key stages below.

Stage 1: establishing the parameters

The first stage in the scenario planning exercise requires setting parameters around the exercise. When engaging in the unknown future there is the potential that the exercise will be become unwieldy and therefore certain criteria need to be established. Issues such as a relevant time frame and also the scope of the exercise in terms of geographic regions, product lines and so on. It is also necessary at the beginning of the process to consider who will be invited to participate in the exercise. Much of the evidence suggests that when scenario planning exercises are limited to the most senior management they will have least impact, as the current strategy of the organization is likely to be a reflection of this group's field of perception. In order to be a truly creative exercise, a broader range of participants is necessary. In particular, middle managers are seen as key contributors given their closeness to the marketplace (Wack 1985a). Shoemaker (1995) even advocates incorporating outside actors such as suppliers, customers, and even academics, who may be able to assist particularly with the next stage in the process, the external analysis.

Stage 2: external analysis

The second stage typically requires building a picture of future trends through some variation on an external audit, such as a PESTEL exercise in which future political, economic, social, technological, ethical and legal environments are considered and projected patterns and trends identified. The 'world of facts', in the form of established product life cycles, political developments such as election cycles, rates of technological development, and so on are collected. Once the data has been collected, the trends and patterns need to be prioritized in terms of their potential importance and likely impact on the future of the organization. As Schoemaker (1995) notes, it is necessary to make economies at this stage in the exercise. It would not be possible to consider every possible variation and thus it is often helpful to identify loosely framed categories of change. For example, rather than anticipating dozens of different market growth rates, it might make more sense to identify low, medium and high categories.

Stage 3: construct scenario options

Having established the critical issues, the next stage is to begin grouping these into collective effects of several patterns developing simultaneously. There are numerous ways of doing this; one might be to group all of the positive and all of the negative issues into separate lists and then create best- and worst-case scenarios as polar opposite positions and then gradually work inward to combine aspects of each until you reach the status quo scenario in the centre. Another is to cluster patterns and trends in terms of likeliness of occurrence into high, medium and low and construct scenarios on those criteria. Importantly, the goal is to consider collections of factors and not simply isolated events. Moreover, as Shoemaker rightly notes, the perception of whether something is positive or negative is largely subjective, depending on the participant's position within the organization. A negative trend for the operations department could be viewed as a positive one for marketing.

Stage 4: developing scenario narratives

Once the various patterns, trends and events have been considered and allocated a specific place, the next task is to work these into narratives – stories that tell of certain imagined futures that can then be used as case studies on which to develop strategic responses. It is not uncommon for consultants to employ novelists and scriptwriters at this stage to add a sense of dynamism and depth to the narratives. How do you tell if the stories that have been developed are fit for purpose? Shoemaker suggests that they should meet the following criteria: first, they must be *relevant* – relevant to the end users who, in this case, are the senior managers or strategic planners. Second, they must be *internally consistent*, by which he means they should be cohesive and well structured stories (that is why professional writers are often employed). Third, they must by *archetypal* – that is, each scenario should be substantially different from the others so that they present significantly different potential futures rather than simple variations on a recurring theme.

Stage 5: developing strategic responses

Once the scenarios have been developed into narratives that tell a story the next stage is to develop a series of strategic responses. This often employs the same tools, frameworks and methods of analysis that would feature in any strategy intervention. That the scenarios are fictions does not prevent them from being treated as real, for the purposes of strategic evaluation, and it is here that the world of facts and the world of perception merge. For Porter (1985) this is also the stage where most scenario planning exercises fail. Much work and emphasis is put on developing the scenarios but if the firm does not create detailed strategic responses to those potential futures then the exercise is largely meaningless.

Evaluating scenario planning

Scenario planning has enjoyed considerable popularity in recent years. Hodgkinson and Healey (2008) suggest that over one third of UK companies engage in scenario planning, with similar levels of take-up in Europe and the USA.

As an approach to developing strategies the scenario planning exercise has a number of benefits. First, it seeks not to predict the future but to imagine several alternate futures. In this sense it placates the desire for rational analysis on the part of the strategic planner but does so in a more creative way that can lead the organization out of its existing mind-sets towards more varied viewpoints and considerations, which in turn can lead to new and unimagined innovations. Second, by focusing on trends and patterns it can lead to a more nuanced appreciation of potential futures, as it requires not just the collection of hard quantitative data but also more qualitative data emerging from intuition, creativity and perception, from a range of organizational members. As Porter notes:

> Scenarios are a powerful device for taking account of uncertainty in making strategic choices. They allow a firm to move away from dangerous, single-point forecasts of the future in instances when the future cannot be predicted. Scenarios can help encourage managers to make their implicit assumptions about the future explicit, and to think beyond the confines of existing conventional wisdom.
>
> (Porter 1985: 447)

Leavy and McKiernan (2009) also suggest that the benefit of the scenario planning exercise, as a tool in the strategist's arsenal, is that it forces senior managers to think not just more broadly but also more deeply about the contextual complexity in which the organization exists. Whereas the SWOT model or 'five forces' (see Chapter 6) largely seeks to reduce complexity, the scenario approach actively encourages complexity which, they suggest, can lead to a more dynamic and more proactive form of strategy-making:

52 Strategy by design 2

'it also goes much further than previous approaches by using narratives and stories as a way of breaking new ground in strategic thinking and questioning assumptions' (Schwartz 1996: 39).

Finally, akin to the soft benefits of planning described in the previous chapter, scenarios often constitute an excellent tool for developing communication and conversation in the organization, exposing organizational members to alternative viewpoints and ways of perceiving the future. In this sense they constitute a key tool of the learning approach, recognizing the inherent unpredictability and instability of the future. For Bodwell and Chermack (2010: 198) this constitutes one of its main benefits: 'Reframed as tools for learning, scenarios are intended to shift the thinking inside the organization and help managers and decision-makers re-perceive the organizational situation and consider numerous ways in which the future might unfold.'

Of course, scenario planning is not without its limitations and, as with the process of SWOT analysis in the previous chapter, it is subject to various kinds of political interference when organizational members are given the opportunity to reflect on the relative position of the firm. As Carter et al. (2008: 77) observe, 'The politics of the organization may make it impossible to contemplate particular futures – some statements may be inadmissible or even unthinkable. Who is participating in the scenario-making programme is also significant.'

Chapter summary

In this section we have looked primarily at the work of Henry Mintzberg as an example of what is termed the emergent or learning approach to strategy. This particular set of ideas acts as a foil against which to consider the value of the more rational, calculated and controlling planning approach discussed in the previous chapter. We have also looked at the idea of scenario planning as something of a middle ground or bridge between planned and emergent strategy.

When read in conjunction with the previous chapter, what we have covered here constitutes one of the major debates within the strategy field: namely, is strategy a conscious, deliberate and rational process or an emergent, dynamic, reactive and pragmatic pattern in action? This begs a number of further questions: who is or should be the architect of strategy? Where in the organization should strategy-making take place? Should there be a clear divide between those who formulate strategy and those who implement it? Where one sits in response to these questions largely reflects one's position in the wider debate. For those who subscribe to the former viewpoint we have the detailed planning processes outlined in the previous chapter on which to draw in order to assist in the process of strategy development. For those who subscribe to the latter view, the descriptive (rather than prescriptive) methods of crafting strategy and umbrella strategies are the preferred weapons of choice.

As you work through the rest of the book you will hopefully see how other strategy writers also occupy positions within this wider debate. Their preferred methods and approaches to strategy reveal their own implicit answers to the questions above. Therefore, it might be useful when reading the following chapter to consciously think about where you would locate each key theorist or approach on the spectrum between rational planning and emergent learning, as it will help you build up a broader picture of the strategy field and permit broader comparisons and critiques to be made. It will also help address that question lurking beneath the surface … what is strategy?

5 Strategy and the multi-business firm

Introduction

As the 1960s gave way to the 1970s, a number of events began to undermine the competitive strength of American business: the economic impact of the oil crisis, repeated cycles of inflation and recession, the political and economic cost of the Vietnam War, and emerging competition from Europe and the Far East. In combination these factors led to a shift in emphasis in strategy in the US, away from long-term planning to more immediate concerns focused both on cutting costs and also on responding to increasing competition. One of the key practices employed at this time were strategies of growth through diversification and acquisition, utilized in order to spread risk. This posed new strategic challenges for the organization – how to interact with these newly created or acquired businesses or divisions and how to manage their activities. This gave rise to what would be termed 'corporate-level' strategy.

While the subsequent years have seen many innovations in the area of corporate-level strategy (such as the Balanced Score Card and 7S framework), keeping with our historically derived account we will concern ourselves in this chapter with the three main contributions that developed during the late 1960s and early 1970s, and which still carry significant currency today. First we will look at the issue of diversification – why firms choose to diversify in the first place and the possible strategies for doing so. Second, we will consider the strategic relationship between the corporate centre and its individual business units using the notion of parenting theory. Third, we will look in detail at one of the most popular methods for managing the diversified corporation, or multi-business firm (MBF), the portfolio matrix. We will conclude by considering some of the benefits and limitations of portfolio approaches to strategy-making.

The rise of the multi-business firm

The rise of corporate-level strategy can be linked to developments at the American company Du Pont in the early twentieth century. Following World War One, in a bid to manage the problem of excess capacity in its factories, Du Pont began diversifying its range of activities away from its primary business in gunpowder production. It had already begun to diversify backwards into manufacturing the chemical ingredients necessary to make explosives in order to meet demand during the war, but as orders started to decline in the war's aftermath, Du Pont found itself with excess capacity and a large holding of businesses. To manufacture the tools of war Du Pont had also seen its workforce grow tremendously, from 5,300 in 1914 to 85,000 by 1918 (Chandler 1962: 84).

It order to address this over capacity, Du Pont began to diversify into unrelated areas of activity. It set up the Excess Plant Utilization Division, which found uses for some of its plants in the manufacture of chemical dyes, paints and other coatings and adhesives. In particular, it capitalized on Germany's defeat in the war to establish itself as a major manufacturer of chemicals – such as lactic acids, alcohol, nitric and sulphuric acids. Before the war, Germany had been the world leader in this industry but post-war America closed off its market to German suppliers and Du Pont was able to become a key supplier very quickly (Chandler 1962).

Despite a relatively rapid expansion of activities, Du Pont tried to maintain its existing centralized structure with a single production department, a single sales department, and so on. But with diversification came complexity – in the range of decisions that needed to be made, the number of different industries entered into, and the competitive environments it needed to consider. Thus, managers who had developed their expertise in the explosives industry now had to make decisions about paints and chemicals. Moreover, as Alfred Chandler (2009) retells in his case study on Du Pont, the newly emerging divisions began to compete with one another for investment, creating semi-autonomous silos that frequently departed from the overall corporate logic in pursuit of their own, more narrowly defined, goals.

In essence, the problem was one of size, from which emerges complexity. As Waterman *et al.* (1980) point out, while small in size a firm can function through close, personal and regular interactions. However, as it grows these are no longer viable and more formal means of communication are necessary. When this happens, you add layers of complexity and structure, which we can relate back to our previous discussion on bounded rationality and muddling through. This is precisely what happened at Du Pont – it became too big to be managed in a functional way. It struggled to operate efficiently under such a system and came close to collapse. The Executive Committee, under the leadership of Irene Du Pont therefore needed to find a new way of managing their expansive range of activities. Du Pont needed to introduce a structure in which overall control could remain centralized while facilitating the need for more localized and specialized decision-making within the separate businesses. Du Pont had already attempted to divisionalize, in 1908, in response to a loss of government orders for military propellants, but met with little success (Chandler 2009). However, by 1921 and in the face of much internal resistance, Du Pont eventually restructured into a multidivisional form (M form) in which each business unit became a discrete operating unit under the control of a single management team (Whittington 2001).

> Unencumbered by operating duties, the senior executives at the general office now had the time, information, and more of a psychological commitment to carry on the entrepreneurial activities and make the strategic decisions necessary to keep the overall enterprise alive and growing and to coordinate, appraise, and plan for the work of the divisions.
>
> (Chandler 1962: 111)

Du Pont's early experiment with multidivisional structures and the subsequent split between corporate and business level strategies laid the foundation for future developments in the field of corporate strategy. In the relative prosperity of the post-World War

II boom in the US economy, we witness an increasing trend towards divisionalization as strategies of acquisition and merger led to more and more multi-business firms (MBFs). It is in this era that we see the birth of the modern giant corporation, reaching its peak in the late 1960s, when General Electric, under the leadership of Fred Borch, had grown to comprise some 46 divisions consisting of nearly 200 separate businesses.

The spread of the MBF and the size of these new corporations were far beyond anything that could have been imagined just 30 years earlier and it required a new logic of strategic management that ushered in a new breed of strategy expert, the consultants. These outside agencies were fundamental in spreading the multidivisional structure in the US during the 1960s and 1970s and it was through the engagement of management consultants that many of the standard tools of corporate strategy, that are still employed to this day, emerged. For example, to help manage its sprawling empire, GE worked with McKinsey and became an early pioneer of portfolio planning management, as a strategy for managing multiple businesses. Second, on McKinsey's recommendation, it reorganized around a structure built on 'strategic business units' (SBUs), each a separate area of activity under the control of a designated management team. Third, working with Harvard Business School it developed and implemented the Profit Impact Market Share (PIMS) database that fed the corporate centre with market data and analysis, which would subsequently inform its strategy formulation. It was also during this period that the title 'chief executive officer' was born, again starting at GE.

Seeing General Electric's success with managing its corporation, others would quickly imitate and repackage these innovations as the late 1960s and 1970s saw a wave of diversification and acquisition activity in the US, and the number of MBFs spread rapidly. Waterman *et al.* (1980) suggest that by 1970 80 per cent of the Fortune 500 had adopted the multidivisional structure. This is staggering when we consider that as recently as the 1950s, some 70 per cent of US companies were still undiversified and secured more than 30 per cent of their turnover from a single core business activity (Whittington 2001). Strategy consulting also became a huge and profitable business for the consultancies, which were able to sell their wares to more and more organizations. We shall return to the story of consultants later but, for now, let us look more closely at the strategic logic of diversification, as it developed during this period.

Diversification strategy

Before considering some of the tools and techniques employed in the management of the multi-business firm, it is worth spending some time thinking about the whole notion of diversification itself, and why organizations choose to adopt such a strategy for growth.

Why do firms diversify?

The rapid rise and spread of the diversified multi-business firm has led many to try to understand why such a strategy is seen to be so valuable. What is the rationale for growth that requires an organization to seemingly move outside of its core activities and into new markets, industries or activities that it does not currently operate in? Below we consider three possible explanations that are linked respectively to: innovation, efficiency and new market entry.

Diversification and innovation

In the late 1950s, Edith Penrose (who we shall hear a lot more about in Chapter 7) wrote a landmark book entitled *The Theory of the Growth of the Firm* (1959/2009) which, while not widely received at the time, later became a seminal text influencing the development of the resource-based view of strategy in the 1980s and 1990s. In this book, amongst other things, Penrose asks the question: why do firms diversify? In other words, when a firm develops a new product, service, technology or some other innovation which does not serve its current market why does it not simply sell that innovation off to another firm and then reinvest the capital in its core activity? Why get involved in unfamiliar activities and markets for which the firm does not currently have a competence or experience? Her answer was simple and most insightful. The answer, she says, is market failure. In other words, the marketplace is very poor at assigning value to ideas, products and services that are in some way new, novel or not currently in existence. Existing players will not offer a price that reflects the true worth of the innovation. As such, the firm has to enter the market itself in order to demonstrate the value of the innovation before others will recognize its true value. Hence, they may need to diversify. Many of the everyday objects we use today were not deemed, at their point of innovation, to have much worth beyond novelty or meeting the needs of a select few: the telephone, the automobile, the computer and the airplane, to name but a few. In each instance the value of the innovation needed to be demonstrated and proven before it achieved sizeable market value.

Diversification and efficiency

A second, and perhaps more familiar argument for diversification centres on the belief that it fosters efficiency gains. In an argument drawn from Transaction Cost Economics, it is argued that for each organization there are activities that can be sourced more cheaply on the open market and others than can be undertaken more efficiently in-house. Thus, when the costs of going to market outweigh the costs of doing something in-house, a firm may diversify in order to take control of that activity. For example, in the 1960s and early 1970s, many automobile manufacturers diversified backwards into component manufacture and forwards into retail. Ironically perhaps, aggressive competition would see a reversal of such strategies in the 1980s and 1990s when much of the manufacturing process was outsourced and selling activities managed through franchising and licensing agreements, automobile companies instead focusing their efforts on research, design and marketing.

In addition, many firms have under-utilized resources that can be made more efficient by diversifying – for example a factory plant that only operates at 70 per cent capacity can be made to operate at 100 per cent capacity when new production processes for new products are introduced (which is precisely what drove Du Pont's diversification strategy of course). The same logic might apply to an under-utilized sales force, personnel department and so on. In short, diversification can sometimes be seen as a more pragmatic strategy for achieving greater efficiency from current resources and capabilities – it's about getting more bang for your buck!

Diversification and new market entry

A third reason why firms diversify relates more to new market entry. In a study on Chilean and Indian corporations, Khanna and Palepu (1999) found that a strategy of diversification for international growth is often premised on leveraging internal markets and competencies in areas such as management capability, information systems, etc. These are deemed especially valuable when diversifying into markets in which there is a scarcity of such capability. International diversification, they also note, permits the financial power of the corporation to be exercised in gaining more attractive terms and conditions than might be the case in a simple joint venture with a domestic company.

Whatever the reason, the initial decision to pursue diversification prompts a second strategic issue and that is, what form of diversification to undertake – should it be *related* to existing offerings, capabilities, and activities or can it be *unrelated* i.e. into completely new business areas?

Diversification: related or unrelated?

According to Leavy and McKiernan (2009) the received wisdom is that a strategy of related diversification is far more valuable (as measured by shareholder returns) than one of unrelated diversification. The arguments for this are straightforward enough: diversifying into a business area, market or industry in which the company already has certain knowledge, experience or capability theoretically allows existing competencies to be leveraged in that new context, thus increasing the likelihood of success and minimizing the costs involved.

While this has a certain logical appeal, there is little evidence to confirm specifically where the advantage of related diversification lies. For example, Porter (1980) suggests that the benefits derive not from within the corporation but are more directly related to the attractiveness of the industry into which the firm is diversifying. In other words, the success of any diversification strategy will be determined more by the forces at play in that new industry than by the internal integration and capability efficiencies realized through the spreading of knowledge, resources, etc. Alternatively, it might also be argued that the benefits of related diversification are context-specific. For example, Virgin has pursued a very effective strategy of diversification into a broad range of markets and industries not even remotely directly related – from travel to finance to communications and more. In this case it is Virgin's corporate logic (and brand power) that drives its diversification strategy rather than its ability to leverage production-related capabilities.

In the 1960s and early 1970s, strategies of unrelated diversification also came about for more pragmatic reasons. The passing of the Cellar-Kefauver Amendment in 1950 restricted the acquisition of firms in the same industry and therefore, in order to grow, many firms had to look beyond their industry's borders to unrelated and possibly unknown markets and products. This in turn gave rise to the conglomerate organization: a large, diversified company consisting of unrelated holdings (Espeland and Hirsch 1990). Whatever the cause, there can be no denying the speed and spread of the diversification wave of the 1960s and early 1970s, especially the popularity of unrelated diversification as a seeming 'quick fix' to growth and risk reduction took hold.

Diversification as empire-building and the personal strategies of the strategist

However, very quickly into the diversification wave of the 1960s and early 1970s, the limits of growth by acquisition became readily apparent. For example, Ravenscraft and Scherer (1987), in a survey of nearly 6,000 mergers undertaken between 1950 and 1977 found that, within ten years, over one third had already been divested (Whittington,

2001). More recent data suggests that up to '78 per cent of mergers and acquisitions fall apart within three years of conception' (Segil 1998: 13). And yet, firms continued to pursue this strategy: why was this? Two particularly interesting arguments have been put forward. First, Whittington (2001) makes the argument that underpinning many acquisitions was not a strategy for growth and expansion but rather a conscious attempt to eliminate competition. He cites the example of General Motors, which in the 1930s and 1940s began acquiring electric tram companies in 45 American cities, including New York and Los Angeles. There was no obvious rationale for such a move given that GM's capabilities were in automobile and bus manufacture. The strategy behind the acquisitions, which were effectively 'written off', only became apparent when GM started withdrawing tram services in many of these cities, thus forcing commuters to rely on its buses and cars in order to get around.

The second argument, as expressed by Mueller (1969) in exploring the merger wave of the 1960s, concerns the widespread practice of unrelated diversification, which, he argued, went against the logic of growth, which should be based on acquisitions that somehow had synergies, i.e. were related to existing capabilities. He notes: 'either the industrial community is literally a sea of synergistic merger opportunities, or that a lot of bad decision-making has been going on with respect to mergers' (Mueller 1969: 644).

Mueller goes on to explore this seeming paradox by employing what he calls the 'growth maximization' hypothesis which, contra profit maximization, suggests that many managers knowingly put firm growth ahead of shareholder return in making acquisition and merger decisions. In other words, managers are likely to sacrifice profit by paying above market value for an acquisition or make 'bad' acquisition choices knowingly if it allows them to readily increase the size of the firm. So why might they do this? One line of thought, pursued by Mueller and others (see, for example, Morck *et al.* 1990; Roll 1986) is linked to what Tony Watson (2003) calls the 'personal strategies of the strategist'. By definition, we might suggest, senior managers are ambitious people who will look to further their own career as much, if not more, than the aims of the organization overall. As such, one explanation for the merger wave of the 1960s might be, in part, a strategy employed by managers to increase their own position, ambition or reward. This is possibly because of the way that reward is administered in many western firms. In short, value is attached to size. The larger the firm, the higher the reward in the form of salary, bonuses, stock options, etc., that senior managers receive. Thus they have a vested interest in growing the firm. Moreover, as Roll (1986) observes, as most managers only get the opportunity to make a few acquisition decisions over their career, there is a limited window of opportunity in which to exercise this form of personal self-interest.

Managers are able to 'get away' with this practice due to the relatively loose oversight through which they operate. As Morck *et al.* (1990) observe, boards of directors give managers 'considerable leeway' (p. 32) in making investment decisions, on the assumption that they are primarily working for the good of the firm. That, after all, is a basic principle of the idea of rational economic man. While it would be wrong to suggest that managers do not pursue the interests of the firm, it would also be wrong to assume that they do not balance this, in some way, with their own motivations and interests. There is simply too much evidence to the contrary.

Whatever the rationale for diversification, once an acquisition has taken place another strategic question presents itself – namely, what is the role of the corporate centre and what is the nature of the relationship between the centre and the individual business units? To address this we employ the notion of parenting theory.

Parenting theory

If we consider the MBF as a collection of largely self-managed, partially autonomous business units, possibly competing in distinct markets in which there may be little to no interaction between them, then from a strategic point of view we need to ask the question: what is the role of the corporate centre? For if each business can operate effectively and efficiently on its own, what value does the centre bring? In this regard, one of the key strategic issues at the corporate level is the need to determine the value-adding activities of the centre or, to use Goold *et al.*'s (1998) more recent term, the corporate parent. For, like any parent, the corporate centre can both help and hinder the development of its offspring.

Borrowing from Goold *et al.* (1998) we can suggest that the corporate parent can add value (and therefore justify its existence) in the following ways:

- Setting direction – the corporate centre is responsible for developing the overall objectives (mission) and direction (vision) that informs all other strategic imperatives.
- Advisory role – the centre serves in an advisory role, counselling individual businesses: offering advice, support, focus, expertise, etc.
- Protector – the centre can often deal more competently with external stakeholders. For example, when Virgin Atlantic was in an industrial dispute with its flight crews in 2011 it was the corporate parent, under the leadership of Richard Branson, that represented the airline with the unions and other stakeholder groups.
- Policing role – the corporate centre can also intervene in, or between, individual business units to deal with disputes, poor performance, conflicts, and so forth.
- Central services – finally, the corporate centre also has its own capabilities and competencies that it can leverage toward individual business units that might not be able to secure them in any other way – these might include financial resources, managerial expertise, and more.

Conversely, all corporate centres in some sense take value away from individual businesses, if only because it is the revenues from the business units that 'pay' for the central services. Moreover, the corporate parent can also destroy value for the individual business unit. For Goold *et al.* this normally arises for two (interrelated) reasons. First, it stems from poor or limited central management. The larger the corporation grows the more central managers have to divide their time between many different businesses and as a result less time can be spent on each. Drawing on the logic of bounded rationality introduced in Chapter 4, this often means that as a result, strategic decisions on resource allocation and other key factors may be reduced to numerical reports on targets met, growth, market share, etc., which seldom tell the full story of a business activity (as we shall see later on).

Second, poor management decision-making is in part related to the information filters that travel up the organization and inform the decision-making that takes place. In other words, the reporting systems employed by the organization will reflect certain concerns while excluding others, such as a concern with return on investment over market share. Moreover, as we will see later, such systems are subject to many forms of manipulation that can present the reporting business in very different lights. In short these systems are 'systematically biased' (Goold *et al.* 1998: 309). Given that important decisions such as resource allocation and investment are often made in response to such reports, they become powerful tools in the arsenal of the business unit manager.

However, assuming that the corporate centre can justify itself as a value-adding entity, the next strategic issue is to determine the nature of the relationship between the parent and individual business unit. Johnson *et al.* (2009) identify three different parenting approaches, each underpinned by its own logic and strategic imperatives.

Portfolio parent

The portfolio parent operates as an agent acting on behalf of outside parties whose primary interest is capital accumulation. This type of conglomerate corporation is typified by a hands-off approach to managing individual businesses and engages in unrelated diversification underpinned by a strategic logic of 'buy low, sell high'. In other words, the portfolio parent considers the individual business as, in effect, a bundle of liquid assets that can be readily bought, sold and broken up in order to achieve maximum financial return. Thus, the role of the corporate parent is to identify and acquire undervalued prospects and then to turn those around and sell them for a higher price. Think, for example, of Warren Buffett's Berkshire Hathaway Group, which owns firms as diverse as insurance brokers, carpet manufacturers, clothing manufacturers, building suppliers, and more. There is no logic underpinning this diverse portfolio other than that of 'buy low, sell high'. This form of parenting was widely employed in the 1970s and in part gave rise to the spread and popularity of the various portfolio matrices that were pitched by the likes of BCG and McKinsey – who provided a strategic tool that focused exclusively on the financial measures of buy, hold and sell.

Synergy parent

A second type of parenting approach, one that became popular in the late 1980s and early 1990s in the west, is that of the synergy parent. Informed by the corporate strategies of Japanese and Pacific Rim firms, the synergy parent seeks to enhance value across business units by building and maintaining a number of *core competencies* (Prahalad and Hamel 1990) that underpin the activities of all of the businesses within the portfolio. One example might be Honda. Honda competes in a seemingly diverse range of unrelated industries from motorcycles and automobiles to jet skis, lawn mowers, and power generators. However, what underpins all these product categories is that, at their core, they are all technologies driven by engines, and it is the *design* and *development* of these engines that is at the heart of Honda's strategy. It is able to leverage this competence in any market in which an engine is a primary component. Thus, for Honda, it is the maintenance and continual improvement of this competence in engine design and the diversification into markets and acquisition of firms that can either benefit from or help improve this competence that becomes the focus of their parenting approach. As such, a lot of time is spent facilitating co-operation and good working practices across business units (this itself a hallmark of a 'Japanese' approach to strategy).

Parental developer

The third category of parent, according to Johnson *et al.* is the parental developer. Much like the synergy parent, the parental developer seeks to maximize the value of certain core competencies, but here the competencies are not those held across the individual business units but of the corporate centre itself. We can think of Virgin in this regard.

Virgin Group has certain competencies in brand management, marketing and general management that it seeks to ingrain into each of the businesses it acquires, or into which it diversifies, and these then become the basis of the business-level strategy. Thus there is a shared dominant logic, or set of underlying beliefs, crafted by the corporate centre and fed into each of the business units.

Having determined the nature of the relationship between the centre and the business units, the next question becomes one of how to manage these sprawling corporate empires? In the 1970s the answer was largely provided by the burgeoning strategy consultancy industry.

The rise of the consultants

As Kipping (1999: 191) observes, management consultants were 'one of the most important carriers or channels for the dissemination of different waves of managerial expertise during the twentieth century'. The earliest consulting practices typically emerged out of engineering firms and were closely tied to the scientific management movement in the early twentieth century (Kipping 1999). Fredrick Winslow Taylor, himself an engineer by training, consulted widely in implementing the methods of scientific management that he had developed and then refined at the Bethlehem steel works. After his death in 1915, loyal followers and competitors alike sought to capitalize on the popularity of scientific management and continued to consult widely. These industrial engineers, or 'efficiency experts' as they were often known (Kipping 1999) soon broadened their remit to include business surveys and auditing work. As McKenna (2012) notes, the creation of the Securities and Exchange Commission (SEC) in 1934, with its mandate to regulate and oversee the stock and securities markets, led many US firms to hire consultancies to audit and certify their activities as protection against shareholder lawsuits. This new role, McKenna suggests, saw a fourfold increase in the number of consulting firms by the earlier 1940s, with over 400 now offering a range of specialist advice and services. By the 1960s, so established had they become that consulting firms were well placed to position themselves as key players in assisting firms with moving to a multidivisional structure.

The popularity of the products and services offered by the major consultancies in the US soon caught the attention of business managers in Western Europe. In this regard, McKinsey & Co. played a key role in assisting many British, German and French firms to move to the multidivisional form in the 1960s, including 22 of the 100 largest British companies (Kipping 1999). As such, McKenna concludes: 'In a very direct and central way, American management consulting firms, and especially consultants from McKinsey & Company, were responsible for spreading the multidivisional organizational model in Europe during the 1960s' (2012: 159).

By the end of the 1960s, however, the widespread success those consultancies had experienced with introducing the multidivisional structure inevitably led to a reduction in new contracts. Once a firm had been divisionalized there was little more for the consultancy to do. Thus, during the 1970s we see the consultancies begin a rebranding exercise, and in particular a breed of new (or newly labelled) *strategy* consultancies begin to emerge, positioning themselves as now being the experts needed to help develop new strategies and new strategy tools to help manage multidivisional structures. At the centre of this new wave would be a small boutique consultancy that would become synonymous with corporate-level strategy, the Boston Consulting Group.

Portfolio management and the contribution of BCG

Bruce Henderson, a former Arthur D. Little consultant, founded the Boston Consulting Group (BCG) in 1963 from the Management Consulting Division of the Boston Safe Deposit Company. In 1964 it had six employees and virtually no market presence. By 1970, it had over 85 consultants and was widely regarded as one of the pre-eminent strategy consultancies (Kiechel 2010). This rapid rise was due in large part to two key interventions that did much to enhance the reputation of not only BCG but also the wider consultancy industry. Those contributions were the experience curve and the growth/share matrix.

The experience curve

BCG's first contribution derived from a study that the consultancy undertook exploring the relationship between production scale and revenue accumulation for the US firm, General Instruments. As retold by Kiechel (2010), General Instruments were struggling to compete in the television components industry. It simply could not match the costs of its rivals and employed BCG to help understand why. John Clarkson, a newly recruited consultant (and future BCG leader) was tasked with the role.

Looking at the production costs and revenues for 24 different commodity industries, including transistors, diodes crude oil, and ethylene, Clarkson found the following rule appeared to apply consistently: costs go down by 20–30 per cent every time product experience (total volume manufactured and sold) doubles. Thus, the second unit will cost 20 per cent less than the first unit (assuming a constant reduction of 20 per cent as production doubles), the fourth 20 per cent less than the second, and the eighth 20 per cent less than the fourth and so on. Assuming the rule applies consistently, the ten millionth unit will cost 20 per cent less than the five millionth, while prices remain constant. The BCG would articulate this relationship through the experience curve, as expressed in Figure 5.1.

The experience curve may look familiar, and for good reason. As conceived by BCG, the experience curve is an extension of the earlier model of the learning curve. Briefly stated, the learning curve suggests that as a worker repeats a task, he/she gets better at it. As they get better at it, they do it more quickly. Thus, over time, they become more

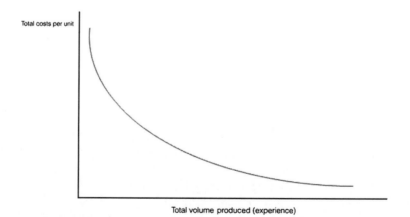

Figure 5.1 The experience curve
Source: Adapted from Lilley *et al.* 2009.

efficient in their labour. BCG's leap was to apply this logic to the whole organization, to all its costs of production. Thus, as the organization produces more, it gets more efficient at doing so and thus realizes the benefits of experience.

The 'discovery' of these economies of experience led BCG to make a number of further suppositions. First, the competitor with the highest market share (by volume) should receive the greatest benefits of experience on the premise that they would be further along the experience curve than their competitors. Second, markets in which experience could be doubled most quickly would be the most attractive to enter (or diversify into) in order to gain the greatest returns most quickly.

BCG was able to effectively translate these findings into a package of strategic interventions that could be sold to clients. Thus, BCG sold the following advice, based on their research into the experience curve. First, they argued for the importance of only operating in markets in which you were (or could become) the market leader by market share (volume). Why? Assuming companies compete on price (as they do in commodity markets), the way to gain an advantage is to ensure that your experience is doubling at a faster rate than your competitors – in this way you will realize greater margins. This necessitates selling a higher volume than your competitor. The position of market share leader would then generate two strategic advantages:

- First, being the highest volume producer would enable a strategy of price-based competition as a barrier to entry, mobility and growth. The market-share leader has the lowest costs and therefore can sustain a price war longer than its competitors (assuming all other factors remain constant).
- Second, the greater margins accrued as a result of the economies of experience mean that the market leader has the greatest capacity to reinvest in marketing, R&D, etc., to further consolidate their lead in the future.

In short, the benefits of economies of experience offer both short-term tactical benefits and a longer-term advantage if the position is maintained. BCG's second piece of advice was to identify those markets in which experience is doubling most quickly. More often than not, this means markets in the 'Introduction' or 'Growth' stages of the Product Life Cycle (PLC). To double experience in a new market is relatively easy compared to doubling experience in a market in the 'Mature' stage of the PLC. As such, the advice from BCG was to focus on high-growth markets where the battle for market share is still being played out and where the benefits of experience can be realized more quickly.

With its empirical grounding there is a great deal of common-sense appeal in the idea of the experience curve but, as noted by Leavy and McKiernan (2009), it has met with mixed levels of success. There are, to be sure, clear examples of the effects of the experience curve in action: for Texas Instruments in calculators, Dell in the home PC market, and even for Ryanair in the airline industry. All have 'proven', at one time or another, the effects of the curve. However, Leavy and McKiernan (2009) also identify a number of limitations of this model. First, it seems that the effects of the experience curve are highly industry-specific and appear to operate most accurately in commodity markets and in markets where there is price-based competition and little variation in product offering. Conversely, in highly branded markets such as retail, the effects seem less consistent.

Second, and perhaps more problematic, the experience curve assumes that all companies learn at the same rate – that is, they realize the benefits of experience and reduce their costs of production in a uniform manner – which ignores the idiosyncratic nature of the individual organization. In addition, there is research to suggest that experience might actually depreciate over time and that recent output, rather than accumulated experience, is the best predictor of current productivity (Devadas and Argote 2006).

Third, a focus on cutting costs and realizing economies of experience can, potentially, result in strategic drift and a failure to attend to changing customer needs, as noted by Abernathy and Wayne in their classic 1974 study on Ford Motors. Despite seeing market share soar from 10 per cent to 55 per cent during its peak in the early 1920s, Ford quickly started to lose market share as it failed to move from its focus on cost. Thus, as Ghemawat continues:

> by its single-minded focus on cost reduction, Ford had sown the seeds of its own downfall. As consumer demand shifted to a heavier, closed body and to a greater emphasis on comfort and styling, Ford responded by tacking on features to the Model T rather than changing models, as General Motors did. Worried about having to replace its massive investment in facilities dedicated to the Model T, Ford continued to build the car until 1927, when customer preferences forced it to close down its plants for nearly a year while it retooled the Model A. In the process Ford lost $200 million and suffered an irreversible decline in market share.
>
> (Ghemawat 1985: 143)

Despite these limitations, for Kiechel (2010) the experience curve's lasting contribution was in ushering in a sea change in the strategy field that forced companies to truly reflect on their costs and on their competitors. Moreover, the experience curve would lay the foundation for BCG's more famous contribution, the growth/share matrix, or the Boston Boxes as they are sometimes known.

Growth/share matrix

In the late 1960s Alan Zakon, one of BCGs consultants, undertook a project with the Mead Paper Company, which was struggling to manage its sprawling business that had entered into a period of rapid expansion via acquisition. In particular, Mead wanted a way to quickly sort out its most efficient and productive businesses and activities from those that were proving a resource drain. Drawing on BCG's previous work on the experience curve, Zakon analyzed each of Mead's activities and came to the conclusion that it was in fact Mead's original paper business that was the greatest drain on the firm. Zakon presented a report which stated that in order to stay in paper, Mead would need to redirect all investment from its other concerns. In effect, Mead would have to inject cash into a dead dog (you will see the relevance of the analogy below).

As such, Zakon made the rather bold recommendation that Mead allow its paper business to dwindle so that it could be managed for cash, which could then be reinvested in higher growth and more attractive businesses. The chief executive of Paper Mead shared this view and, on receiving the advice of Zakon and his team was reputed to reply, 'That's terrific – dress it up' (Kiechel 2010: 57). Zakon did so and thus was born the growth/share matrix. At its most basic level, the growth/share matrix sought to address two of the key questions Mead was asking:

- What businesses should we be in?
- How should we allocate resources between these businesses?

The growth/share matrix draws on two essentially financial measures of business success in order to answer these questions and, in doing so, provide the corporate centre with a quick and easy overview of the current state of its portfolio. The two key measures are *market share* and *market growth*. Market share, which incorporates the experience curve, serves as a key indicator of relative competitive position under the assumption that the competitor with the greatest market share must be realizing the greatest benefits of experience. Market growth, in essence, maps the PLC onto the market to indicate the speed at which economies of experience can theoretically be achieved. This sounds more complicated that it is and is better expressed through BCG's simple two-by-two growth/share matrix (see Figure 5.2).

Let us unpick this matrix in a little more detail. On the vertical axis is market growth, only here the four or five-stage product life cycle has been replaced with just two measures – high and low growth. The point of equilibrium suggests that a market that is growing at more than 10 per cent per year is considered to be high growth whereas anything growing below that is considered low growth. Of course 10 per cent growth is incredibly high and BCG would later revise such optimistic figures. On the horizontal axis, we have relative market share. At the point of equilibrium we have a market share exactly equal to the next largest competitor. Given that only one company can, by definition, have the highest market share then by extension only one company can be situated on the left of the line and thus be considered to have high market share. All others, have a relatively low share (relative to the market leader by volume).

These two measures led BCG to identify four types of business unit to be found within any corporate portfolio:

- Stars;
- Cash cows;
- Question marks (also known as 'problem children' or 'wild cards')
- Dogs.

For each type of business unit, BCG recommended a specific strategy and we shall consider these below (for purposes of brevity, and in true consultancy style, these will be presented as a series of bullet points).

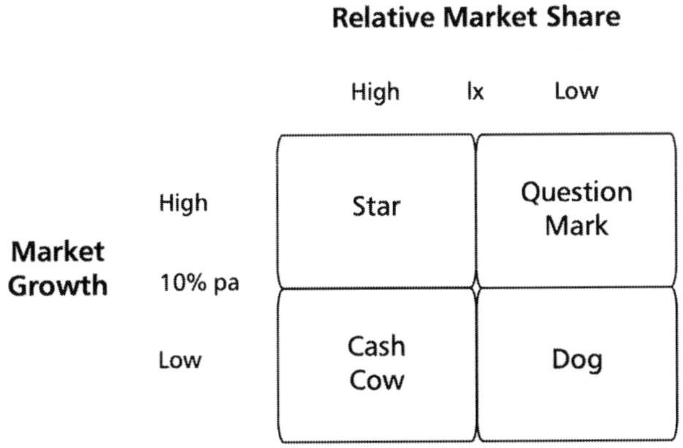

Figure 5.2 The growth share matrix
Source: Adapted from Stern and Deimler 2006.

Stars

- Stars have a high market share and operate in a high-growth market.
- They will generate a lot of cash due to the effects of experience but also consume a lot of cash because of the associated costs of competing in a new market (R&D, marketing, etc.). Therefore, they may be self-sustaining but are less likely to return positive cash sums for the corporation.
- Despite being cash neutral, stars represent the best opportunity for investment as, if managed carefully, they could be the cash cows of the future.
- Strategic advice is therefore to invest to fund future growth and maintain market share. Utilize the benefits of experience to lower prices to force out competitors.

Cash cows

- In answer to the question of how to fund stars, the answer comes primarily in the form of cash cows.
- Cash cows are former stars that have maintained their market share as the market has matured and thus become 'low growth'.
- These businesses produce a positive cash balance on the basis that they generate a lot of cash as market leaders but need to spend little cash because little reinvestment is necessary in a mature market.
- The strategy therefore is to ration new investment and maintain prices in order to 'milk' the cow for all the cash you can in order to fund stars and also those question marks deemed worthy.

Question marks

- Question marks are low-share businesses in high-growth markets. As such there is potential opportunity for returns but there is a question mark over why they are not returning a positive cash sum.
- Their position in high-growth markets means they need a lot of investment but their relative share means they are not generating a lot of cash, thus they have a negative net contribution and therefore are the most problematic businesses in the portfolio.
- There are two strategic options here: invest for future growth in the belief that the business can capture market share and become a star. Or, alternatively, manage for cash and withdraw. This does not constitute a cut-and-run strategy but rather indicates that prices should be gradually increased or maintained such that the business actively prices itself out of the market. Why? To make the highest return, of course.

Dogs

- Operating in low growth markets with relatively low market share, dogs are seen as the least attractive businesses in the portfolio. This despite the fact that they may be generating a neutral cash contribution (in the same way as stars).
- In BCG terms the business is worthless and should be liquidated for cash to fund stars and preferred question marks.

The balance portfolio

Based on the rationale outlined above, the advice of BCG was to operate a 'balanced portfolio'. Every corporation needs a balance of the four business types as each serves a function in the wider corporate logic. A corporation full of stars would not survive for long, as there would be no cash available to fund their development. A suitable blend of cash cows and question marks and dogs are necessary to provide the necessary funds to invest in stars. Without careful management of the portfolio, BCG argued, there are natural market tendencies that come into play to the detriment of the firm. Namely, cash cows and question marks naturally degenerate into dogs if not managed carefully, and stars can become question marks as new competitors with new capacity enter the market. As described in Figure 5.3.

Recognizing that both success and disaster sequences come about through direct managerial involvement, a new role for corporate managers – the role of managing the portfolio to ensure success and avoid disaster – was proposed by the consultancies. Thus, questions of investment, resource allocation, and which companies to invest in and which to divest became the core concerns of the corporate centre. As Stalk *et al.* (1992) observe, 'A company must behave as an investor, not as an operator, if it is to achieve its potential' (p. 263). Although subtle at first reading, the notion of the corporate centre as an 'investor' would come to have profound effects on the logic and direction of strategic management as more and more companies diversified and larger and larger corporations grew.

The firm as a bundle of liquid assets

The spread of the large corporation and the logic of the portfolio approach gave rise to a new dominant logic that came to govern the way business was thought about, regulated and managed. At the heart of this new dominant logic, Espeland and Hirsch (1990) argue, was the language and practice of finance and accounting, with the firm positioned as investor. Prior to the merger wave of the 1960s the dominant logic of American business

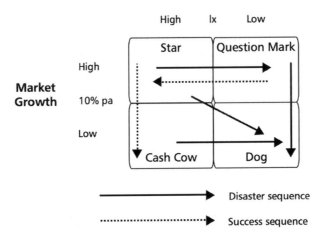

Figure 5.3 The growth share matrix
Source: Adapted from Stern and Deimler 2006.

was production: the role and function of a business predominantly to make and sell products. Thus, the logic of production, of operations and of sales dominated the language and practice of business and strategy. This called for a cadre of managers skilled in production, marketing and sales. However, as Espeland and Hirsch (1990) go on to say: 'The men who created and sustained the conglomerate movement were a different type of businessmen operating under a new business philosophy. They were more financiers than managers, concerned with deal-making more than with day-to-day operation of the companies they bought' (p. 78).

Thus there was a shift in emphasis from a logic of 'industrial capitalism' to one of 'financial capitalism' (ibid.) and with it a new conception of the firm – not as an organic entity full of human beings creating things and building things but as a 'bundle of liquid assets' (Espeland and Hirsch 1990: 79) that could be readily bought, sold, broken-up, merged, dismantled and sold off for scrap subject to the needs of the investor. This new logic, in turn, led to a rethinking of many corporate goals and operating practices. As Espeland and Hirsch (1990) note, the logic of production directs goal-setting towards units sold and experience acquired; to a logic of survival and of profits achieved through producing better, cheaper and more valuable products and doing so better, faster, cheaper or to a higher standard than competitors. Great emphasis has to be placed on a wide range of stakeholders; not just shareholders, but also employees, suppliers, and customers too. By contrast, they suggest, the logic of finance reimagines the firm as a 'stream of assets' (p. 88) with little direct correlation between production and output but instead as various costs or valuable sources of quick money. Survival is less relevant, especially where the liquidation of the firm can in itself yield a high return, which can then be used to acquire other assets. By extension, the primary focus is on the shareholder whose funds are needed in order to secure new assets and whose primary motivation is their financial return. Employees and managers skilled in finance become the most valuable and highly prized human resource.

In this regard, the portfolio matrix became a key tool in the financialization of the firm. By considering only two financial measures of the firm – that focus on potential earnings and costs – internal markets could be created within the corporation and each business unit measured by its net return, outside any wider strategic considerations or imperatives. BCG drew explicitly on this financial logic by conceiving of the corporation the way an investor might conceive their personal portfolio as 'a differentiated holding of interests in businesses with variety of potential risk and opportunities' (Morrison and Wensley 1991: 108). Interestingly, in the first rendering of the growth/share matrix the four quadrants employed the language of finance to express the four types of business unit, as 'sweepstakes', 'saving accounts', 'bonds' and 'mortgages' respectively (Espeland and Hirsch 1990). However, they were soon changed to make them more managerially accessible and appealing.

Putting it all together: the portfolio planning process

In sum then, the portfolio approach treats each business unit as a semi-autonomous entity which requires specific levels of investment and from which a positive net contribution is expected. The process of portfolio management requires first the allocation of activities and resources into coherent and meaningful groups, which may require the merging of formally discrete businesses or operating units. Following McKinsey & Co.'s recommendation to GE, these groupings became known as *strategic business units* (SBUs). SBUs constitute the basic building blocks of many multi-business firms. The boundaries around the business units establish what activities will receive the focused attention of a single management team, and will be aggregated together for performance measurement and reporting purposes (Morrison and Wensley 1991). Drawing on the logic of the experience curve, Haspeslagh (1982) suggests that the key criteria for identifying groups of activities within a single SBU rests on the test of whether the value it can create vis-a-vis its competitive market is sufficient to sustain competitiveness. In other words, if we group these activities together, will we have a business unit that can compete successfully in the marketplace?

Each SBU should then be plotted on the portfolio matrix in order to determine, at a glance, its cost position relative to its competitors, while also being able to consider the attractiveness (growth potential) of the market in which it competes. Strategic decisions about resource allocation and investment can then be made with regard to each SBU, and a suitable strategic goal or target set. This, in essence, is the portfolio approach.

What value the portfolio approach?

By the mid-1970s the growth/share matrix was in use in over 100 US businesses. So confident was Henderson in the analytic power of the two-by-two matrix that he boldly proclaimed: 'Such a single chart, with a projected position for five years out, is sufficient alone to tell a company's profitability, debt capacity, growth potential and competitive strength' (Henderson 1973: 6, cited in Morrison and Wensley 1991: 110).

While a little ambitious perhaps, it was certainly the case that the growth/share matrix rapidly gained in popularity and numerous other consultancies produced their own variation on the portfolio matrix. Perhaps best known was the GE/McKinsey matrix which produced a three-by-three model measuring market attractiveness against business strength to produce its own range of buy, hold and sell strategies. Other examples include BCG's later growth/gain matrix, a competitive advantage matrix, a market definition matrix and even a 27-option share/strategy matrix. Take-up of these matrices was also widespread with some 45 per cent of the Fortune 500 believed to be employing portfolio management by the end of the 1970s (Haspeslagh 1982). So lucrative did the business of portfolio interventions become that at Bain & Co. the revealing of the matrix to a company's board was known as the 'million dollar slide' because 'a single image that captured and conveyed so much information about a company's strategic situation was worth a million dollars in consulting fees' (Kiechel 2010: 65). Clearly, the portfolio approach struck a chord with the prevailing managerial logic of the day, but what were the perceived benefits of this approach and what are its main limitations? To these questions we now turn.

The perceived benefits of a portfolio approach to strategy formulation rests largely on a series of conveniences. First, there is simplicity to the approach. Because data on only two variables is required, such analyses can be very quickly put together and decision-makers can see, at a glance, the current state of the portfolio – which businesses are preforming well, where the weaknesses are, and so on. It therefore facilitates more rapid decision-making. Following this logic, Jack Welch as CEO of GE in the 1980s famously insisted that the only objective for each business was to be number 1 or number 2 in their market, or risk being divested. Second, against some of the basic premises of the dominant logic of strategic planning, this approach delegated considerable autonomy to the business level. With the relationship with the corporate centre primarily a financial one, the everyday workings of the individual business were largely left to individual management teams. Third, the tool is extremely versatile. It does not just speak to managing a portfolio of businesses but can also be used to manage product or brand portfolios and even territories, distribution channels, customers, etc. Indeed, today, the Boston Boxes are as likely to be used as a tool of marketing strategy as one of business strategy.

Despite these perceived benefits, numerous authors have offered a wide range of criticisms of the portfolio approach, and a number of those are summarized below.

Lack of direction

The portfolio approach, much like the planning approach, says little about how to achieve the strategy. It is only focused on the end result. According to Haspeslagh (1982) the process is essentially 'sterile'. By which he means that key issues such as how best to define a group of activities into an SBU, how the SBU should then develop a business-level strategy within the constraints imposed by the corporate centre are left unanswered. In this regard, Hayes and Abernathy (1980, cited in Ghemawat 2002) argued that portfolio management encouraged a short-term focus on financial returns rather than a long-term strategic orientation. This in turn led to a culture of quick deals and fast returns rather than a commitment to long-term resource investment – something that would come back to bite American business as Japan and the Asian Tigers rose to dominance in the 1980s.

Over simplified?

The approach, in its simplicity, is perhaps too simplistic to be of any real value. Does it really make sense to base strategy on just two financial measures? Moreover, what are the implications of doing so? For example, according to BCG's original measures, some 70 per cent of UK business would be classed as dogs (Pearson 1999) because of the rigours of the measures of growth and share.

Context-specific

Relatedly, it seems there was some evidence to suggest that the strategic recommendations that the portfolio approach produced were matrix-specific. As reported by Ghemawat (2002), in a study of 15 SBUs that were subjected to four different matrices, in only one case did the SBU fall into the same category in each of the four matrices. Thus, the decision on which matrix to use could potentially have significant ramifications for the corporation and for the individual business units.

Problems of definition

Another limitation of the approach is in defining the various key measures. For example, BCG had to revise many of its indicators of market growth because they were simply too high and thus many of the organizations to whom they were selling their advice were seemingly a little too low on stars and problem children. Equally difficult to define is the market itself. Given that this is the key variable on which everything else rests, market definition is highly important. Pearson (1999) tells the story of managers of dog businesses simply redefining their core market more narrowly, more broadly, or in whatever way so required in order to magically reimagine themselves as stars or problem children, thus not only saving themselves from immediate liquidation but also suddenly in contention for greater investment. Thus, much of the success of the business unit seems to come down to the savvy and political skill of the business unit manager.

Impact on people

Perhaps one of the main criticisms levelled at the portfolio approach is reflected in its underlying logic that sees the firm as a bundle of liquid assets. From such a perspective there is little room for sentiment, or even consideration of the human impact of buy, hold and sell strategies. Moreover, there is a potential motivation issue – how, for example, do you motivate the manager of a cash cow business who sees all of its profits returned to the centre to be allocated to other businesses that are not performing as well? Equally, what is the impact of internal mergers in which a cash cow or star has to absorb a problem child or dog and suddenly sees its own position negatively affected?

Connections within the portfolio

Another more practical problem with the portfolio approach is its frequent failure to accommodate the interconnectedness of business units (Leavy and McKiernan 2009). Business units may, for example, share production facilities, key personnel or locations. Many dog businesses, while not valuable as stand-alone entities, may perform an important role in the portfolio in relation to other businesses or in sustaining the credibly of the portfolio as a whole. For example, if we take the university as a corporation then many of the most 'prestigious' departments would, in BCG's terms, be classed as dogs but are necessarily retained in order to demonstrate the standing of the university. Alternatively, dogs may be retained for more tactical reasons to keep competitors at bay.

In short, there are numerous abstract as well as more practical limitations with the portfolio approach that redress some of its perceived benefits. Indeed, the perceived benefits of its simplicity and versatility might be seen as a direct cause of some of the limitations stated above.

Chapter summary

The rapid rise of the corporation, and the conglomerate form in particular, posed new questions and problems for regulators, investors, government and managers. Regulators struggled with questions of whether and how to limit the power of corporations and to what extent they were reducing, through legal means or otherwise, competition, in the same way the big corporations of the nineteenth century had done. Investors initially struggled with how to make investment decisions and managers faced the operational challenge of managing a portfolio of twenty or thirty different business units. Such challenges were debated in the business press, on Wall Street, in business schools, and in the upper echelons of government. This in turn led to the need for new economic thinking as many of the long-standing beliefs about industry behaviour were undermined, such as the notion of barriers to entry – pulled down by simply acquiring an existing competitor. As Espeland and Hirsch (1990) claim, these new corporate empires 'defied traditional boundaries and standard business policy' (p. 77).

While the portfolio approach began to lose favour by the end of the 1970s, it offered a number of initial responses to these challenges that would shape future developments in the field: industry choice, positioning, and buy, hold or sell decisions are clearly important parts of strategy. Moreover, even simple models like the growth/share matrix make clear that the determinants of success are to be found in the interaction of internal resources and external circumstances. While corporate-level strategy continues to be a fundamental component of the strategy field, by the 1980s attention had shifted from the corporate level down to the level of business, or competitive, strategy and to the contributions of a certain Michael Porter and his ideas on industry analysis.

6 Creating strategy from the outside-in

Introduction

By the early 1980s it had become apparent that the extolled virtues of portfolio strategy had not delivered on the promised achievement of sustainable competitive advantage and the US was increasingly losing out to foreign competitors who were now outperforming US companies on US soil: 'It was the powerful and dramatic impact of foreign competition, particularly from Japan, that jolted awake most American managers, and with them, students and analysts of management and firm behavior' (Bartlett and Ghoshal 1991: 5). It seems that American business, buoyed by decades of stability and growth, had been unable to anticipate the emerging competition from the East. Or was it that they simply believed that the threat was not serious? Kiechel reminds us of Henry Ford II's famous remarks on the entry of Japanese automobiles into the US car market in the 1980s, dismissing them as 'those little shitboxes' (Kiechel 2010: xii).

While Japan was regularly held up during the 1980s as the greatest threat to American business, it was not long before the Asian Tiger countries of Singapore, Taiwan, South Korea and Hong Kong would also emerge amid the wider move towards an increasingly globalized world. As Bartlett and Ghoshal (1991: 5) go on to say:

> What followed was a decade when managers, consultants and academics alike made 'global' one of the most overused adjectives in the business lexicon. As we were flooded with definitions and analyses of global competition, global strategies, and global organizations, it became increasingly clear that rather than representing a special case, the study of industries, strategies and organizations in their global context needed to be regarded as the norm.

In this context, the focus of strategy researchers, academics, consultants and practitioners turned increasingly toward the external environment and to the opportunities and threats present therein.

Enter a young Michael Porter, recently described by Fortune magazine as 'the most famous and influential business professor who has ever lived' (Colvin 2012: 70). His 'five forces' industry analysis is at the heart of many strategy courses and a great many strategy textbooks too. He has advised companies, governments and international bodies on issues of strategy and continues to be a highly sought-after speaker on the conference circuit. Porter's contributions span four decades and it would be impossible to do justice to the wide range of his work in the limited space we have here. Instead, and in keeping with the chronological narrative that is at the heart of this book, we will focus primarily on just three of Porter's main ideas – industry (five forces) analysis, generic strategies and the value chain. Porter's work on these themes throughout the late 1970s and early 1980s culminated in two seminal texts, *Competitive Strategy* (1980) and *Competitive Advantage* (1985). In these texts, Porter addresses perhaps the most fundamental strategic question – namely, why are some firms more profitable than others? Then, by extension, why are some industries inherently preferable to others?

When read collectively, the ideas in Porter's early works produce quite a coherent, self-contained approach to strategy that addresses these fundamental question by considering issues of both external and internal analysis as well as important advice on strategic positioning. Such an approach has come to be known as the 'outside-in' approach to strategy, in which strategy develops as an internal response to the opportunities and threats in the outside world. Despite this underlying logic, Porter's ideas are seldom presented in this way in the strategy literature. In many textbooks, for example, the five forces appear in a chapter on external analysis, his generic strategies appear in business-level strategy chapters, and his value chain in internal analysis chapters. This significantly dilutes the connections between these three components. Thus, in this chapter of the book we shall put the pieces of the puzzle back into place and present a more coherent overview of Porter's contribution, which in turn allows for a more detailed and sophisticated treatment of his work to develop. Specifically, we will do the following. First we shall briefly outline industrial organization economics as the theoretical basis on which Porter's contributions are built. Then we shall present each of the three key components of his approach sequentially before 'putting it all altogether' to provide a practical example of the outside-in approach to strategy. We will then briefly consider some of the ways in which Porter has extended his core arguments by looking at his work on national competitiveness and also his work on strategic groups, or clusters. We will finish with an evaluation of Porter's contribution to the field.

Theoretical underpinnings: industrial organization economics

Porter's work is underpinned by a firm base in classical economics, specifically a strand of economics that focuses on industry forces called 'industrial organization' economics (IO economics from hereon in). The origins of IO economics date back to the first half of the twentieth century and were originally developed in order to assist the US government in constructing policies to both encourage and control competitive forces in competitive markets. Policy-makers needed to understand the dynamics of industries in order to ensure that they developed appropriate regulatory legislation that would neither unnecessarily inhibit competition while also restricting the opportunities for monopolistic dominance. Two of the key contributors to this strand of literature were Edward Mason (1949) and his doctoral student Joe Bain (1956). Based on statistical analysis of hundreds of industry across the world Bain and Mason found a recurring relationship between key determinants of industry structure and the performance of individual firms. They developed this into the 'structure-conduct-performance' (SCP) model. Briefly, this suggests that it is the *structure* of an industry (with its underlying competitive forces – such as barriers to entry, levels of product differentiation, size and number of existing competitors, etc.) that determines the *conduct* of firms competing within that industry (pricing strategies, propensity to innovation, product strategies, etc.). The conduct of those firms, within the limits of the structure of the industry, then shapes the *performance* of that industry as a whole. Performance, in this regard, according to Porter (1981), refers to economic measures such as innovativeness, profitability, efficiency, employment levels and so forth.

Put simply, from this perspective it is believed that the industry in which a firm competes has a stronger influence on the firm's success than what goes on inside the firm itself (hence an outside-in approach). Such a claim went against much of the received wisdom and research at the time, which was much more focused on the individual firm. IO theorists put forward the argument that industry was the more important side of the equation. Their claim rested on a number of further assumptions about the nature of the firm:

1 Most firms in most industries control similar resources and pursue similar strategies and therefore there is relatively little difference between them (in this regard IO economics shares some of the characteristic assumptions of both the planning and portfolio approaches).
2 Resources are highly mobile across firms and thus a resource-based advantage cannot be sustained in the long term.
3 Organizational decision-makers are rational and will seek to maximize returns for the organization by adopting profit-maximizing strategies. All other considerations are secondary.

Taking all of this into account, the process of strategy-making, from this perspective, should be to identify the underlying competitive forces in the industry, exploit any opportunities and weaknesses for best advantage and, if necessary, restructure the organization in pursuit of that advantage ... and this is precisely what Porter advocated in the late 1970s and early 1980s (and still does to this day).

The contribution of Michael Porter

Michael Porter was born in Ann Arbor, Michigan in 1947, the son of an army officer. A career academic, he obtained his PhD from the Economics Department at Harvard University, having previously completed an MBA at Harvard Business School. His doctoral thesis entailed an extension and refinement of the ideas of IO economics discussed above and would provide the foundation for the five forces framework. Whereas much of the IO literature was written from a public policy perspective and therefore aimed at regulating competition and excess profit, Porter's interest was in business policy and how industry analysis could be used to maximize profit at the firm level.

Within the confines of the Economics Department, Porter's work was well received, with one of his papers even winning the department's prestigious 'Wells' prize (Kiechel 2010). However, on completion of his doctorate Porter decided to return to the Business School where, in his own words, 'they hated' his ideas (ibid.) for being too abstract and too prescriptive. However, in line with the mandate of the Pittsburgh conference with its call for a more scientific approach to strategy, Porter persevered and soon attracted more attention. The extolled virtues of planning and of portfolio balancing acts had not delivered on the promised achievement of sustainable competitive advantage and the US was increasingly losing out to foreign competitors who were now outperforming US companies on US soil. Porter's argument about the importance of industry and his suggested shift in attention away from the corporate level to the business level, with its focus more on the down and dirty practice of competitive strategy, seemed to provide new solutions to old problems.

In priming his contributions on the importance of industry analysis, Porter (2008) provides a critique of earlier strategy approaches that we will briefly review here. First, Porter argues that portfolio management is not strategy. It is an important activity, to be sure, but it is simply a resource allocation activity. Strategy, he suggests, takes place at the SBU level, where decisions are made about where to compete and how to compete. Second, diversification is not a strategy but a means of achieving one (i.e. the actual strategizing takes place once the diversification has taken place). Third, he argues that market share is the wrong measure of performance. Industry leadership, he argues, is an *effect* of good strategy – it is an outcome not a strategy in itself. Instead, Porter prefers to focus on the *attractiveness* of an industry (in relation to its underlying structural forces). After all, he notes, you can have a high market share but if it is in an unattractive industry then it is likely to yield lower returns than a market follower competing in a more attractive industry. Fourth, Porter also takes issue with the focus on market growth rate. A common mistake, he suggests, is to assume that fast-growing industries are the most attractive. Far from it, he suggests. Fast-growing markets tend to be the most unattractive because of the costs involved in entering, such as high R&D costs, high marketing costs, etc., and because of the strong competitive forces as firms 'jockey for position'. Other structural forces, such as powerful suppliers, are also more common in fast-growing markets as competitors fight for scarce supplies while production ramps up. Porter gives the example of the home PC industry, which grew rapidly throughout the 1990s but has consistently been one of the least profitable of industries. Porter is quite clear in this regard:

> Industry structure drives competition and profitability, not whether an industry produces a product or service, is emerging or mature, high tech or low tech, regulated or unregulated. While a myriad of factors can affect industry profitability in the short run – including the weather and the business cycle – industry structure, manifested in the competitive forces, sets industry profitability in the medium and long run.
>
> (Porter 2008: 80)

Drawing from this critique, and building on his foundation in IO economics, Porter makes the following claims:

- The strategic goal of an organization is to maximize its profits and competition eliminates profit.
- Underlying competitive forces determine the overall profitability of an industry.
- Some industries are more attractive (profitable) than others.
- Even in unattractive industries, some firms are more profitable than others and this is due to the way they position themselves within the industry.
- Strategy should be about identifying (and where possible only competing in) attractive industries and (in either scenario) positioning the firm in such a way that it can secure a sustainable competitive advantage and achieve above-average returns.

On the basis of these claims, Porter developed a series of strategy tools and frameworks that he believed would assist senior managers in achieving sustainable competitive advantage: industry analysis (1980); generic strategies (1980), and the value chain (1985). In the next part of this chapter we will look at each in more detail.

Industry analysis

On the basis of a large-scale quantitative survey of hundreds of different industries undertaken by IO economists, Porter suggests that there are consistently five underlying competitive forces that are present in every industry and which determine the structure of that industry. The relative strength of these five forces will determine how attractive (profitable) the industry will be. While other variables such as the distinction between product/service offerings, the industry life cycle, technological innovation, etc., can influence profitability in the short run, none of these remain constant over time or across industries.

As outlined in Figure 6.1, Porter's five forces constitute both a horizontal and a vertical dimension of competition. The horizontal dimension replicates the manufacturing process from the acquisition of raw materials through production and selling. At each stage there are forces that can be either powerful or weak – these are represented as the power of the *suppliers* to the industry, the competitive *rivalry* among existing firms competing in the industry, and the power of the *buyers* who acquire or consume the offerings. In each relationship the firm competes with these forces to retain value. Thus, it competes with its suppliers who seek to raise prices up on the industry or drive quality and quantity down, it competes with rivals for a share of the value created in the industry, and it competes with buyers who will always try to pay less for more. On the vertical dimension Porter identifies the forms of competition that can take profitability away form the current industry – these come from the threat of *new entrants*, that might disrupt the current competitive forces, and from the threat of *substitute* products or services that can displace the current industry's offerings.

Let us look at each of the five forces in turn.

Threat of new entry

New entrants can take profitability away from the industry in a number of ways. First, where demand is limited, a new entrant will effectively compete for an existing slice of the pie thus taking revenue away from existing competitors. It can often also ignite price wars as incumbents try and defend against the threat. Where the new entrant has diversified from an existing market or industry then it may be able to leverage existing capabilities in this new industry, bringing with it new technology, innovation, new capacity

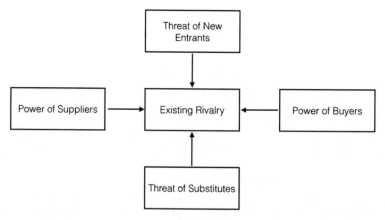

Figure 6.1 The five forces
Source: Adapted from Porter 1980.

or some other disruption that might require existing rivals to respond. Much of the assessment of the threat of new entrants comes from the height and strength of the barriers to entry that can be raised against it. Common barriers to entry include economies of scale, scope and experience; product differentiation; resource requirements; switching costs; and access to key resources, distribution channels, etc.

Let us take as our example the home PC industry, which Porter has identified above as an unattractive industry. We might suggest that one reason for this is that the barriers to entry are very low. It is quite easy to set up in this industry with a little know-how and minimal investment. Setting up a workshop in the garage or back room, building machines in a build-to-order arrangement from pre-purchased parts widely available on the internet and then sold through a website, for which payment is taken in advance, makes for a very low-cost business model and is evidenced by the large number of very small PC competitors that populate the web – which, incidentally, is how Dell first started, and it still retains many of the above features in its current business model. By contrast, the entry barriers into something like the pharmaceutical industry would be incredibly high, with massive capital investment in facilities, patents, technology and personnel. Indeed, so high are these barriers that the strategy of acquisition and merger tends to be the preferred method of growth in this industry, thus further restricting the possibility of new entrants.

In addition to barriers to entry, we also need to consider barriers to mobility or growth because, in the business environment of the twenty-first century, this can be a more important measure. If we return to our PC industry example, the threat of new entry is very high but the ability of firms to grow in this industry is less viable. Interestingly, since the 1980s just four or five key players have dominated the PC industry at any one time but these have not remained the same over time. Instead, the common strategy in this industry is for powerful new entrants to acquire existing players rather than build up their own position. Thus, the current leader in the industry, Lenovo, only started competing in this market in 2005 and did so by acquiring IBM's established PC business. Acer, another dominant player today, established itself in the US market in 2007 with its acquisition of Gateway Inc. It also acquired Packard Bell in 2007 to spread its reach into the European market. In response, Hewlett Packard acquired Compaq to establish a defence against these new entrants.

Barriers to mobility, Porter (1980) suggests, are a powerful explanatory factor for understanding why early entrants into an industry may pursue different strategies to late entrants: early mover advantage translates into a strong position that cannot easily be overcome by later entrants. Thus, in the 1970s and 1980s Sony's remarkable ability to bring to market many innovations in consumer electronics meant that despite lower-cost models quickly being introduced by competitors, none could displace Sony as the gold standard in consumer electronics throughout this period.

The power of suppliers

Suppliers can reduce profitability in an industry when they are able to charge higher prices to the industry, have control over key components vital to the industry, or possess key technologies or resources that they can withhold, limit or remove. Powerful suppliers pass on costs to the industry, thus reducing profitability. A supplier group is deemed to be powerful if:

- It is dominated by a few companies and is more concentrated than the industry it is selling to;
- It is not obliged to contend with other substitute products for sale in the industry;

- the industry is not an important customer of the supplier group;
- the supplier's product is an important input to the buyer's business;
- the supplier group's products are differentiated or it has built up switching costs;
- the supplier group poses a credible threat of forward integration.

(Porter 1980: 27)

If we return to our PC industry example, three of the key components necessary to build this product are the microprocessor, the graphics card and the operating system. Each of these components is controlled by one or two key suppliers: Intel and AMD in processors, Nvidia and ATI in graphics, and Microsoft in operating systems. Even here, things are becoming slightly less clear, with Intel now producing graphical capabilities on their processor chips and ATI being owned by AMD. In each instance, these suppliers have been able to leverage up prices in the industry while limiting the speed at which the industry can launch new products which, in a largely undifferentiated market, are driven by the launch of new processors, graphics cards or operating systems. Indeed, Microsoft's dominance of the market for operating systems has seen it squeeze more and more profit from the manufacturers as it has continued to raise the price of licensing its software over the years. The only viable alternatives are open source software which, while gaining in popularity, are still only a faction of the install base overall. In addition, each of these key suppliers has gone further by not only supplying this industry but establishing themselves as brands in their own right. If we take Intel as our example, the famous 'Intel Inside' advertising campaign came about at a time when few people really understood the components in their PC and this had the knock-on effect that manufacturers were happy to continue using Intel's older and cheaper chips, thus forcing prices down on Intel. In response, a young MBA graduate at Intel, Dennis Carter, persuaded CEO Andy Grove to explore the possibility of branding the chips so as to draw end customers' attention to the Intel inside. With a modest budget and little confidence, Carter went about devising a suitable campaign. It worked. The end consumer understood the message and began to push manufacturers into supplying the latest chips in their PCs. In that moment, Kaplan (2013a: 79) argues, 'Carter had shifted the power ... from the PC makers to a key supplier'. Arguably Microsoft had been doing this for years and it was not long before Nvidia and ATI followed suit in relation to graphical processors.

The power of buyers

Here we need to distinguish two key buyer groups – customers in the supply chain and end consumers. In the case of end consumers, assessments of power rest largely on the notion of switching costs – how easy is it for a consumer to switch between offerings within the industry and/or between the industry and its substitutes. The easier it is, measured in relative cost saving, the more powerful they are deemed to be. Other key indicators include the standard economic measures such as their concentration, geographic spread, individual purchase power, etc. Where consumers are deemed to be powerful they can exercise their right to switch as a means of driving down prices or demanding higher quality – each of which draws profitability away from the industry. In the case of our PC industry, we might anticipate the end buyer to be very powerful, with most manufacturers using the same core components there is little to differentiate offerings at a technical level. Thus, competition becomes increasingly about price, service and additional features with a view to building brand loyalty. Customers in the supply chain (e.g. retailers) also constitute a buyer group and while they share many of the characteristics above we can also add other measures such as threat of backward integration into the supply chain.

The threat of substitutes

Porter defines a substitute as a product or service that 'performs the same or a similar function as an industry's product by a different means' (Porter 2008: 84). In this regard, it is important to distinguish between rivals who compete in the same industry and substitutes that are provided by a different industry. Thus, in the manufacture and sale of PCs, Dell and Asus are rivals. However, a substitute for the PC might be a tablet or a smartphone. In theory, existing rivals could make these products but they constitute, in Porter's frame, a separate industry and therefore are classed as substitutes.

Porter notes that substitutes are an ever-present threat in any industry and are therefore often easy to overlook. This was very much the case with the tablet computer. The PC industry failed to appreciate the disruptive innovation that was the Apple iPad and by the time they had realized what was going on the tablet market had grown substantially and was drawing customers away from the traditional PC industry. Why was this? The answer takes us to a second key issue in substitution, namely on what basis do customers make the distinction between rivals and substitutes? For Porter, the idea of substitutes derives from the customer's need and therefore the use value of the offering. Thus, if a customer's need is to surf the web, do some email and play a few games then a tablet or a smartphone makes an enticing substitute for a PC. However, if the need is music or video creation then a tablet or phone may not be a substitute (although the speed at which tablet technology is developing means this may not be the case for much longer). If we conceive of the PC as a productivity tool then we might still see the tablet or phone as a substitute, but we could also see a typewriter or pen and paper as a substitute. If the PC satisfies an entertainment need then a games console or a TV may constitute a substitute. As we can see, substitution is a messy concept and this perhaps explains why it is so often overlooked.

Existing rivalry

Existing rivalry addresses the competitive practices among existing players in the industry such as price-based competition, differentiation, new product launch, etc. In short, all of the tactical moves necessary to keep the strategy in place. Where there is a high degree of rivalry, either in the sense of a relatively large number of rivals competing for limited business or where there is a desire to outperform others, these activities will all drive profitability out of the industry as rivals compete to gain and retain business. Of all the bases on which rivalry can take place, Porter warns that price-based competition is the most dangerous as it can result in a 'zero-sum' game in which firms may be driven out of the industry altogether through accepting lower and lower margins. This is important as Porter does not advocate the elimination of competition in pursuit of profit. Rather, he suggests that competition is healthy and necessary for industry performance. The question is how to occupy a more attractive position that your rivals.

Critical lessons in successfully applying the five forces

Despite the seemingly straightforward nature of this framework, it is not uncommon to miss a number of its finer points, necessary for successful application. We shall briefly review some of these below.

A tool of industry analysis

The first key point to take away is that Porter's framework is aimed at the industry level NOT the firm level. Many mistakenly apply the five forces to an individual firm – focusing on the firm's own buyers, suppliers, rivals, etc. While it is highly likely that this is frequently what happens in practice, it is to fundamentally misunderstand the outside-in approach to strategy. Porter is not primarily interested in firms – they are just one more competitive force. For Porter it is the industry forces that matter because it is the industry that determines competition.

Defining the industry

A second key issue in the five forces analysis is defining the industry itself. This is a lot harder to do that it first appears. It is perhaps useful to begin by distinguishing the market from the industry – the former refers to a system of exchange in which competing goods and services are offered and purchased; the latter refers to the whole system of production necessary to produce the goods and service that are exchanged in the market. Definitions of industries often draw on either supply-side or demand-side factors, i.e. the similarity of the raw materials, production processes, finished goods, etc., that define an industry or, conversely, the degree to which consumers view one product as satisfying the same need as another. Porter defines an industry as 'the group of firms producing products that are close substitutes for each other' (cited in Spender and Kraaijenbrink 2011: 34).

In addition, Porter (2008) seeks to distinguish the boundaries between industries through the notion of *scope*. First, the scope of a product or service in meeting a particular need. Thus, if the industry structure for two different products is very similar or the same then they should be treated as one industry. If there are fundamental differences in the two then they should be treated separately. Second, there is the issue of geographic scope. Most firms compete on an international level and if the industry structure is replicated across a number of different countries then it makes sense, he suggests, to treat this as one industry whereas if the industry structure is different in each country these are best treated as separate industries, for the purposes of analysis. However, as Porter observes:

> The extent of differences in the five forces for related products or across geographic areas is a matter of degree, making industry definition often a matter of judgment. A rule of thumb is that where the differences in any one force are large, and where the differences involve more than one force, distinct industries may well be present.
> (Porter 2008: 91)

Despite these best attempts, defining an industry for many goods and service is still incredibly difficult and it is therefore unsurprising that Porter picks relatively straightforward examples in his work – the 'airline industry', the 'automobile industry'. But what industry does Apple compete in? Or Amazon? Or Google? Is there just one industry definition that captures the range of activities in which each is engaged? As an aside, Porter's definitions and examples also tend to reflect his target audience. The five forces is not an economic model but a managerial framework intended to help managers create strategy. Thus his definitions are perhaps more accessible and meaningful to the manager than to the economist.

Why only five forces?

A common criticism of industry analysis is Porter's insistence on only five forces. In particular, critics have suggested that there are at least three other forces than need to be integrated: government, technology, and complementors (complementary products or services that are mutually co-dependent, such as Microsoft and Intel in the PC industry). In response, Porter explicitly outlines his continued defence of the 'five' forces. He argues that government is an external force that impacts the industry as a whole and therefore cannot be considered as a discrete force in its own right – government policies inform all of the forces in different ways and on multiple levels. On technology, Porter suggests that this is not an indicator of an attractive or unattractive industry and therefore is not a key force of industry structure – there are plenty of mundane, low-tech industries that are very attractive while there are many high-tech industries that are not very attractive (such as the PC industry, as seen above). Thus, he argues, there is no direction correlation between technology and profitability. Regarding complementors, he makes the argument that they are neither inherently good nor inherently bad for the industry but, like government, operate on numerous levels and therefore reside outside the industry structure.

Confusing substitutes and rivals

Another common error in interpretation, one that frequently goes hand-in-hand with a failure to recognize this as an industry-level framework, is to confuse and conflate rivals and substitutes. Competitors are rivals. Substitutes are those industries (not competitors) that offer a product or service that may satisfy the same buyer need. Of course there is no absolute threshold for substitutability thus we need to talk in terms of close and broad substitutes. For example, the video-games industry is a close substitute for the PC industry if the need is game-playing. Equally, a broad substitute for game-playing might be watching a movie or going to the cinema, if the need is entertainment. Needless to say, Porter offers less messy examples but the issue remains the same – the level of substitution is considered at an industry level and not at a firm level.

A tool of analysis not description

Finally, as Porter states, the five forces is an *analysis* – an active process. Thus, it is not enough simply to produce a detailed list of forces culminating in a tick list against each of the five forces but rather, for Porter, the five forces is a dynamic framework and interest lies not in the current profitability but in potential future profitability – after all, strategy is a forward-looking discipline. It is not enough to simply describe the key forces; rather, the goal is to analyze them in order to better understand the underlying drivers of profitability in the industry – both present and future – to understand where power lies and to identify weaknesses or gaps that can be exploited.

The attractiveness test

Having collected data and assessed each of the five forces, the goal is to draw a conclusion on the relative attractiveness of the industry. For Porter an industry is attractive if it yields the potential for long-term profitability, which in turn is measured in terms of the long-run return on invested capital (Porter 1980). The mistake here is to assume that the most attractive industry is one in which there are no competitive forces and therefore one in which a monopoly position is possible. For Porter, writing in 1980s America and somewhat revealing of his neoliberal persuasions, competition is necessary and healthy: it is the plane of competition that determines how attractive the industry will be. Thus, Porter advises looking at the underlying drivers of change in the industry that will determine profitability in the future. Questions such as:

- Why is current industry profitability what it is? What is propping it up?
- What is changing? How is profitability likely to shift?
- What limiting factors must be overcome to capture more of the value in the industry?

(Magretta 2012: 58)

Understanding these underlying drivers then allows the firm to *position* itself in such a way as to defend against the competitive forces while also exploiting any potential weaknesses that are uncovered. The concern with positioning led Porter to his second contribution in this period, the generic strategies.

Positioning and the generic strategies

Having identified the relative attractiveness of the industry the next stage in a Porterian strategy process is to identify a position of 'best fit' from which to compete. Such a position should allow the firm to defend against the five forces while also providing an opportunity for exploiting any weaknesses. Thus, if industry analysis addresses the question of where to compete, generic strategies address the question of how to compete. The great mistake here, Porter argues is to compete to 'be the best'. For Porter there is no 'best' in the singular, rather there are a number of different customer needs that can be satisfied by a range of different value propositions. Being 'the best' he suggests is a common business goal but a poor basis on which to build a strategy as it leads to a 'zero-sum game' in which competitors all converge on the same strategy with the same goal and thus drive profitability out of the industry. Magretta (2012) highlights the airline industry as a classic example of competitive convergence:

> If American Airlines tries to win customers by offering free meals on its New York to Miami route, then Delta will be forced to match it – leaving both companies worse off. Both will have incurred added costs, but neither will be able to charge more, and neither will end up with more seats filled. Every time one company makes a move, its rivals will jump to match it. With everyone chasing after the same customer, there will be a contest over every sale.

(Magretta 2012: 24)

Instead of this, Porter advocates the need to pick a position in the industry in which competition can be avoided or exploited. Building on his work on the importance of industry structure and attractiveness, Porter suggests that there are two bases on which sustainable competitive advantage can be achieved: *cost leadership* or *differentiation*. These combine with the scope of the business – whether it services the whole industry (*broad*) or just one part of it (*focus*) to create four generic strategies, as outlined in Figure 6.2. Failure to pick, and stick to, one of these strategies means that, in Porter's famous term, the company is 'stuck in the middle' and will never realize anything but mediocre results.

Cost leadership

Cost leadership is about becoming the lowest cost producer in the industry. This is not the same as offering the lowest prices (although the two do often correlate). The strategic focus is on lowering internal costs such that the margins that can be generated are greater than the industry average. This type of strategy therefore puts the emphasis on achieving economies of scale, scope and experience; on high-volume production; and on closely monitoring all operating costs.

So how does cost leadership defend against the five forces? A successful cost leadership strategy defends against the five forces in the following ways:

- Existing rivals are weakened by the economies of experience that derive from higher volume sales. Rivals will resist competing on price as it confers a price-based advantage to the cost leader – only the cost leader can compete effectively on price.
- Threat of new entrants is reduced by using price as a barrier to entry to force new competitors out.
- Threat of substitutes is negated by the ability to rapidly enter substitute industries due to large reserves accrued. Alternatively, prices can be lowered to bring buyers back.
- Power of suppliers is reduced by being able to absorb price increases with less impact than the industry average rival. Alternatively, bulk purchasing can force suppliers to offer more favourable terms (lower prices).
- Power of buyers is limited when they are price sensitive.

(Ireland *et al.* 2011)

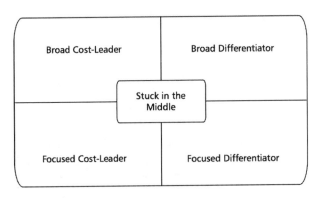

Figure 6.2 The generic strategies
Source: Adapted from Porter 1980.

Of course, such a strategy does not come without risks. In the case of cost leadership, Porter (1980: 45) identifies the key strategic risks in the following ways:

- Technological changes that make obsolete past investments or learning. For example, Sony's Betamax format lost the video wars against VHS but then won the DVD war with its Blu-ray format against HD DVD. In both instances the low-cost manufacturers of those obsolete systems were unable to reposition as easily as differentiated competitors.
- Low-cost learning by industry newcomers or followers, through imitation or through their ability to invest in state-of-the-art facilities. As there can only be one cost leader, the strategy is under continual challenge and once the advantage is lost the firm has no other basis on which to achieve competitive advantage – as experienced by numerous US firms in the 1980s and 1990s who were displaced by even lower-cost South Korean competitors, such as Samsung in the home electronics market.
- Inability to see required product or marketing change because of the attention placed on cost. For example, Ford's failure to recognize changing customer tastes in the growing car industry in the 1920s allowed its rival, General Motors, to overtake it while Ford had to close its factory for 12 months in order to retool and move away from its one-car-for-all business model.
- Inflation in costs that narrow the firm's ability to maintain enough of a price differential to offset competitors' brand images or other approaches to differentiation. Thus, the pursuit of cost leadership may eventually come at the cost of achieving an acceptable level of service for buyers. For example, budget airline EasyJet experienced consumer backlash when it removed what were felt to be too many standard features and charged for too many essentials, such as drinking water or the use of toilets. Wal-Mart has faced similar opposition for having too few staff in stores, a key cost saving.

Differentiation

Differentiation, by contrast, involves providing some perceived benefit or feature that distinguishes the offering from that of competitors and for which a premium price can therefore be charged – if it helps, think about it through the logic of branding. The point of differentiation will vary widely – it might be tangible, such as a particular product design, delivery system or product feature, or it might be intangible, such as a certain brand proposition. As Clegg *et al.* (2010) note, in most instances it will be a combination of tangible and intangible features that provide an overall point of differentiation. Thus, we might suggest that Apple, as a differentiator offers a particular product design and product features combined with, for some, a trusted brand reputation, a particular buying environment and a certain level of after-sales service.

A position of differentiation thus allows a firm to defend against the five forces by leveraging the loyalty it is able to garner for its product or service and to pass costs on to the customer who is already willing to pay a price premium. In short, its premium position acts as a defence against each of the five forces – it can be leveraged as a barrier to entry, can be used to pass cost increases levied by suppliers on to the customer, and can be used to mark out a clearly defined value proposition against rivals and substitutes.

Porter (1980: 46) identifies the key risks of differentiation as follows:

- The cost differentiation between low-cost competitors and the differentiated firm becomes too great for differentiation to hold brand loyalty. For example, branded food goods are being increasingly exchanged for cheaper supermarket 'own label' alternatives by customers looking to make economies.
- Buyer need for the differentiating factor falls. This typically occurs where the industry converges on a largely undifferentiated offering. We can refer back to our example of the PC industry above where issues such as price and promotion increasingly influence consumer choice when presented with rows of rather generic and undifferentiated black boxes.
- Imitation narrows perceived differentiation. This might be as a result of industry maturity but a growing counterfeit culture has also accounted for numerous failures to maintain a premium position. For example, in the UK the fashion brand Burberry, a focused differentiator providing expensive, high-end fashion wear had its image destroyed as counterfeit goods flooded the market and the brand became associated with less aspirational characters in British society in the 1990s.

Focus

Focus simply means serving one segment of the market – this might be a particular segment of customers, focused product lines, specific distribution channels, etc. However, to compete effectively in such a niche, Porter suggests that there needs to be either unmet or unusual customer need or a unique production or delivery system. Otherwise, the focuser is unable to offer anything that the broad-based competitor cannot, and the latter can probably do it more efficiently or effectively as they are able to leverage their broader customer base. In short, the focus strategy requires doing something not just differently, but differently to the industry norm. For Porter, the risks of focus include:

- the possibility that the cost differential between broad-range competitors and the focused firm widens to eliminate the cost advantage of serving a narrow target or to offset the differentiation achieved by focus;
- the differences in desired products or services between the strategic target and the market as a whole narrows;
- Competitors find submarkets within the strategic target and out-focus the focuser.

(Porter 1980: 46)

Despite its commonsense appeal it is worth noting that, unlike the industry analysis framework that preceded it, Porter provides no empirical grounding on which to base these ideas. Indeed, although appearing as chapter 2 in the 1980 text, the discussion of generic strategies was the last chapter that Porter wrote and did so almost as an afterthought. As Kiechel recalls the story: 'Porter decided that he 'needed to say something about positioning', about how a company should seek to locate itself within an industry, given the array of those forces: 'Having taught cases, I knew that one had to have something to say about the firm, and firms are all different' (Kiechel 2010: 132).

The generic strategies are also the most criticized component of Porter's approach to strategy, with numerous examples of highly successful companies actively pursuing both cost leadership and differentiation with continued success – IKEA, Toyota and Coca-Cola, for example. In fact, in the contemporary business climate there are few companies that do not seek to do things differently while also trying to reduce costs. For example, despite charging premium prices, Apple enjoys some of the highest industry profits in its various markets due in large part to its cost management strategy. For example, in 2010 Apple sold just 17 million iPhone handsets compared to over 400 million sold by Nokia, Samsung and LG. Yet Apple received 39 per cent of the industry profit from these 17 million. The 400 million sold by its competitors returned only 32 per cent of the industry profit (O'Reilly 2010).

So sustained has the critique been that Porter has recognized the possibility of such *hybrid* strategies but, somewhat belligerently, argues that they only exist in unique situations and are never defendable in the long term (Porter 1985). Specifically, Porter argues that there are three conditions under which a hybrid strategy can be achieved. First, where all competitors are stuck in the middle and no one firm has a clearly defined competitive position. However, he goes on to say that such a state of affairs is likely to be only temporary for, as one firm chooses a generic strategy it will begin to realize the benefits of this trade-off and achieve above-average returns. This will push competitors to follow suit. Second, cost leadership and differentiation can be combined and sustained when cost position is heavily influenced by market share as in the case of many commodity markets where there is little brand differentiation and where buyers and sellers have something close to perfect information. Third, cost and differentiation can be combined when a firm has developed a new innovation or technology and thus is able to leverage first-mover advantage to differentiate itself based on its innovation while selling more of its product. For Porter, there are few industries in which this is sustainable over the long term as the process of reverse engineering and the practice of imitation begin to erode that advantage.

However, if we look beyond the semantic debates then the underlying point that Porter is making is an important one. Ultimately, what he is saying is that firms need to do something different in order to create a sustainable position over the long term. Doing things differently might sound like common sense but in many industries, and certainly when Porter was developing these ideas, competition was often a zero-sum game in which the aim was to beat the competition and to be the best in the industry. Don't forget, being the best, as defined by being market share leader, was core to the prescription on the portfolio approach. However, for Porter competition need not be zero-sum. There are many positions available in an industry which allow many competitors to thrive, but a desire to all compete for the same tag 'be the best' results in what Porter call 'competitive convergence' in which a race to the same position becomes in itself a force that drives profitability out of the industry.

Another key lesson we can draw from Porter is the importance of making trade-offs. Any strategy is as much about what you don't do as what you do. Trying to be 'all things to all people', Porter (1985) has argued, leads to strategic mediocrity and industry average returns. If you try and serve all customers groups in all product categories you will fail to carve out a unique value proposition. The most successful companies, he suggests, are those that consciously make trade-offs and knowingly sacrifice potential avenues for profit in order to maintain a robust value proposition. In a sense we can see this as a response to the failures of the diversification wave of the previous decade – the attempt to do more and more leading to lower levels of profitability. In a similar vein and writing at a similar time, Peters and Waterman (1982) suggest that firms 'stick to the knitting' – in other words, do what they are best at.

From Porter's work on the generic strategy and on positioning we can draw the following lessons:

- positioning should be determined in relation to industry structure;
- do things differently – don't get stuck in the middle;
- dare to make trade-offs – trying to be all things to all people, Porter claims, leads to strategic mediocrity.

At the heart of Porter's thesis on positioning is the need to develop a meaningful, unique and sustainable *value proposition*. The value proposition, Porter argues, is the response to three fundamental questions:

- Which customers are you going to serve?
- Which needs are you going to meet?
- What price can you charge that will be acceptable to both customer and the firm?

(Magretta 2012: 96)

The simplicity of the value proposition is that it captures all of the different aspects of Porter's strategy process in one simple statement. The decision on what value proposition to pursue should reflect the underlying drivers of profit in the industry, as understood through an industry analysis, and should impart on the firm a particular position in that industry, based on the underlying logic of the generic strategies. In contemporary business language we often refer to this as the firm's *business model*. As Teece notes:

> The function of a business model is to 'articulate' the value proposition, select the appropriate technologies and features, identify targeted market segments, define the structure of the value chain, and estimate the cost structure and profit potential. In short, a business model is a plan for the organizational and financial 'architecture' of a business. This model makes assumptions about the behaviour of revenues and costs, and likely customer and competitor behaviour. It outlines the contours of the solution required to earn a profit, if a profit is available to be earned.
>
> (Teece 2009: 24)

The pursuit of a generic strategy based on cost leadership or differentiation and informed by the competitive forces in the industry frequently necessitates a certain degree of restructuring of the organization. Following Chandler (1962), Porter subscribes to the notion that structure follows strategy. To achieve structural alignment, in 1985, Porter offered a tool of organizational analysis and, in doing so, addressed the claim by many of his critics that his work was too focused on the external environment. Porter's contribution was the *value chain*.

The value chain

In 1985, Porter followed up the book *Competitive Strategy* with *Competitive Advantage*. The main theme of the 1985 text was the value chain. The purpose of the value chain is to address specifically the issue of how to implement the generic strategy. In this regard

88 Creating strategy from the outside-in

Porter claimed that his aim was to: 'build a bridge between strategy [formulation] and implementation' (Porter 1985: 3). Porter views the firm as a collection of 'discrete, but interrelated economic activities' (Porter 1991: 102) such as manufacturing products, shipping goods, making sales and processing orders, and argues that what connects these activities is the value they produce when combined: this he terms the value chain. As shown in Fiugre 6.3, the value chain seeks to break down the internal workings of the firm into discrete value-adding activities in order to understand how they can contribute to the competitive advantage being pursued through the generic strategy.

The value chain is broken down into primary and support activities. Primary activities reflect those different stages necessary to manufacture and sell products right through from acquiring and shipping in raw materials to offering customer support after a sale has been made. These *primary* activities (note again Porter's preference for a manufacturing model of the organization) are supported by a range of activities that include personnel management, infrastructure, technology and procurement policies. The vertical dotted lines indicate that each support activity, save for structure, link directly to each primary activity. The firm's infrastructure is seen as an overarching activity that informs all primary and support activity. On the right-hand side we have the label 'margin' which refers to the revenues accrued less the costs of performing the value chain activities, in other words the *profit* margin. However, it is important to note that the identification of margins is not simply the equation of price–cost. The margin is a reflection of the value the firm can add to the product such that it can charge a particular price. Thus, it may cost £10 to build a widget but if it is then sold for £15 there must be some way of accounting for that margin. In Porter's value chain this is represented by the value-adding activity that is drawn from the value proposition outlined in the identification of a generic strategy. Let us explore the value chain in more detail.

Primary activities

Maintaining his preference for an industrial model of the firm, Porter (1985) identifies primary activities as those required to manufacture and sell a product. Thus the primary activities replicate the manufacturing process and consist of the following value-adding activities:

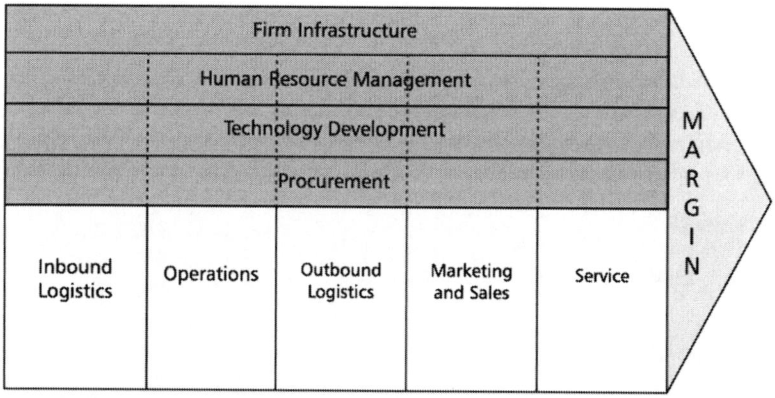

Figure 6.3 The value chain
Source: Adapted from Porter 1985.

- Inbound logistics – the acquisition, receiving, storing and distributing of materials and inputs into the production process.
- Operations – activities required to turn raw materials into final products such as machining, assembling and packaging, quality control and testing.
- Outbound logistics – storing and shipping finished goods to distribution centres or customers.
- Marketing and sales – advertising, sales force management and all activities required to communicate with customer and end consumers.
- Service – the activities involved in supporting customers with their purchase post sale. This might include after-sales care, repair services, and warranty management.

(Porter 1985: 40)

Support activities

Primary value-adding activities are complemented by a number of company-wide support structures that influence each activity:

- Procurement – the activities involved in acquiring the raw materials necessary to produce the product. Such purchasing activities may be activity-specific or company-wide.
- Technology development – every value-adding activity makes use of technological know-how to achieve ever more efficient processes. As Porter (1985) notes, technological development can take many different forms, from basic research and design to product improvements to developments in production processes to the use of new technologies to communicate with customers and suppliers.
- Human resource management – here Porter refers primarily to the recruitment, training, development and remuneration policies employed by the firm. HRM can add value through recruiting, training and compensating a work force best equipped for the needs of the primary activities.
- Firm infrastructure – this consists of a number of activities such as general management, strategic planning, financial control, and so on.

(Porter 1985: 41)

Activity types

Within each category of primary and support activity, there are three 'activity types' that play a different role in achieving competitive advantage:

- Direct – activities directly involved in creating value for the buyer, such as assembly, parts machining, sales force operation, advertising, product design, recruiting, etc.
- Indirect – activities that make it possible to perform direct activities on a continuing basis, such as maintenance, scheduling, operation of facilities, sales force administration, research administration, vendor record-keeping, etc.
- Quality Assurance – activities that ensure the quality of other activities, such as monitoring, inspecting, testing, reviewing, checking, adjusting and reworking. Quality assurance is not synonymous with quality management because many value activities contribute to quality.

(Porter 1985: 43–4)

In sum, the purpose of the value chain is to identify the varied activities of the organization and determine to what extent they add or take away value. Or, to put it another way, do these activities contribute to the basis of the firm's pursued position and competitive advantage. In order to do this, every activity undertaken within a firm has to be captured within the value chain analysis, which can make it an exhaustive exercise, as Porter notes: 'Every machine in a factory, for example, could be treated as a separate activity. Thus the number of potential activities is often quite large' (1985: 45). Perhaps an even greater challenge is in trying to measure, or quantify, value itself. Pearson (1999: 150) provides the following example to illuminate the problem:

> Take, for example, the automobile – a very typical Porter industry and example – in amongst the firm's various activities is the part where the wheels are attached to the car. It may be easy to measure the 'costs' of this process but how do you assign 'value'? What value is a car without wheels? – A crude example but it makes the point. In short assigning value appears easy in theory but fails to reflect the more fuzzy nature of reality.

We might level the same question at less crude examples. For example, one of Porter's identified support activities is human resource management, but again how do we add value to this function? How do we quantify the value added from recruitment, training and grievance processes?

Such unanswered concerns have led many to downgrade the importance of the value chain, which was soon replaced by more sophisticated treatments of the internal environment arising out of the emerging resource-based view of strategy, which we shall hear about in the next chapter of the book. Others have questioned its continued relevance. Brusoni et al. (2009) suggest that in an increasingly networked economy in which firms frequently work together, seeing each one as a separate and isolated entity is no longer meaningful: the firm has been displaced by a network of interconnecting activities, they suggest. Others have questioned whether fundamental aspects of organizational life – culture, motivation, leadership, communications, etc. – can be captured through this rather clinical process, which lends itself much more to visible and quantifiable activities (see Aktouf et al. 2011).

However, once again we may suspect that much of this dismissal comes from a limited reading of the value chain. When located in the context of a wider Porterian strategy process – and if one takes the time to read the actual 1985 text rather than a brief entry in a textbook – it can be found to provide valuable insights into the organizational restructuring necessary to achieve a generic strategy. So let us take the time to explore this in a little more detail.

For Kiechel (2010), much of the power of the value chain comes from its attention to linkages. By connecting the various constituent parts of the organization together through the logic of value-creating activity, as opposed to the more common approach of reporting lines, hierarchy, etc., it is possible to begin to unpack where value lies in the organization and how different activities either contribute to the value-added activity or take value away. Thus, a firm may have an outstanding marketing department but if it is unable to produce products worthy of such promotion then there will be little value to be gained. Porter was also keen to point this out, discouraging proponents of the value chain from seeing each activity as separate and discrete – a common feature of many organizational structures. In this regard Porter advocates a need for synergy between value-adding activities, recognizing that performance in one activity area can have an effect, positive or negative, on other activities. For example, a periodic discount sale in a retail store needs to be communicated through marketing and backed up by operations to ensure sufficient stock levels and capable logistics systems. Witnesses to events such as 'Black Friday' sales in the US and the Boxing Day sale in the UK are often testament to the failure of such coordination. Think also, for example, of the synergy needed at Amazon when it offers its 'Prime' customers next-day, or in some instances same-day, delivery. This requires significant coordination both within the value chain and across the value network, employing external delivery firms to ensure the goods are collected and delivered on time.

Kiechel further suggest that the value chain reflects the wider enthusiasm for quality management and the efficiency systems that came to be known colloquially as the Japanese management approach in the 1980s. Remember, the 1980s was a period of intense competition, with many American firms losing out to international competitors – Japan in particular. As a result, a lot of attention was paid to the Japanese way of doing things and while some explain Japanese success as a result of strategic intent, or strong cultures, or a focus on innovation, there was also an influential stream of literature that focused on operational excellence, out of which a wider audience came to learn about total quality management, just-in-time production, lean manufacturing, and so on. In many respects, Porter's work on the value chain can be seen as an example of this latter literature.

The value chain and strategic fit

Perhaps the most important linkage between the value chain and the positioning strategy is that of *strategic fit*. Put simply, Porter's argument is that it is insufficient simply to ensure a lean, efficient and margin-generating value chain. It must be explicitly tied to the value proposition that is at the heart of the positioning strategy. As such, the test of value and the activities that need to be focused on are those that facilitate the firm's delivery of its value proposition. Hence, there must be *fit* between the firm and its strategy. So how might this work in practice? Let us take first the generic strategy of cost leadership.

Cost leadership and strategic fit

Optimizing the value chain in pursuit of cost leadership typically requires producing a fairly standard product with features or benefits that appeal to the industry average buyer. Due to its standardized nature it tends to be lower priced. Therefore, the firm needs to sell higher quantities than the industry average, at lower price, in order to realize above-average returns. In order to do this it needs to consider each activity in the firm as a cost centre. Porter warns that a common mistake when pursuing a cost-based strategy is to focus too heavily on production as the primary cost centre. In fact, he suggests, substantial, if not the majority of costs occur in support activities and other stages in the value chain, in particular, in marketing, sales, service and technology development. Indirect costs also tend to draw profitability away from the low cost producer. Therefore, Porter proposes a methodical process of value chain analysis in order to achieve a low-cost strategy. These steps require the firm to:

- diagnose the cost drivers of each value activity and how they interact;
- identify competitor value chains, and determine the relative costs of competitors and the sources of cost differences;

- develop a strategy to lower relative cost position through controlling cost drivers or reconfiguring the value chain and/or downstream value;
- ensure that cost-reduction efforts do not erode differentiation, or make a conscious choice to do so;
- test the cost-reduction strategy for sustainability.

(Porter 1985: 118)

So how might this translate into practice? Let us take a number of value chain activities as examples:

- Operations – typically, a low-cost producer will undertake a series of transaction cost analyses in order to determine which manufacturing activities to retain in-house and which to outsource. In a global context, with manufacturing capability and low-cost labour typically focused in certain geographic regions, for many low-cost producers outsourcing will be a key cost saving. This may well apply to logistics and sales too.
- HR costs will frequently centre on retaining staff in order to keep recruitment costs down, focusing on standardized training, remuneration and reward schemes that can be reliably controlled and predicted. This does not necessarily mean a low wage. Perhaps the most famous example here is Ford's introduction of the $5 day. By 1913, Ford's Model T motorcar was becoming hugely popular and thanks to the introduction of the moving assembly line at the Highland Park plant Ford was able to manufacture the car more and more speedily. However, the knock-on effect of this was that the workforce, reduced to completing mundane repetitive tasks for hours on end, had become increasingly frustrated and many left, resulting in a very high turnover of staff (up to 370 per cent per annum according to Taylor 2013b). This, in turn, slowed down production. In order to combat this issue Ford summoned a press conference on 5 January 1914 to announce that not only was he reducing the working day and increasing the number of shifts but that he was doubling the daily rate of pay to $5 (although strict criteria applied). Despite adding more than $10 million to the wage bill it had the desired effect: turnover dropped from 370 per cent to 16 per cent and productivity went up 40 per cent (Taylor 2013b).
- As research, design and marketing are typically high-cost centres these will normally be kept to a minimum and the firm, in its offering, will typically offer an imitation product rather than positioning itself as an innovator or first-mover, due to the high costs involved. Indeed, it was such strategies that in the 1970s and 1980s allowed firms such as Samsung, Kia, Daewoo and LG to establish themselves in a range of consumer electronics markets.
- Organizational infrastructure tends to be relatively flat with few layers of management and instead a more classic Taylor-inspired notion of a few brains and many bodies.

Differentiation and strategic fit

By contrast, a differentiation strategy requires an integrated set of value-adding activities that produces a unique or in some way non-standard product for which a price premium can be charged. However, even the differentiator needs to be aware of costs and thus there is still an attempt to limit spending wherever possible. A typical value chain may therefore focus on R&D, marketing and service as key customer-facing activities. Indeed, it is quite common for firms to outsource all activities other than design and marketing – the clothing and apparel industries being prime examples. Outsourcing then brings its own costs in ensuring supply levels, quality control, etc., that can add significant indirect costs to the differentiator, especially where the point of differentiation is focused on a particular promise of quality. Support activities tend to focus more on building an infrastructure that is customer-centric and thus the quality of employees will be a key factor, for which high HR costs may be incurred. Likewise, R&D will potentially be a high-cost centre as innovation is increasingly a key aspect of differentiation strategies.

Value networks

As well as drawing attention to the activities within the firm, Porter also locates the value chain within a wider value network or value system. Recognizing that firms do not operate in isolation, Porter was keen to point out the interconnections between firms and numerous outside agencies. For example, suppliers provide key resources necessary for the manufacture of products by the firm; thus they indirectly contribute to value-adding activity. For Magretta (2012), managing suppliers and buyers in the value network can be as important strategically as managing the internal value chain. She gives the example of McDonalds' to illuminate this point:

> For example if you want to build a fast food business around consistent, perfect French fries, as McDonald's did, you can't make excuses to customers because the potato farmer you buy from lacks proper storage facilities. Customers don't care who's at fault, they only care about the quality of their fries. So McDonald's has to perform specific activities to make sure that, one way or another, all the potato growers from whom it buys can meet its standards.
>
> (Magretta 2012: 85)

This work on the value network and on the linkages between firms and industries would prove to be one of the key foundations for Porter's later work on national competitiveness.

Porter's further contributions: expanding the logic of the outside-in approach

While Porter is still probably best known for his work on the five forces and on industry-level analysis, he subsequently moved to extend the logic of the outside-in approach to both a broader and a narrower competitive environment. In two subsequent works he introduced the notion of the competitive advantage of nations, a direct corollary of industry analysis albeit now at the national level, and also localized the logic down to the group level through his notion of clusters and strategic groups. Let us briefly review each of these later contributions as a way of situating Porter's work and as an indicator of how the logic of the outside-in approach can be strategically repositioned at different levels of analysis.

The competitive advantage of nations

In the late 1980s Porter was invited by then US president Ronald Reagan to join a commission established in order to investigate US competitiveness. In many ways the commission was set up to try and address the question of Japan, which had continued to strengthen its economy at the cost of American competitiveness. Both the US government and US firms desired to understand the remarkable power of the Japanese economy and of Japanese firms across a range of industries in which the US had previously been either unchallenged or at least dominant.

Based on a survey of 12 different nations at three points in time, Porter concluded that while there is a global movement of goods, materials, labour, capital, etc., location was still a key determinant of relative competitive advantage. This in turn leads to different, often strikingly variable, levels of national productivity and output. The data appeared to suggest that across a wide variety of different industries, global industry leadership was consistently located in just one or two countries. Drilling down further, Porter hypothesized that each nation has a number of attributes that can be leveraged to improve the economic standing of its key industries. Whereas five forces underpin industries, at the national level Porter (1990: 77) identifies four attributes or conditions:

1. Factor conditions – the nation's strategic position in relation to factors of production, such as skilled labour or infrastructure, necessary to compete in a given industry.
2. Demand conditions – the nature of home-market demand for the industry's product or service.
3. Related and supporting industries – the presence or absence in the nation of supplier industries and other related industries that are internationally competitive.
4. Firm strategy, structure and rivalry – the conditions in the home nation determining how companies are created, organized and managed, as well as the nature of domestic rivalry.

Factor conditions

Taking first factor conditions. In standard economic theory these usually refer to inherent factors of production – classically land, labour capital and raw materials. Porter refers to these as the basis of *comparative* advantage. However, in the late twentieth-century business environment Porter preferred to identify factor conditions that lead to *competitive* advantage, i.e. not those that are inherent to the nation but to those that it actively nurtures and creates. Basic factors of production, he suggests, can be acquired through the global marketplace. Thus, having a highly educated workforce does not automatically create skilled workers, nor does access to a raw material necessarily produce a capability to extract and make best use of that resource. Moreover, an abundance of resources can make a nation wasteful (Yetton et al. 1992). Rather, Porter suggests that these factors of production need to be nurtured through, for example, the building of world-class research institutes or through government policy, incentives and regulations that enable a country to capitalize on its store of inherent resources. In each instance, innovation is required to make best use of factor conditions.

In pointing to the success of the Japanese economy Porter suggests that it was in part the lack of natural resources that forced the Japanese government and economy to innovate in the period after World War II, not for growth but for mere survival. During World War II the Japanese economy and infrastructure had been decimated. Moreover, the country had few natural resources on which to begin to rebuild. Therefore it was dependent not only on outside intervention but also on making more out of what it had available. A number of writers have thus suggested that initiatives such as lean production, just-in-time and total quality management owe just as much to the needs of Japanese firms to function within the limits of extreme resource scarcity as to any innate capacity for innovation.

Demand conditions

While globalization may imply a reduction in emphasis on home demand, Porter suggests that a strong and robust home market is crucial to global economic success. He suggests that nations most frequently achieve a competitive advantage in industries in which there is strong home demand, the focus on the home market building a competitive advantage that can then be exported, especially where the home market represents 'the world's most sophisticated and demanding buyers for the product or service' (Porter 1990: 79). In short, the home market constitutes a benchmark for global buyer behaviour. This is especially true, Porter suggests, where the home nation has a strong influence on wider social and cultural trends at a global level. Hence, US domination in the global fast food industry reflects not only a strong home demand but also a wider global taste for American fast food. Similar arguments can be made for the US entertainment industries.

Related and supporting industries

Related and supporting industries are an important factor in national competitiveness on account of the cumulative effects enjoyed by a value network in which collaboration, reliable and strong supplier relationships, and complementary industries drive the industry forward. In the late nineteenth century, for example, Chicago became a key industrial zone due to its strategic position as a meeting point of numerous railway lines. This location led Chicago to establishing itself as a key centre for the slaughter and processing of meat. Cattle were shipped in from the agricultural states in the Mid-West, slaughtered, processed and then railed out to the growing industrial cities such as New York. Soon after, a number of related and supporting industries popped up that could make use of the 'spare parts' – tanneries, glue factories and canneries (Clegg *et al.* 2010: 16).

A more contemporary example might be that area of California known as Silicon Valley, with its concentration of high-tech firms, technology start-ups and technology research institutions such as Stanford University. Detroit, historically a location for the manufacture of US automobiles, is now becoming home to a burgeoning motorcycle industry.

Firm strategy, structure and rivalry

The final condition, firm strategy, structure and rivalry, addresses the culturally specific forms of organizing and managing in different nations. Porter notes, for example, that the Italian nation is dominated by small and medium-sized enterprises often privately or family owned. This dominant model has led to international success for Italian firms in high-end and luxury goods that tend to be produced in small quantities – clothing, accessories and apparel, for example. In contrast, the German preference for engineering, science and precision has created organization structures and management systems that have led to Germany's competitive advantage in engineering, optics and chemicals. The assumption being, therefore, that other nations would not be as competitive in these industries due to their differing structures, so that Italy has never found much success in chemical engineering and Germany is not well known for high-end fashion houses.

As with his industry analysis, Porter sees the role of government as informing and shaping all four conditions rather than being a condition in its own right. For Carter et al. (2008) this continued downplaying of the role of government is a reflection of the dominance of the neoliberal economic and political ideology of the time, as encapsulated by Reagan's mode of government. Thus, government's role is to provide the necessary legislative and regulatory environment in which domestic competition can flourish rather than engage in state-sponsored interference. Porter's work on national competitiveness also drew his attention to regional or local competition and this in turn produced his contribution of clusters, or strategic groups.

Strategic clusters

Porter defines clusters in the following way: 'Clusters are geographic concentrations of interconnected companies, specialized suppliers, service providers, firms in related industries, and associated institutions (for example, universities, standards agencies, and trade associations) in particular fields that compete but also co-operate' (Porter 2008: 214). While Porter formally locates clusters within the 'related and supporting industries' aspect of the framework, he is keen to suggest they are in many ways best conceived of as interlinking all four conditions. Examples of regional clusters include automobile manufacture in the Kanto region of Japan (Rumelt 2011) and the concentration of life science research in the Boston area of the United States. The latter, Porter suggests, has come about due to the presence of world-leading scientific universities such as MIT and Harvard, a number of elite teaching hospitals and a concentration of biotech companies (Snowdon and Stonehouse 2006). The concentration of these related activities and institutions allows for collaboration and the cross-fertilization of ideas, research and practices that can lead to more rapid innovation than might be the case elsewhere.

When talking about clusters, and in something of a reversal or at least a partial change of direction from his earlier work, Porter seems much more amenable to the notion that firms can and do work together rather than necessarily being in a perpetually competitive state. A cluster, he suggests, typically includes a group of competitors, upstream and downstream activities, and a range of supporting and complementary industries, services and institutions.

In their review of Porter's work on national competitiveness and clusters, Yetton et al. (1992) suggest that what underpins these complimentary levels of competition are two underlying forces, namely *pressure* and *proximity*. Pressure, they suggest, is the key driver of innovation and an absence of pressure is what often leads to inertia and hubris. Thus, nations such as the USA, with its vast reserves of factor conditions and long periods of unrestricted growth, failed to recognize and react promptly to the innovation emerging from Japan because of a lack of perceived pressure, until it was too late. Pressure, however, is also what helps explain Japan's economic ascendency: pressure to rebuild the economy, society and national pride after World War II. Constrained by a scarcity of natural resources on which to do so drove the Japanese to innovate, not just in product design but in management practices, collaboration, and so on.

Evaluating Porter's contributions to the strategy field

Despite some of these ideas being over thirty years old and given the rapid changes in the business environment in the intervening period, Porter's work appears to have stood the test of time: at least in the sense that it occupies a central position in the literature on strategy and in management education. As such, it is important to identify the contribution he has made while also being sensitive to the limitations of these tools and techniques for strategy-making.

We might begin our evaluation by reminding ourselves of the context of emergence in which Porter's work arose, coming as it did at a time when the US was facing increasing competition from overseas, when national markets were maturing and when the strategy tools of the past were proving unsuccessful in realizing sustained competitive advantage – in short, it could be said that he was in the right place at the right time to shift the strategy agenda. Moreover, there was a clear 'fit' with the prevailing economic and political ideology of the time, which facilitated the more rapid take-up of his ideas.

Second, a major contribution of Porter's work was to fundamentally shift the strategy terrain away from a focus on the internal environment and on to the external environment. Historically, strategy had been very inwardly focused and, while this may have been productive in a context of stable markets and more localized forms of competition, there was a lack of sensitivity to wider external forces. Porter's work shifted emphasis to the external environment at a time when external forces were undermining the traditional boundaries and bases of competition in the US.

Third, Porter's introduction of IO economics and, for the first time, a real attempt to locate strategy within more deeply rooted and robust academic theory rather than being primarily practice-based, was a major contribution. It laid the ground for an economics-based understanding of strategy that still pervades the field (we will see how both the resource-based view and value innovation approaches are underpinned by economic theory). This grounding in theory, along with quantitative methodologies, again served as a field-altering contribution (note also that Porter's work directly succeeds the Pittsburgh conference and 'spoke' to the rebranding that was proposed there).

A fourth contribution was Porter's argument that competitive forces operate at numerous levels of analysis: local, industry and national. Finally, Porter makes a very real contribution in his stressing the importance of making trade-offs and the need for a disciplined, methodical approach to strategy formulation. Indeed, underpinning his tools, frameworks and methods was some rather sound strategic advice: dare to be different, make trade-offs and ensure that there is fit between the activities of the firm.

While not dismissing this enviable contribution we must also be aware of some of the limitations in not only Porter's work but also the wider logic of an 'outside-in' approach to strategy. Henry Mintzberg, Porter's long-term sparring partner, identifies what he describes as three 'concerns' with Porter's work and the whole 'positioning' approach: concerns about methodology; concerns about focus; and concerns about application (Mintzberg et al. 2009). Concerns about methodology turn on the continued emphasis, in Porter's work, on strategy as a rational, controlled process. In this sense we can draw a direct line from the basic premises of the planning approach to Porter, some 20–25 years later. Porter still sees the CEO as the chief strategy architect and reaffirms a belief in a quantifiable, numbers-driven approach to strategy formulation. In this regard, a number of critics have suggested that the five forces framework, based as it is on the 'fallacy of pre-determination', is too static and provides only a snapshot of an industry at a particular point in time. Moreover, as Porter himself acknowledges, completing a 'full-blown industry analysis is a massive task, and one that can consume months' (Porter 1980: 368) and thus probably unachievable for many firms, and maybe even undesirable or obsolete in fast-moving, dynamic industries. While Porter's ideas were originally developed by drawing on data produced in a period of relative stability and growth, the contemporary marketplace no longer reflects these conditions. However, even in the context of dynamic and turbulent environmental change Porter is adamant that industry behaviour is still relatively stable over time and that, even where change does occur, the five forces remain consistent (Magretta 2012).

A second concern, that of focus, suggest that Porter's work, because it is so deeply rooted in economics and quantitative methods, fails to recognize the qualitative, the social, the cultural and the political aspect of organizational life and strategy-making. Aktouf et al. (2011) argue that Porter's belief in the rationality and logic of managers and consultants simply does not accord with the widely held acceptance of the boundedly rational nature of human decision-making. Even computer simulations, they argue, are incapable of the kind of analysis Porter prescribes. Others have also suggested that the emphasis on the external environment as the starting point for strategy formulation is equally problematic. As we shall see in the next chapter, proponents of the resource-based view argue that an inside-out approach to strategy is more likely to lead to sustainable competitive advantage than an outside-in approach. In this regard, critics suggest that the power and presence of individual firms can sometimes be more influential than the industry structure.

Finally, Mintzberg expresses a concern about applicability. There is a strong emphasis in Porter's work on big business, established industries and mature markets. Hence he is able to demonstrate the applicability of his ideas through carefully chosen case studies. It is much harder to apply these ideas to industries marked by turbulent or dynamic market conditions. His work also fails to address the interconnectedness of industries and firms. His value chain concept, which he extends to an industry level, is still premised on a manufacturing logic, but many firms now actively work with competitors, suppliers and buyers, making for much more complex and networked relationships that are not so easily captured through the tools and techniques discussed above. O'Shaughnessy (1996) extends this line of critique to the *Competitive Advantage of Nations* by suggesting that the analysis, key factor conditions, and case studies were all based on developed industrial societies. The theory would have to be 'radically reformulated' (p. 14) in order to have relevance to emerging or developing industrial societies.

Chapter summary

In this chapter we have considered an approach to strategy that has come to be known as the outside-in approach. Underpinned by IO economics, this approach assumes that it is the external environment and, in particular the industry, that shapes the competitive landscape and limits the strategic options of the individual firm. The firm's activity is restricted, or enabled, through the dynamic interplay of the competitive forces that drive the industry forward. As such, the firm frequently needs to reorganize in order to meet the challenges of the external environment. Perhaps the most widely recognized example of this approach can be found in the work of Michael Porter. Both Porter and his work gained huge popularity in the 1980s, with the five forces becoming the dominant model of strategy analysis in many MBA programmes. Porter was also often recruited by both firms and governments to consult on their strategy development. Indeed, he was invited by President Ronald Reagan to lead a commission into US competiveness, out of which would come one of his other main contributions, *The Competitive Advantage of Nations* (1990).

However, by the early 1990s Porter's ideas were beginning to lose some of their appeal. The belief in the restrictive nature of the industry and the recommendation to find a position of fit was increasingly rejected. The continued success of Japanese firms and the growing influence of the emerging Asian Tigers could not be explained away in Porterian terms. These firms were simply not competing on the same playing field and were not playing by the same rules. It *appeared* from a western viewpoint that these competitors, who were seemingly always first to market with new innovations, technologies and products, were far more focused on what was going on inside the firm and were less worried about 'the industry'. As such, by the early 1990s, US academic attention began to shift eastwards and inwards and so developed a preference for inside-out strategies and the importance of resources and capabilities as a basis of competitive advantage.

7 Creating strategy from the inside-out

Introduction

The forces of globalization, quickening apace throughout the 1980s, led to a change in the language of strategic management by the early 1990s. Discussions of global markets, global firms, global brands and global industries began to take centre stage and a strategic focus only on local or even national levels became increasingly untenable as many industries and markets became truly global. As they did so, American businesses were exposed to management and organizational practices that did not accord with the main tenets of western management training. There were new players on the scene and they were not conforming to the rulebook of industry analysis and long-range planning. Innovations in digital technology and computer processing power led to radical innovations in manufacturing processes and the introduction of many new goods and services. As a result, Collis and Montgomery (1995: 118) observe, 'at the business-unit level, the pace of global competition and technological change has left managers struggling to keep up' (Collis and Montgomery 1995: 118).

As such, the (broadly speaking) domestically focused strategic approaches of positioning and diversification were becoming less and less meaningful and strategy practitioners and researchers looked elsewhere for inspiration and for the elusive answer to the problem of achieving sustainable competitive advantage. Moreover, evidence started to gather suggesting that firm performance within industries and even within clusters did not necessarily conform to the prescriptions laid down by Porter (Teece *et al.* 1997). Elsewhere, *Rumelt's* (1991) detailed and damning critique of industry analysis suggested that intra-industry differences in performance were often far greater than inter-industry performance. These and other studies suggested that what went on inside the firm seemed to be a more reliable predictor of performance than industry factors. Developed throughout the 1980s but gaining more widespread appeal and recognition in the early 1990s, the resource-based approach to strategy and, on a more practitioner-orientated level, the works of Gary Hamel and Coimbatore Krishnarao (known as C. K.) Prahalad, developed as a counterbalance to the previous focus on the external environment. In this chapter we will consider these works as an example of an 'inside-out' approach to strategy-making. We begin by briefly reviewing some of the main theoretical underpinnings of the resource-based view (RBV) of strategy before undertaking a more detailed study of some of the key contributions of Hamel and Prahalad, namely: strategic intent, core competence and strategy as stretch and leverage. We will finish our discussion by introducing the notion of network-level strategy, which forms an important complement to Hamel and Prahalad's ideas.

Theoretical underpinnings: the resource-based view (RBV)

To put it simply, the RBV's central argument (*contra* Porter) is that it should be the internal environment (and not the external environment) that takes primacy in the strategy formulation process. Specifically, the way in which the firm configures its unique collection of resources, competencies and capabilities creates certain strengths and weaknesses that inform the strategic options available to the firm. These factors, proponents argue, are far more influential and important than those of industry structure or any other outside forces. In order to explore this claim in more detail we shall look at some of the key contributions underpinning this approach. Specifically, we shall introduce the work of Edward Chamberlin (1933), Edith Penrose (1959/2009), Birger Wernerfelt (1984) and Jay Barney (1991).

Edward Chamberlin

Edward Chamberlin was an economist at Harvard University in the first half of the twentieth century and is credited with making one of the earliest contributions to the inside-out view of strategy (Barney 1986). Chamberlin's (1933) argument is that the resources and capabilities possessed by competing firms in an industry are heterogeneous. They may overlap at times but they are specific to the individual firm. Thus there is limited resources mobility or homogeneity at an industry level. Moreover, the unique way in which these resources and capabilities are combined will be the key determinant of how successful (profitable) the firm might be.

In this regard we can draw a number of parallels between IO economics and Chamberlinian economics, with the former underpinned by a belief in resource homogeneity and the latter in resource heterogeneity. Second, IO economics maintains a belief in resource mobility, in contrast to Chamberlin's belief in the embeddedness of resources. Third, and by extension, IO economists subscribe to an outside-in approach (industry structure shapes firm performance) whereas Chamberlinian economists subscribe to an inside-out view (firm behaviour shapes industry performance). Of course, these two viewpoints are competing sides of one coin and both recognize the importance of the match between internal and external environment; where they differ is in where they lay greatest emphasis, and in this regard they adopt fundamentally opposing views on the strategy formulation processes.

Edith Penrose

In the 1950s Edith Penrose built on the work on Chamberlin and others (e.g. Robinson 1933) in her work on the theory of the growth of the firm. An economist driven from America by McCarthyism, Penrose's ideas would only later come to wider acclaim when they were employed by the likes of Birger Wernerfelt (1984), who drew upon Penrose in shaping the RBV theory of strategy in the 1980s. Penrose subscribed to many of the views of Chamberlinian economics, conceiving of the firm as a bundle of 'productive resources' under the conscious control of its management. Indeed, her working definition of the firm was as an 'autonomous administrative planning unit' (Penrose 1959/2009: 13). Conceived as such, Penrose also defined resources in a broader sense than had previously been the case, moving beyond tangible assets such as machines, labour and land towards resources such as managerial expertise, know-how and entrepreneurial skill (Barney and Clark 2006).

Penrose also argued that these resources and the competencies and capabilities they create, or 'services' as she preferred to call them (Penrose 1959/2009), constitute the main limiting factor regulating a firm's activities. In other words, the firm can only compete in areas in which it has a current capability, or where its resources can be combined in such a way as to provide a specific service. As such, it is not the resources that matter so much as how they are combined and put to use: 'The services yielded by resources are a function of the way in which they are used – exactly the same resource when used for different purposes or in different ways and in combination with different types or amounts of other resources provides a different service or set of services' (ibid. p. 22). Thus, resources constitute a boundary or limitation around what the firm can do. Such resources are immobile, she claims, because they are embedded in firm-specific knowledge and are not in the possession of a single individual. Therefore they cannot be easily transferred, even when a key architect of a firm leaves to work for a competitor. As she goes on to say: 'experience-based knowledge is proprietary because it cannot be transferred to new managers quickly, and it cannot be purchased in the market … experience itself can never be transmitted' (cited in Kor and Mahoney 2004: 187).

Moreover, the same set of resources held by several firms will not lead to similar levels of performance, as suggested by IO economics, because of the idiosyncratic and unique way in which each firm will deploy those resources, leading to different innovations, processes and products. How can this be so? For Penrose, the key limiting factor is human, and specifically managerial: 'The availability of top managerial and technical talent serves as the bottleneck for a firm's growth *rate* in a particular period of time' (ibid.: 184).

Furthermore, and crucially as a primer for our discussion on Hamel and Prahalad, Penrose argues that it is the embedded competencies and capabilities achieved through the existing resource base, that will direct future growth – firms should diversify only into markets and industries in which they can capitalize on their current capabilities. This limitation she saw primarily as an outcome of the tacit knowledge embedded in the firm, which in turn would limit the speed of learning that any firm could enjoy. Thus, much of her work was about articulating the foundations of this tacit knowledge and the path dependencies within the firm that limit as well as facilitate its growth.

Birger Wernerfelt

The term 'resource-based view' was first coined by Birger Wernerfelt in his 1984 article of the same name. Wernerfelt sought to translate Penrose's earlier arguments into a workable theory for strategy. In doing so, he made the following arguments:

- The organization constitutes a unique bundle of resources on which sustainable competitive advantage can be built.
- Key resources include not just tangible artefacts such as buildings, technology and people, but also knowledge, brand image and technical skills.
- Out of these resources, strategic capabilities can develop (e.g. technological resources, combined with skilled staff and operational processes can lead to a manufacturing capability).
- Unique products and unique industry positions stem from the firm's resource base, and the idiosyncratic way in which they are combined to produce specific capabilities.

Barney and Clark (2006) observe that Wererfelt's initial aim with this article was to provide a complement to Porter's work on industry analysis. Hence, they suggest, Wernerfelt chose the word 'view', as in resource-based *view*, rather than 'theory' or 'framework' to reflect the fact that he was 'viewing' the same competitive environment as Porter, albeit from the vantage point of the firm's resources rather than industry forces.

Although these ideas seem eminently sensible today, in the original article they were presented in a rather theoretical and abstract form, thus leading to a relatively narrow take-up (Newbert 2007). Indeed, Wernerfelt (1995: 171) acknowledged as much, suggesting that his original outline of the RBV was somewhat 'terse and abstract'. As such, it was not until the early 1990s when a number of other academics and practitioners sought to develop the RBV into a more practical and workable strategy framework did the ideas gain more widespread recognition. In this regard, Jay Barney's work was seen as a key catalyst.

Jay Barney

In the early 1990s, Jay Barney (1991) developed the central ideas of Chamberlain and Penrosian economics and combined it with Wernerfelt's *view* to provide a more detailed resource-based strategy approach. In particular, Barney sought to articulate what made certain resources strategically more valuable than others and, subsequently, how these could be nurtured for competitive advantage. In doing so he produced the VRIN framework, in which he argued that strategically important resources should be:

- Valuable (making a specific contribution to strategic goals or processes);
- Rare (or unique and therefore hard to acquire);
- Imperfectly imitable (difficult for others to understand, replicate or acquire);
- Non-substitutable (offering a point of differentiation).

Numerous additions, variations and alternatives to this basic framework have since been proposed such that we can now talk about a broadly defined resource-based approach to strategy, one that has established a substantial following in the academic literature. We might summarize the key tenets of the RBV in the following way:

1. Every organization is conceived of as a bundle of unique assets, resources and capabilities that emerge through the path dependent and causally ambiguous processes and practices that are the key markers of organizational life.
2. The unique configuration of resources and capabilities permits the firm to manufacture products or provide services in a way that is to a greater or lesser extent unique and which constitutes a barrier to imitation.
3. Based on the belief that the external environment is too volatile, turbulent and ephemeral to build a strategy in response to it, the RBV advocates building a strategy around unique resources and capabilities and then searching for market opportunities where these can be exploited. Thus strategy develops from the inside out.
4. Only this approach, proponents suggest, can lead to sustainable competitive advantage over the long term and in the face of an inherently unknowable future.

Dynamic capabilities

A more recent contribution to the RBV has been the notion of dynamic capabilities as put forward by Augier and Teece (2008). Dynamic capabilities proponents, while sharing many of the same theoretical beliefs as the wider RBV and subscribing to an inside-out logic, suggest that in the context of the twenty-first-century business environment it is not enough to just build and strengthen an existing resource base as, over time, these resources will erode. This is especially the case, both literally and figuratively, in relation to tangible resources. Instead Teece and others advocate building and maintaining *dynamic capabilities*, which create repeated short-term advantages that respond to the ever-changing environment. Barney describes dynamic capabilities in the following way:

> dynamic capabilities refer to the particular (nonimitability) capacity business enterprises possess to shape, reshape, configure, and reconfigure assets so as to respond to changing technologies and markets and escape the zero-profit condition. Dynamic capabilities relate to the enterprise's ability to sense, seize, and adapt in order to generate and exploit internal and external enterprise-specific competencies, and to address the enterprise's changing environment.
>
> (Teece 2009: 87–8)

To build a strategy around dynamic and intangible resources requires a focus on knowledge, patent acquisition, technical expertise, and so on that can be leveraged to identify and capitalize on innovation and changes in industry landscapes proactively as they happen. For example, as applied to the production process, the capability to operationalize batch production, faster production cycles and quicker retooling of machines allows the firm to more rapidly respond to market change.

The RBV in practice

As Clegg *et al.* (2010) note, in order to undertake a resource-based approach to strategy-making, the strategist needs to be able to:

1 identify the current bundle of resources possessed by the firm and assess their individual strategic importance;
2 identify the current capabilities possessed by the firm.

This is a much more difficult task than at first appears. While it might be relatively straightforward to identify tangible resources such as facilities, financial resources and numbers of trained staff, it is much harder to quantify their specific strategic importance. Even more difficult is to identify intangible resources such as knowledge and technical understanding. Moreover, understanding exactly how bundles of resources combine to create certain capabilities is even harder. How for example, might a firm determine the range of resources that lead to a capability for innovation? Capabilities are often only recognized after the event, or are rationalized on a post hoc basis to make sense of activities or performance levels that were unexpected or unplanned – how else can we know if a resource is valuable unless it has proven to be so in the past? Thus, a common critique of the RBV is that it is tautological: in this case we know we have strategic capabilities because they have proven to be so in the past.

A further challenge with implementing the RBV is that, despite its theoretical coherence, there are few workable tools and techniques that can be applied in a practical context in order to capitalize on this theorizing (Barney et al. 2001). Those that are available are frequently highly complex and beyond the bounded rationality of the time-pressured manager trying to muddle through. Barney and Clark (2006: 14) suggest that more workable methods are in development but that 'it may take many years to refine this measurement technology and complete the data analysis.'

A criticism that has hampered the pursuit of a unified and marketable (in the consultancy sense) theory of the RBV is confusion and lack of consensus over relevant terminology. Porter, for example, is quick to question the imprecision in the RBV:

> What is a competence? What is a capability? What makes a firm unique? ... I have come to the conclusion that the problem with the competence-resource approach is that it often comes across as vague and allows companies to make exaggerated claims about their resources and competencies without validating those claims with proper analysis.
>
> (Cited in Stonehouse and Snowdon 2007: 266)

Just a quick review of some of the literature gives a flavour of the difficulty: whereas Wernerfelt and Barney both talk of the RBV, Hamel and Prahalad talk about the core competence approach and Teece posits the dynamic capability approach. Where some talk about resources others say assets or even 'invisible assets' (Itami 1987); for some these combine into competencies, for others capabilities, for others again into distinctive competences or absorptive capacities or valuable heuristic processes (cf. von Krogh and Roos: 1996). This in turn leads to numerous theories of competitive advantage such as '"resource-based theories of superior performance", "capability theories of superior firm performance", "dynamic capability theories of superior performance", "competence theories of superior performance", and "knowledge-based theories of superior performance"' (Barney and Clark 2006: 23). Few managers have the time or inclination to survey this minefield of confusion in order to develop a workable solution to the problem of strategy, and who can blame them.

Finally, in a contemporary context, it seems that few resources really achieve VRIN status, at least not for a sustainable length of time. Backward engineering and patent purchasing can make it very difficult to maintain a unique resource base for long.

For these kinds of reasons, and despite solid foundations and thorough empirical testing in research contexts, the RBV has never really taken off as a managerial framework for doing strategy. This is not to deny the underlying logic of the resource-based approach. The difficulty is more in its execution. At least, that is, until Gary Hamel and C. K. Prahalad joined forces (or continued their relation, Hamel being Prahalad's doctoral student) to present a more managerially acceptable, more practically implementable version of the resource-based approach. They called theirs the *core competence* approach. Combined with their ideas of *strategic intent* and strategy as *stretch and leverage* it offers a self-contained strategy process of the kind that we discussed in the previous chapter through the work of Porter. Therefore, as in the previous chapter we will present these ideas as a collective whole. Before doing so let us review Hamel and Prahalad's critique of the strategy field, on which their contribution is then built.

Hamel and Prahalad stake their claim!

Hamel and Prahalad introduce their work with the following observation:

> As 'strategy' has blossomed, the competitiveness of Western companies has withered. This may be coincidence, but we think not. We believe that the application of concepts such as 'strategic fit' (between resources and opportunities), 'generic strategies' (low cost vs. differentiation vs. focus), and the 'strategy hierarchy' (goals, strategies, and tactics) have often abetted the process of competitive decline. The new global competitors approach strategy from a perspective that is fundamentally different from that which underpins Western management thought.
>
> (Hamel and Prahalad 1989: 63)

Basing their argument on examples drawn primarily from Pacific Rim firms (from Japan and the *Asian Tiger* countries of South Korea, Taiwan, Singapore and so on), Hamel and Prahalad argue that western firms were woefully unprepared for the conditions of global competition that arose in the 1980s and, as a result, were increasingly losing out to overseas competitors who appeared to be competing, successfully, under a different set of rules. To substantiate their claim they address what they see as a number of fundamental errors in western strategic thinking. First, in a familiar argument, they challenge the separation of formulation from implementation in the process of strategy-making, believing that such hierarchical separation fosters an 'us versus them' attitude in the organization. Hamel and Prahalad argue for wider involvement in the strategy process, underpinned by their belief in the value of a developing a 'strong culture' (Peters and Waterman 1982).

Second, they reject the premise that the external environment dictates firm performance: against the portfolio approach they challenge what they see as the *relativity* of concepts such as 'mature' and 'low growth' markets observing that, in the 1970s for example, many US companies considered consumer electronics to have become a mature market ... after all nothing could beat the colour television! The impact of this belief and the scaling back of R&D in these areas left the market wide open for overseas competitors to both dominate and transform the industry with advances such as handheld electronics, personal video equipment and then into the realm of mobile phones, mobile computing and so on. Against Porter, they see his advice on positioning as a passive strategy. They suggest that industry structure is shaped by the industry leader, and therefore you need to be that industry leader rather than seek some safe position of fit and hope to be left alone.

Hamel and Prahalad also level criticism at the RBV. They argue that focusing on current resources and capabilities is the wrong way to approach the strategic value of the internal environment. Competing on existing resources will not achieve sustainable competitive advantage. Instead, resources must be stretched and leveraged to perform beyond current capability in order to address the challenges of tomorrow.

In short, Hamel and Prahalad call for a rethinking of the existing assumptions of western strategic management. They argue that:

> In the long run, competitiveness derives from an ability to build, at lower cost and more speedily than competitors, the core competencies that spawn unanticipated products. The real sources of advantage are to be found in management's ability to

consolidate corporate-wide technologies and production skills into competencies that empower individual businesses to adapt quickly to changing opportunities.

(Prahalad and Hamel 1990: 81)

In order to achieve this, Hamel and Prahalad advocate a 'strategy process' that begins with a vision, which they term *strategic intent*. Achieving the goal of a strategic intent requires the building of certain *core competencies*. This will invariably require a sizeable *stretch* for the organization and thus there will be a need to *leverage* existing resource and capabilities in order to achieve the above. Let us look at each of these in turn.

Strategic intent

Hamel and Prahalad introduced the notion of strategic intent at a time (the late 1980s) when the language of mission statements and visions were popular amongst managerial élites. However, they were also keen to distinguish their concept from these more familiar labels, although it was still intended to be an articulation of the firm's overall goal. What distinguishes strategic intent from mission and vision is that it describes a desired *leadership* position, specifically a global leadership position. Strategic intent, they argue, is marked by three underlying characteristics:

1   Strategic intent captures the essence of winning (in this regard it also normally means taking on a much bigger competitor, i.e. the current market leader).
2   Strategic intent is stable over time (unlike missions and visions, strategic intent is a long-term goal, typically a 10–20 year ambition).
3   Strategic intent sets a target that deserves personal effort and commitment (this claim draws on the corporate culture logic informing their work, strategic intent can and should be a motivating force).

As examples of strategic intent we might cite the following:

- Komatsu, who set out to 'Encircle Caterpillar';
- Canon, who sought to 'Beat Xerox';
- Honda, who aimed to 'Yahama wo tsubusu! (roughly translated: We will crush, squash, slaughter Yamaha!).

Hamel and Prahalad are keen to point out that strategic intent is 'more than simply unfettered ambition' (1989: 64) and suggest instead that it should be considered (what we earlier termed) an umbrella strategy. Also note the competitive, even war-like, language employed. Indeed, across their work Hamel and Prahalad regularly play to the masculine militaristic undertones of the strategy field.

As an umbrella strategy, strategic intent displaces the more formal strategic plan and articulates the firm's strategic objectives in a more open and flexible way. As a planned objective, strategic intent is, to evoke one of the many analogies employed by the authors: 'like a marathon run in 400-metre sprints. No one knows what the terrain will look like at mile 26, so the role of top management is to focus the organization's attention on the ground to be covered in the next 400 meters' (Hamel and Prahalad 1989: 86). Thus, it is about setting short and medium-term goals which contribute in some way toward the final objective – for now it might be about developing a new product range, the next goal might be to enter a new market, the next to consolidate existing markets, and so on. However, the goals that are set must be ambitious – after all, global leadership does not come easily. The quest for global leadership will inevitably require benchmarking against, and then outperforming, the best in class. For most firms this will require a sizeable *stretch*.

Strategy as stretch

> Current capabilities and resources will not suffice. This forces the organization to be more inventive, to make the most of limited resources. Whereas the traditional view of strategy focuses on the degree of fit between existing resources and current opportunities, strategic intent creates an extreme misfit between resources and ambitions.
>
> (Hamel and Prahalad 1989: 67)

At the heart of strategic intent is what Hamel and Prahalad call strategy as stretch. In other words, making existing and often limited resources work much harder than might otherwise be the case. It is only through stretch, they suggest, that Japanese firms in the post-World War II period could achieve their remarkable rise to economic dominance. A country blessed with few natural resources and an infrastructure decimated by the war, it was necessary for the Japanese economy, under the conditions of such scarcity, to get more out of their limited resources. Thus they had to make them work harder, smarter, leaner – to stretch them.

Such an approach to strategy relies much more on active employee participation and commitment than the traditional and hierarchical top-down structures more prevalent in the west. Instead, Hamel and Prahalad advocate something frequently referred to as the Japanese organization structure (Aoki 1990). Reviewing the rapid rise to dominance of a number of Japanese firms during the 1980s, Aoki sought to understand the importance of organizational structure as a key determining factor. Conducting research on both US and Japanese firms, Aoki identified what he saw as two distinctive structures that seemed to differ on a number of fundamental issues. In the US he found a form of organizing that he labelled the 'H-mode', characterized by hierarchical separation of planning from implementation and an emphasis on the 'economies of specialization' in which each business unit was treated as a separate semi-autonomous entity, with little collaboration between them (the classic portfolio model). Such a structure, he suggests suited the business conditions of the US in the post-World War II era in which stability and growth allowed for the benefits of long-term planning and the responsiveness inherent in a portfolio structure to be realized. There was little need for 'learning at the operational level' (Aoki 1990: 8).

By way of contrast, during the same period Aoki sees an organizational structure developing in Japan, which he calls the J-mode, characterized not by hierarchy but by horizontal coordination and not by specialization but by the 'sharing of ex post on-site information', what we might refer today as collaboration (Aoki 1990: 8). This alternative structure, which emphasizes learning at the operational level, he suggests grew out of necessity as Japanese firms had few resources to work with and had to make them work harder (i.e. they had to stretch them). It was out of this dual combination of conservation and stretch that production systems such as kanban emerged, along with initiatives in quality control and employee involvement programmes. For Aoki, they were born out of necessity but developed into key characteristics of the Japanese way of doing business:

A view of competition as encirclement rather than confrontation, a propensity to accelerate the product development cycle, tightly knit cross-functional teams, a focus on core competencies, close links with suppliers, programs of employee involvement, and so forth are elements of a managerial approach typically labelled as "Japanese".

(Hamel and Prahalad 1994: 16–17)

Hamel and Prahalad suggest that a deep understanding of Japanese operational practices, and in particular the logic of strategy as stretch, does much to 'demythologize' the success of Japanese firms during this period. Their rapid and impressive growth a result not 'from the sacred soil of Japan' but from the operational benefits of strategy as stretch (Hamel and Prahalad 1994: 170–1). However, pursuing a strategy of stretch requires a certain buy-in from organizational members and in this regard Hamel and Prahalad (1989) recognize the need to build a strong, supportive culture through which strategic intent can be realized. Specifically, they suggest the organization's culture needs to reflect the following characteristics:

1 Competitor focus at every level of the organization. This is achieved through the use of competitive intelligence and of benchmarking different functions and roles against the best in the industry. Ford, for example, would show employees videos of the production line at Mazda (then its strategic partner) in order to demonstrate the possibilities of lean production.
2 Providing employees with the skills they need to work effectively. In this regard strategic intent is employee-focused, which takes us some distance from the Taylorist view of the employee as docile body. Thus, attention is given to recruitment, training, development, and so on.
3 Giving the organization time to digest one challenge before launching another. This is a reflection of Japanese culture. The urgency and short timeframes of western culture are one of the key impediments to realizing strategic intent. Recall that the average strategic planning round is 12 months whereas strategic intent is a 20-year goal.
4 Establishing clear milestones and review mechanisms. Critical self-reflection is a key component of strategic intent, acknowledging failure and success. Again, the more immediate relationship between success and reward in western management practice tends to discourage identifying failures as learning experiences.
5 Creating a sense of reciprocal responsibility. At the heart of the culture needs to be reciprocity. Whereas the western corporation is often built on internal competition, at the heart of the 'Japanese way', at least as authors such as Hamel and Prahalad appropriated it, was a shared commitment and culture of trust and shared responsibility. In a sense, we can see horizontal integration, as described by Aoki, as an example of this.

The added benefit of a strategy based on stretch is that it also creates the kind of tactical deception so widely advocated in those ancient military manuals of strategy we discussed in Chapter 2. The firm with few resources looks weak and thus will often be ignored by large competitors, who frequently identify threats by the quantity of resources possessed rather than the way they are used. That is, they look at resources rather than resourcefulness. Hamel and Prahalad identify this as a key weakness in western approaches to strategy formulation:

To the extent that challengers even register on the radar screens of leaders, they produce such small 'blips' that they are easily ignored. Yet if there is one conclusion to be drawn from the endless shifting of competitive fortunes it is this: Strategy resource positions are a very poor predictor of future industry leadership.

(Hamel and Prahalad 1994: 140)

Core competencies

Hamel and Prahalad argue that the route to achieving strategic intent and of putting into practice 'stretch' is to invest in core competencies. They define core competencies as: 'the collective learning in the organization, especially how to coordinate diverse production skills and integrate multiple streams of technology' (Prahalad and Hamel 1990: 82).

As examples of core competencies we can consider the following:

- Sony in electronics and miniaturization (as evidenced in its range of personal consumer electronics in the 1970s and 1980s – the Walkman, Discman, miniature televisions, portable radios and so on);
- Honda in engine design (used in end products from automobiles, motorcycles, power generators, lawn mowers, jet skis, jet airplanes and more);
- Samsung in screens and displays (used in computers, televisions, mobile phones, etc.);
- Toyota and its just-in-time and lean production systems (enabling it to produce small batches of a wide variety of models more efficiently than its competitors).

But how do competencies differ from resources or capabilities as defined by the resource-based view? In this regard Hamel and Prahalad suggest a number of distinguishing features:

- Unlike resources, competencies do not diminish with use but improve the more they are utilized.
- Few companies will be able to build more than five or six core competencies. Any more than that and they are just operational capabilities.
- A core competence typically has a technological component. For example, Fed Ex relies on a careful integration of barcode technology, wireless communications, real-time tracking systems and network management to achieve its competence in delivery service.
- Hamel and Prahalad (1994) also distinguish a competence from a resource in an accounting sense. Competencies do not show up on the balance sheet, they say. Thus a brand cannot be a competence; rather it is the ability to manage and maintain the value of the brand that would constitute a competence.

To determine whether something is a core competence, it also need to pass three tests:

1. It should provide access to a wide variety of markets. Thus, Honda's competence in designing and manufacturing engines allows it to compete in any industry in which a motorized engine is a key component – this includes cars, motorcycles, lawn mowers, generators, jet skis and air conditioning units.

2   It should make a significant contribution to the end user. Volvo's core competence in car design makes theirs some of the safest and most robust cars available, which is very attractive to families with young children.
3   It should be difficult to imitate. In other words, it needs to exhibit the attributes of path dependency and causal ambiguity discussed earlier. As an example we might cite Apple, which continues to dominate a range of mobile devices industries with its innovative designs that, while frequently imitated, have continued to confound competitors.

This in turn begs the question: what is the relationship between these underlying competencies and the products and services actually offered by the firm? To explain this relationship Hamel and Prahalad employ the metaphor of the *competency tree* to imagine the diversified corporation in the following way:

- The trunk of the tree and the main limbs are the core products. Hamel and Prahalad define a core product as an intermediate product between the competence and the end product and it typically constitutes a core technology utilized in a range of end products. Thus, LG's digital screens are a core product that it then embeds in numerous end products including televisions, monitors and calculators. In many instances, a core product will also be developed for customers further up the supply chain; thus, LG's screens are used by Apple in their computers and by numerous TV brands.
- The smaller branches of the tree are the business units. In contrast to the portfolio approach in which the SBU is the starting point for strategy development, Hamel and Prahalad see them as having only secondary importance. They are channels through which core competencies and core products are transformed into end products for separate markets and are thus bound together much more closely that is typical in the kind of multidivisional structure we described in Chapter 5.
- The leaves or fruits of the tree are the end products, the brands that are offered to the customer.
- The roots of the tree are the core competencies. They nourish and feed the whole organization and are also the source of new product development. Also, as roots they are partially hidden from sight and constitute the hidden part of the organization, as embedded in operational activity.

A colourful analogy indeed, but it also permits Hamel and Prahalad to communicate some more serious findings about the changing nature of competition, as discussed below.

From core competence to core products

The oft-neglected link between core competence and end product is the core product. These are what Hamel and Prahalad describe as the physical embodiment of the competence. In the case of Canon, its core competence in mechatronics allows it to develop a range of core products such as miniature motors, lens systems and laser engines. These in turn open up a wide range of end product categories such as cameras, printers, copiers and digital video recorders. Thus, there is an inherent logic from competence to core product to end product. Too many western companies, Prahalad and Hamel argue, are focused only on end products, on the fruits of the tree, and fail to recognize the strategic value and importance of core products (it is worth pointing out that much of Hamel and Prahalad's argument rests on their fairly narrow interest in technologically based manufacturing industries).

Moreover, they suggest that much of the academic theory on strategy is also focused too heavily on end products: 'Issues of positioning, experience curves, order-of-entry, pricing, cost and differentiation, competitive signaling, and barriers to entry are typically discussed in the context of a single product or a closely related line of products. Likewise, competitive battles are usually described in product terms: Coke vs. Pepsi, MS vs. Apple' (Hamel and Prahalad 1994: 221). By way of contrast, Hamel and Prahalad look at the success of Japanese and Pacific Rim countries in battles for core products in pursuit of manufacturing share, rather than brand share.

Manufacturing share vs. brand share

Hamel and Prahalad's second argument is that too many western companies are focused on brand share only. It is brands that are well known, receive media attention and are experienced by consumers but, in the battle for global leadership, it is manufacturing share that matters most, they suggest. Thus Canon may have had a relatively small share of the desktop printer market but, at the time of their writing, Hamel and Prahalad suggested it had some 84 per cent world manufacturing share in printer engines – controlling core technologies often means you control the industry and pace of innovation. We can see similar examples of this if we return to our industry analysis in the previous chapter. Both Intel and Microsoft control two of the core technologies that make up a PC and to a large extent PC sales are driven by the release of new processor chips, thus allowing for new models of PC, and new operating systems. Where Porter would describe this as constituting a powerful industry force, Hamel and Prahalad see it as the ability to develop core competencies and core products. The end result is the same – both influence and shape the PC industry – but with different causal explanations.

Watch out for surprise competitors

Related to the above point, Hamel and Prahalad note that Pacific Rim competitors have been aware of the benefits of establishing manufacturing share leadership for some time. Thus, in the 1970s and 1980s many US (manufacturing) companies, driven by a logic of diversification and value chain-based efficiencies, began outsourcing many of their core processes to low-cost suppliers, many of them based in the emerging Asian Tiger countries. For example, in South Korea, companies such as Daewoo, Kia and Samsung became primary component builders for many US automobile and consumer electronics manufacturers, making the products that would then be stamped with the western firm's brand logo. Unable to compete head-on but acting as OEM-suppliers, these Korean firms were not only enabled to understand their (future) rivals' technologies and processes but, once they began to compete in end-product markets, also found themselves in the enviable position of being both supplier and competitor. Moreover, many US rivals had become so dependent on these supplier relationship that they no longer had the capability to efficiently take manufacturing processes back in-house and therefore found themselves effectively funding their competitors through supplier contracts and having to expose these supplier/competitors to their latest designs and innovations.

These supplier/competitors, not having to invest as heavily in R&D, could then employ those technologies and offer lower-cost alternatives ... now, that's what I call strategy!

The tyranny of the SBU

In order to achieve a core competence-based strategy, Hamel and Prahalad also warned against the 'tyranny' of the strategic business unit logic that had underpinned western approaches to corporate strategy since the 1970s. Instead they argued for the need for a *strategy architecture* that allows for the cross-fertilization and sharing of competencies across the corporation. In this regard we can locate Hamel and Prahalad's work as an example of synergy parenting. The primary failure of the western corporation, they suggest, is the internal competition that portfolio management encourages in which SBU managers become protective of their own area while competing internally for additional resources and investment. Moreover, through the practice of growth via diversification, existing resources become fragmented, decoupled and weakened. The result, Hamel and Prahalad argue, is 'imprisoned and under-leveraged competencies' (1994: 244). Against this they argue for the need for resource *leverage*.

Strategy as leverage

As well as stretching resource and competencies to make them work harder, another key component of Hamel and Prahalad's thinking is the need to leverage existing resources and competencies to multiply their use value. Hamel and Prahalad (1993, 1994) suggest that there are five arenas of resource leverage:

- **Concentrating resources** through *converging* all effort on the realization of the strategic intent and staying *focused* on that goal without the temptation to drift.
- **Accumulating resources** through processes of *extracting* and *borrowing*. By extraction Hamel and Prahalad, following the same logic as the emergent perspective, recognize that the firm is a reservoir of experience, tacit knowledge, new ideas and innovation. By facilitating employee participation (through practices such as quality circles), resource efficiency can be extracted where it might otherwise be ignored or left idle. Likewise, through strategic partnerships, resources and technologies can be shared, borrowed, studied, learnt from and improved. A strategy well employed by Japanese and South Korean firms through the 1970s and 1980s in collaborative partnership with US firms.
- **Complementing resources** through *blending* and *balancing*. Successfully integrating, or blending skills and resources across the firm are key to realizing the benefits of strategic intent. Thus, although many western firms had far greater capital and expertise, this was often spread thinly across a corporate structure built on internal competition, as was the case at Ford and GM. Toyota, by contrast was able to integrate skills and resources across the corporation to build core competencies and core products. Balancing resources, for Hamel and Prahalad, involves ensuring that the firm always has 'a strong product-development capability; the capacity to produce its products or deliver its services at world-class levels of cost and quality; and a sufficiently widespread distribution, marketing, and service infrastructure' (Hamel

and Prahalad 1993: 81). Failure in any of one of these three areas can destabilize the whole strategy architecture.

- **Conserving resources** through *recycling* and *shielding*. Recycling simply means re-using the same competency over and again. Thus, Sharp re-cycles its competence with digital screens in products ranging from televisions to monitors to calculators, etc. The same applies to Honda with its engines. Shielding resources is crucial to ensure their long-term sustainability and, assuming the core competence has passed the three tests and is thus embedded in the organization through path-dependent and causally ambiguous practices, it will not be easy for competitors to identify and replicate.
- **Recovering resources** from the marketplace in the shortest possible time so that they can be redeployed and the profits realized used to fuel the next round of R&D and new product development. The methods of lean production served Japanese automobile manufactures well in recovering their invested resources. Hamel and Prahalad (1994) observed that the major US car manufactures typically took on average eight years to develop a new product line; in Japan it was just 4.5 years. Thus, those invested resources could be recovered in the form of revenues much more quickly, alongside maintaining a more frequent release cycle.

Putting it all together: building a strategy architecture

The ability to build cross-functional core competencies in pursuit of strategic intent is not without its challenges as it takes a significant restructuring of not only the organization but attention to leadership, culture and the everyday routines of the organization. To facilitate this kind of shift, Hamel and Prahalad construct the notion of a strategy architecture; a structure through which a competence-led strategy can develop. Hamel and Prahalad describe it in the following way: 'Strategic architecture is basically a high-level blueprint for the deployment of new functionalities, the acquisition of new competencies or the migration of existing competencies, and the reconfiguring of the interface with customers' (Hamel and Prahalad 1994: 118).

Following the overall logic of their strategy process, Hamel and Prahalad suggest that a strategic architecture should take the form not of a detailed plan but rather a map outlining key information such as major goals, a guiding paradigm for strategy development, and the identification of core competencies to be acquired, built or leveraged. The capstone of the strategic architecture is of course the strategic intent, the end point on the map that we are trying to arrive at, and the strategy less a set of specific directions than a compass bearing indicating the general trajectory of the journey. To continue with Hamel and Prahalad's colourful analogies, if the strategy architecture constitutes the map and strategic intent the destination and bearing, then stretch and leverage provide the fuel to get there. They provide the vocabulary, logic and paradigm for operating practices that can lead toward the realization of strategic intent.

Building such a strategy architecture necessitates a different form of leadership than the top-down hierarchy we are more familiar with in the strategy literature. The role of leadership moves from one of directing the organization to one of facilitator – facilitating collaboration, cross-fertilization, innovation. It is about creating the structures, policies and operating practices that allow for more open forms of communication – middle-up and bottom-up as well as top-down. In this regard we see an implicit avocation of many of the major tenets of transformational leadership agenda, a theme well explored and very popular at the time that Hamel and Prahalad were developing their own ideas (Bass 1990). As an example, Table 7.1 outlines Canon's own path to realizing its strategic intent to 'Beat Xerox' (courtesy of Lilley, personal communication).

Drawing all of the above themes together, what Hamel and Prahalad advocate is an approach to strategy focused on accomplishing a very specific goal through flexible means under the conditions of resource scarcity. The heart of such a strategy rests on focusing on the foundations (or roots) of the organization, its unique abilities – its core competencies – in order to create a portfolio of products and services that can achieve sustainable competitive advantage. All other activities become secondary. In fact, to achieve a strategic intent often necessitates a need for greater collaboration with suppliers, buyers and other organizations that can undertake those activities necessary, but not core, to the organization. Thus we also see increasing talk about network-level strategy at this time.

Network-level strategy

Hamel and Prahalad's call for a firm to focus only on its core competencies also led them to recommend greater use of collaborative arrangements. They suggested two key forms of collaboration: those in which the firm could learn new skills, methods and practices; and those with best-in-class collaborators to whom non-core activity could be outsourced. Working with buyers, suppliers and even competitors in these ways, they suggest, would enhance the development of core competencies in the longer term: 'Using an alliance with a competitor to acquire new technologies or skills is not devious. It reflects the commitment and capacity of each partner to absorb the skills of the other' (Hamel *et al.* 1989: 134). Aside from the more familiar practices of joint venture, licensing arrangements and

Table 7.1 Xerox's path to achieving strategic intent

Step 1:	*Establish strategic intent to 'Beat Xerox'*
Step 2	Identify existing core competencies
Step 3	Understand Xerox's technology and patents in order to identify the necessary core competencies
Step 4	License the technology to gain market experience and begin to acquire the core competencies not already owned
Step 5	Invest in R&D to improve on the existing technology to acquire and start to exploit core competencies, primarily to achieve cost reductions, e.g. by standardizing components (to save cost and improve efficiency), improving ease of maintenance and replenishment, etc.
Step 6	License out own technology to fund further R&D and thus further consolidate the core competence required to 'beat Xerox'
Step 7	Open challenge, first by attacking markets where Xerox were weakest, e.g. Japan and then Europe
Step 8	Finally, innovative, rather than imitative, attack on markets where Xerox were strongest, e.g. by selling rather than leasing, distributing through office equipment retailers rather than direct, and focusing promotion on end-users rather than corporate functional heads
Result	Between 1980 and 1988 Canon grew by 265% and became the world manufacturing share leader in copier engines

franchising agreements that have been utilized as strategic devices since the 1970s, by the 1990s more integrated forms of collaboration such as 'strategic outsourcing', 'business networks' and 'co-opetition' had become increasingly common. But why, we might wonder, would firms want to collaborate, especially if this means potentially revealing some of their most treasured processes and practices?

Why collaborate?

Clegg *et al.* (2010) suggest four common reasons why firms might want to collaborate. First, and perhaps most pragmatically, it can be used as a strategy to gain *access to resources* the firm does not currently possess. For example, Intel, Microsoft and Nvidia collaborate as each has firm-specific capabilities and resources that the others depend on to ensure the smooth operation of the final consumer product ... which none of them actually make thus warranting additional collaboration with PC manufactures further down the supply chain.

Second, collaboration can also be used as an opportunity to *learn from* suppliers, buyers and even competitors. In the 1980s, General Motors entered into a collaborative agreement with Toyota to co-manufacture automobiles for the US market. In the process, Toyota was able to learn about 'doing business in America' with its very different regulations, competitive practices, labour laws, etc., and GM was able to learn about Toyota's famed production processes.

Third, in some cases collaboration is a requirement of doing business and might be the only way of *gaining market entry*. Thus, many US companies wanting to compete in Japan and South Korea in the 1970s and 1980s were only permitted to do so if they formed a collaborative agreement with a local company.

Finally, collaboration can be a means of *overcoming trade barriers*. Import quotas and tariffs can often prove extremely costly, as US firms discovered when trying to operate in China in the 1990s, and it was only by partnering with local firms, which could act as distribution channels for their goods, that such barriers could be overcome. In short, collaboration is highly strategic, both in the imperatives behind it and also in the way in which collaborative arrangements play out, as we shall see below when we consider some more recent examples of collaborative agreement.

Strategic outsourcing

One of the most common forms of collaborative agreement in recent years has been strategic outsourcing (although how this differs from regular outsourcing is unclear – yet one more example of the rhetorical weight of the word 'strategy' being employed to add meaning to something that was already occurring, perhaps?). Outsourcing itself is certainly not new. Ford Motor Company was outsourcing both supply and retail activities as early as the 1930s. However, as Leavy and McKiernan (2009) note, in the current age of globalization the imperative to outsource has become that much greater. Increased competition from new and emerging competitors, who seem able to do things smarter, cheaper and faster than established players, are lending increasing weight to the arguments made by the likes of Hamel and Prahalad that firms need to, in the word of Peters and Waterman (1982) 'stick to the knitting'. In other words, work out what they do best and do it relentlessly while outsourcing all other activities, ideally to similarly placed best-in-class firms.

Leavy and McKiernan go on to suggest four reasons why strategic outsourcing is seen as increasingly important to company survival, beyond the more obvious financial savings. First, it allows for greater *focus* on the things the company does well. Nike is great at designing and marketing sportswear so why does it need to concern itself with the messy process of actually manufacturing, distributing and selling its branded goods when there are others willing and able to do this for them? Second, it allows the firm to achieve *scale without mass and complexity*. Samsung, for example, in response to a rise in demand for one of its latest gadgets, can rapidly increase production by simply outsourcing to even more third-party manufacturers with little residual cost to itself, i.e. it does not have to acquire the production facilities and manage manufacture itself. Third, Leavy and McKiernan note that outsourcing has been a crucial component of the more recent strategic approach of *disruptive innovation* (Christensen 1997). We shall discuss these ideas in the next chapter but suffice to say that disruptive innovators, such as IKEA, have both relied on and also effectively utilized outsourcing as a fundamental component of their strategy. Finally, outsourcing enables *strategic repositioning* far more efficiently than might otherwise be the case if the firm were saddled with large quantities of assets such as staff, buildings and stock. This benefit has particular relevance for the contemporary phenomenon of internet start-ups that seem to exist as little more than websites and which primarily act as conduits through which goods and services pass. As such, when a market dries up or is no longer viable the firm simply packs up (closes the website down) and re-imagines itself in some new guise to service some new market.

Despite this convincing strategic rationale there are, of course, risks with outsourcing. For example, Leavy and McKiernan note that one of the main dangers is in the loss of existing resources and capabilities that are no longer maintained by the firm and will be difficult to recapture in the future. Such a firm might, in the future, be locked out of an industry because it no longer has the necessary capabilities to compete there. We have seen this happen time and again across a range of industries from automotives to consumer electronics. As a cautionary tale, Leavy and McKiernan tell of General Electric's early outsourcing agreement with Samsung in the newly emerging microwave oven market of the 1980s:

> In the early 1980s, GE was still investing heavily in its own manufacturing capability in the US, when it decided to outsource the production of some of its models [of microwave] at the small-to-medium end of the range to Samsung, which at that time was little known outside of Korea. While the initial contract was for just 15,000 units, GE quickly found itself on a steep dependence spiral that ultimately saw it ceding most of the investment and skills initiative in microwave production to its outsourcing partner within just two years. For Samsung, the arrangement allowed it to scale up its production and engineering at a rate that would not have been possible without the access it was given to GE's consumers, and this one small outsourcing contract set the stage for the later emergence of the Asian partner as a global powerhouse in consumer appliances.
>
> (Leavy and McKiernan 2009: 157)

As well as more formal outsourcing arrangements, recent years have seen increasing interest in the value of business networks and the practice of co-opetition.

Business networks and co-opetition

Writers such as Hagel *et al.* (2008) suggest that advances in digital communication have facilitated far greater interaction between firms and led to the establishment of more closely linked business networks. Indeed, Leavy and McKiernan anticipate that in the coming years and decades, the main basis on which competition will play out will not be firm against firm but network against network. The current computing platform wars between Google, Amazon, Microsoft and Apple give us a glimpse of this future, in which locking a consumer into a particular platform becomes a key part of the strategy.

Astley and Fombrun (1983) also identify what they term 'collective strategy' in which firms, and sometimes competitors, work together to produce a new industry standard, from which all will benefit. As an example we might observe Intel's recent activity in working with PC manufacturers to produce a range of what it calls 'Ultrabooks'; thin, lightweight mobile computers. This move, and Intel's subsidizing of each unit produced, was a direct response to the unanticipated success of Apple's MacBook Air range of notebooks. Thus, PC manufacturers and suppliers came together to form a collective strategy aimed at disrupting, even displacing, Apple's lead in that market. This more explicit attempt to engage in collaboration against a 'common enemy' has been termed 'co-opetition' by Brandenburger and Nalebuff (1996): a combining of the words *compete* and *cooperate* in which firms, in one way competitors, form a cooperative agreement in order to tackle a particular issue or take on a shared enemy.

Assessing Hamel and Prahalad's contribution to the field

In considering their work on strategic intent, core competence, stretch and leverage, and collaboration in the late 1980s and throughout the 1990s we can identify a number of substantive contributions that Hamel and Prahalad have made to the field of strategic management (they would continue to contribute ideas both together and separately in the future). Their first contribution was to develop a strategy approach that had wide applicability. While their focus was on global leadership and they used hand-picked high profile case companies to support their claims, their underlying argument about identifying an out-of-reach, long-term goal that can potentially act as a motivating force and then shape the organization to relentlessly pursue that goal has a lot of strategic appeal. Moreover, the accessible language and style through which they made these arguments made Hamel and Prahalad's strategy approach a useful managerial frame through which to pursue a resource-based approach to strategy development. In this regard it makes a genuine contribution to the inside-out approach.

Second, Mintzberg *et al.* (2009) note that these ideas have much wider applicability than some of the previous approaches we have looked at. Setting aside the quest for global leadership, the underlying message is one that has direct relevance to small and medium enterprises, as well as global players. Indeed, Mintzberg *et al.* (2009) suggest that this type of approach is often most successful in start-up firms. It is also highly applicable for firms in trouble and in which strategic turnaround is necessary. The reason being, and a further contribution to note, is the transformational nature of the approach. In other words, this approach to strategy is not about fitting in to existing structures, rules and conventions but thinking and working 'outside the box' in order to shake up companies, industries and markets.

Third, it is the first of the strategy approaches we have looked at that puts people at the heart of the strategy process. Unlike planning, portfolio and positioning strategies, Hamel and Prahalad's work, drawing on the main principles of the learning approach, recognizes the commitment and motivation of those involved as being crucial to the strategic success of the firm.

Fourth, and perhaps reflecting the context of its emergence, this approach also captures another contemporary development in that it lends itself very well to network-based strategies, with its perceived attendant benefits of both the tangible outcomes of collaborative agreements and the opportunities for learning that collaboration facilitates. It can also be linked to other popular themes in the late 1980s and early 1990s such as the notion of transformational leadership and strong cultures.

However, there are also limitations and challenges with this approach. First, in its recognition of the importance of people in the strategy process in takes a very unitarist perspective in the sense that it assumes that all organization members are working towards the same goals (that of the CEO in effect, as it is they who define the strategic intent). There is little room in this account for the power and politics of organizational life. Second, the risks of pursuing a strategic intent are very high: core competencies are difficult to develop and by extension, difficult to unlearn (as they are intended to manifest themselves as a dominant logic in the organization) and if, for some reason, the strategic intent is no longer desirable, then the core competence can become a 'core rigidity' (Pearson 1999), limiting further development in the firm. Other concerns about this approach, drawn from a portfolio perspective, suggest that the pursuit of strategic intent through the building of core competencies both limits the responsiveness of individual business units – who will always be restricted by their need to stay within the confines of the strategic intent – and also limits acquisition and diversification strategies that again will presumably only be pursued if they are deemed to contribute toward the building of a core competence. Perhaps this is why it is a 20-year goal, and whilst such slow and patient growth may be advisable it does not accord with some of the basic principles of western (strategic) management practice.

Chapter summary

In this chapter we have considered the work of Hamel and Prahalad as an example of an inside-out approach to strategy. Underpinned by a resource-based logic and drawing on the success of Japanese and South East Asian firms in the 1970s and 1980s, they propose an approach to strategy that begins with a desired leadership position encapsulated in a strategic intent that is then realized through the building of core competencies. Their work also lends itself to network-based strategies and taps into the wider corporate culture literature that was proving equally popular during the same time period. In the final chapter we shall look at an approach to strategy that in many ways builds on Hamel and Prahalad's work (and to which they themselves have contributed) but which also moves beyond some of its limitations outlined above: it is called the value innovation approach.

8 Creating strategy through value innovation

Introduction

> While the positioning and competency approaches have dominated the strategy field since the early 1980s, the last decade or so has seen a shift in emphasis away from the field's traditional focus on competition to a newer strategic logic of value innovation. Driving this shift has been the growing recognition that traditional routes to marking out and defending competitive space are becoming less and less effective as entry and mobility barriers are relentlessly assailed in market after market, switching costs are all but disappearing in many instances, and competencies tend to lose their market relevance more rapidly than before.
> (Leavy and McKiernan 2009: 146–7)

As indicated in the quote above, the business landscape of the twenty-first century seems no longer to accord with the prescriptions that have dominated the strategy teaching, research and practice agenda of the past 40 years. Faced by an external environment increasingly marked by conditions of turbulence and complexity (Mason, 2007), firms are being forced to rethink their current perspectives on the nature of markets, competition and strategy. As such, the strategy field has begun to shift attention to the importance of knowledge, innovation and technology as a basis for competitive advantage. Captured by the term 'value innovation' this approach to strategy is marked by two key characteristics. First, and most fundamentally, it seeks to draw strategy's attention away from competitors and onto customers. This is a novel move when we look back at the ideas we have discussed throughout this book; they have all been focused more on less explicitly on beating competitors, and while this achieves the outcome of serving greater numbers of customers, this often appears as a secondary concern. Second, and related to this, value innovation approaches seek to eliminate competition by making it irrelevant. By focusing primarily on the relationship between the firm and its customers (and ensuring that they are receiving greater value than they might find elsewhere), traditional conceptions of competition in strategic management are turned on their head – we are no longer interesting in trying to beat Xerox or crush, squash and slaughter Yamaha!

In this chapter we shall come to a better understanding of this new strategic approach by doing the following. First, we shall briefly review the ways in which value has been conceived in the strategy literature and introduce some of the key characteristics of the value innovation approach. Then we introduce the work of Joseph Schumpeter as a key theoretical underpinning and, in particular, discuss his idea of creative destruction. Second, we shall examine three of the most prominent value innovation approaches to strategy, as identified by Leavy and McKiernan (2009): specifically, we shall look at Kim and Mauborgne's (2004) 'Blue Ocean Strategy'; Christensen's (1997) notion of 'disruptive innovation;' and Prahalad and Ramaswamy's (2004) work on experience innovation and the co-creation of value. We will conclude our study of strategy by drawing out a number of connections between the various strategy-making approaches that we have considered throughout the book. We will consider the possibility that they constitute a more holistic view of strategy that can help us finally come up with an answer to the question, 'what is strategy?'

Perceptions of value and the limits of a dominant logic

One of the key proponents of the value innovation approach has been C. K. Prahalad. Most closely associated with the co-creation and experience innovation approaches in particular, he also draws attention to the failure of many firms to recognize the important connections between value and innovation. Too many firms, he suggests, are trapped into a narrow way of thinking about value and that blinds them to the possibilities of innovation. He refers to this as the failure of a *dominant logic*.

So what is a 'dominant logic'? A dominant logic, Prahalad (2004) suggests, is comparable to the DNA of the firm. It is embedded in the way things are done – its standard operating procedures, decision-making processes, communications methods, organizational structures, and so on. Others might think of it as the culture or ethos of the firm. For Prahalad, the dominant logic is a result of past performance – it is a present attempt to replicate the successes of the past. Thus we institutionalize that which has worked for us before on the assumption, or the hope, that it will continue to be a source of competitive advantage in the future. As such, the dominant logic becomes the lens through which present and future challenges, opportunities, etc., are considered, evaluated and pursued. The trouble is, Prahalad argues, that over time this logic becomes so embedded in the working of the organization that it can become hard to break free from. It becomes a 'dominant rigidity' limiting scope for change, and in a fast-moving business environment this can be very dangerous. As we shall see throughout this chapter, many large, powerful firms have been toppled by small start-ups and much of the causal explanation seems to rest with the 'blinders of a dominant logic' (Prahalad 2004).

Before we get into the detail however, let us explore a little more how the notion of a dominant logic links to the role and importance of value in the wider sense. In Table 8.1 Kim and Mauborgne (1997) offer a comparison of the traditional dominant logic on value creation

Table 8.1 Competing logics on value creation

Dimension of strategy	Conventional logic	Value innovation logic
Industry assumptions	Industry conditions are given	Industry conditions can be shaped
Strategic focus	Beat the competition	Avoid the competition
Customers	Retain, expand and segment your customers	Search for commonality
Resources and capabilities	Leverage existing resources and capabilities	Find new resources and capabilities
Product and service offering	Determined by market/industry structure	Look beyond traditional boundaries

and situate this against the assumptions emerging out of the value innovation approach to strategy-making:

For Kim and Mauborgne (1997) then, there are two competing dominant logics when it comes to understanding value. The conventional logic, which they see being present in most large western firms, and the logic of value innovation, which they advocate. In a sense, we can see this table as Kim and Mauborgne's quick and easy critique of the existing strategy field, as they saw it at the end of the twentieth century. Let us look at each in turn.

Industry assumptions

Levelling what appears to be a standard criticism at Michael Porter, Kim and Mauborgne argue that one of the great blinders of western management practice is to accept that industry forces are given, or fixed, as advocated by the outside-in approach. Accepting the logic of IO economics and adopting strategies of best fit within pre-given industry forces, they suggest, is one of the great failings of western strategy. You cannot hope to innovate, and to win, by playing by the existing rules of the game. Instead, value innovators, they suggest, ignore existing industry structure and seek to re-imagine the industry in their own model, just as Amazon have done in the book retail industry or EasyJet did in the UK airline industry.

Strategic focus

The dominant logic at the heart of many firms is 'beat the competition'. Thus the strategic focus and much of the competitive advantage involves competing against, with a view to out-performing, the competition. But for what purpose? It seems that competition and beating others has become ingrained in the strategy mindset, at least since the 1970s. Value innovators, however, take stock and pause. They question the combative nature of business and instead focus their energies on customers, not competitors. By doing so, they seek an exchange relationship with the customer that makes the competition irrelevant – a strategy successfully employed by IKEA when it entered the Swedish furniture industry. Whilst the competition are swimming around in the bloodied waters of red oceans, value innovators bathe in the cool and calm waters of blue oceans.

Customers

A more strategic focus on creating value for customers rather than trying to outperform competitors leads to a different logic of the customer itself. The conventional logic, Kim and Mauborgne suggest, is to maintain and expand the existing customer pool. Focusing on serving more and more customers with higher and higher value products and services. This kind of approach has led to a customer dominant logic that seeks to provide increasingly tailored services and product offerings, a form of mass customization such as that found at Dell or Starbucks. However, against this powerfully embedded logic, value innovators look for commonality across customers and seek to offer products and services that appeal across customer groups. A classic example here might be the smart phone industry with many competitors seeking to out-do one another with more and more features and more and more phones to suit every imagined need or want. Apple, by contrast, releases just one handset (with minor variations) per year and yet continues to exhibit some of the strongest sales in the industry. In an era in which the dominant logic is mass customization, the success of the iPhone is testament to this competing logic: what binds customers is greater than what divides them.

Resources and capabilities

The influence of the RBV of strategy has led many firms to focus heavily on their current resource base. However, as forewarned by Hamel and Prahalad, the danger of focusing on existing resources and capabilities is their inability to respond to future and unanticipated events. Thus capabilities can become rigidities. Value innovators are not afraid to 'start again', to reimagine the firm and replace existing resources and capabilities, irrespective of their previous value. As an example, Kim and Mauborgne cite Virgin Music's move from small high street music stores to the mega store format in the late 1980s. Recognizing that a key resource to high street retail is floor space and seeing that small stores cannot, for this reason, be turned into mega stores, Virgin took the bold move of selling-off the entire chain. It then reinvested that capital into building, gradually over time, the larger mega stores that, until the rise to dominance of digital music downloads, were the first choice for many in the UK high street music retail sector. Without being willing to start again, this business model would never have been possible.

Product and service offering

Whereas the conventional, and conservative, logic of value is based on the premise of existing, and discrete, products and services determined by existing market and industry structures and boundaries, value innovators seek to look beyond such boundaries. Instead, they look to combine products and services to offer complimentary and integrated value propositions. Thus Google is not just a search engine but has combined social media, productivity, communication, entertainment and information into a complete package of integrated products, programmes and services. This kind of 'platform' strategy has been central to the success of many value innovators, as we shall see throughout the chapter.

In summary, then, what is argued by proponents of the value innovation approach is that a dominant logic around how value is created and maintained has developed historically within western business firms, shaped, in no small part, by the prescriptions of strategy theorists, consultants and managers. While such a logic might prove useful under conditions of stability and growth – which allow attention to be focused on building and sustaining a specific value proposition – in the current competitive era, defined by complexity and turbulence, it is not sustainable in the long term. Value innovation, they propose, offers an alternative approach, one more suited to the conditions of the early twenty-first-century business environment. Before embarking on such a strategy approach, however, the incumbent firm needs to break free from the blinders of the conventional logic. But how does it do this? Prahalad (2004) suggests a number of possible practices that can be implemented to instigate the kind of change of logic needed. Specifically, firms need to focus on next practices, experimentation, and looking beyond conventional borders.

Breaking free from the blinders of a dominant logic

Focus on next practices

One failing of many businesses, Prahalad suggests, is focusing too much on best practices, or benchmarking. That is, industry leaders are held up as benchmarks against which we measure our own performance. The trouble with this practice, however, is that the industry leader sets the performance level for the industry and strategy becomes about competing to attain that level. Prahalad advocates instead searching for 'next practices'. Next practices, as the name suggests, means looking for approaches that are not yet in existence. It is thus about pioneering new approaches – and in this sense we can see a link back to Prahalad's work on strategic intent. As a good example of next practices we might cite Toyota's 'just-in time' production methods, which set new standards for manufacturing, or eBay's innovative business model for auctioneering. Focusing on next practices not only avoids the competitive convergence inherent in all competitor benchmarking, but also necessitates a more experimental approach, which is the second condition of breaking away from the dominant logic.

Experimentation

For a firm to hope to develop next practices or discover new, uncontested market space, experimentation is a necessity. However, many firms, operating with increasingly scarce resources, are reluctant to invest in ideas and projects for which there is no quantifiable return. History repeatedly tells us, however, that it is the experimenters and risk-takers that typically produce the break-through products in any industry or market. While Prahalad does not recommend excessive risk-taking, he does advocate 'low-cost' experimentation that allows a firm to learn (i.e. discover) new ways of working that can lead to innovation and change. You may recall the account of 3M's invention of the Post-it note as an example of an emergent strategy back in Chapter 4 of this book. While the final use for the technology emerged from unplanned events, the very development of the adhesive gel itself was an outcome of 3M's broader approach to innovation, one that dates back to the company's beginnings at the turn of the twentieth century. As retold by Colvin (2012), Minnesota Mining and Manufacturing (3M) was founded by five businessmen with no experience or expertise in either mining or manufacture.

They were reckless and clueless and the result was a swift withdrawal from these industries and entry into another unknown territory: sandpaper production. During the 1920s, one of its young employees, Richard Drew, was delivering a consignment of sandpaper to an automobile garage and happened to get into conversation with one of the mechanics about the poor quality tape they used to protect car body parts during repairs – it often left a sticky residue or else pulled the paint away when removed. Drew went back to 3M and quietly set about thinking up a solution to this problem. The result was 'masking tape'. Launched in 1925, masking tape remains a ubiquitous product to this day and is one of 3Ms greatest inventions. Drew's tinkering led then-CEO William Knight to enact a policy in which 3M engineers and scientists could dedicate a portion of their time to private projects of this sort. The '15% rule', as it came to be known, has become one of the most famous corporate policies of all time and has led to numerous inventions and, for 3M, billions of dollars in revenue. Today, firms like Google, Samsung and Apple have emulated such experimentation at the fringes.

Look beyond the borders of industries

As also recommended by Kim and Mauborgne, Prahalad advocates the need to look beyond existing market and industry boundaries for new sources of innovation and value. The satisficing of multiple needs in a single product or service is increasingly seen as a key requirement for many consumers. Phones that also operate as handheld computers, games consoles that also function as entertainment hubs, and one-stop shops are all examples of such mould-breaking products and services. Not only should firms look to combine industry offerings, they should also search for new ones or, more specifically, uncontested market spaces – 'blue oceans', as Kim and Mauborgne refer to them. Here, firms can establish market presence and build up a strong customer base free, at least for a time, from competition.

Looking beyond geographic borders

Finally, Prahalad advocates rethinking key target markets for the expansion of sales and new product development. The dominant logic of western firms, he argues, is to focus on high-end geographic markets where individual customers spend more per transaction. Against this he advocates a potentially highly profitable approach involving a larger number of lower-spending customers. By targeting 'the bottom of the pyramid' firms can achieve profits (while supposedly also helping many of the world's poor) through the 'marketization of social welfare' (Munir *et al.* 2010). As noted by Kolk *et al.* (2013), the idea of the bottom of the pyramid was first proposed by Prahalad, with Lieberthal (1998) and then Hart (2002). It became more popular following the 2002 publication of Prahalad and Hammond's *Harvard Business Review* article, 'Serving the world's poor, profitably' (Kolk *et al.* 2013).

The simple principle behind the strategy is to target not the top of the economic pyramid, which Prahalad defines as markets in which GDP per capita is more than $10,000 per annum, but instead the bottom of the pyramid, where GDP per capita is less than $2 a day. What is the strategic rationale for this?

> Technologies have spread rapidly in these emerging economies, as new technologies such as the wireless phones and Internet leapfrog the traditional infrastructure of landline communications systems. Three years ago there was no text messaging in India. Today a housewife in India uses 60 messages per day. What this is doing to social life is phenomenal.
>
> (Prahalad 2004: 178)

The relative speed at which new technologies roll out, as described in the quote above, leads Harjula (2007) to suggest that the bottom of the pyramid is an ideal testing ground for value innovation propositions – where an absence of competition and a lower level of expectation matched with lower price point converge meeting the criteria that Christensen in particular identifies as key to a disruptive innovation strategy. Others are more sceptical, suggesting that such a strategy, under the guise of CSR (corporate social responsibility) is nothing more than a smokescreen for exploiting the world's least well off with the technologies and consumer products of the privileged west (Davidson 2009). However we might view such initiatives, it certainly seems to be the case that proponents of the value innovation approach are at least thinking more creatively about issues of competition and firm performance. Perhaps part of the impetus for doing so comes from the theoretical underpinnings that inform this body of work.

Theoretical underpinnings: Schumpeterian competition

Where the outside-in approach draws on the logic of industrial organization (IO) economics and the inside-out approach of the theories of Chamberlin and Penrose, value innovators find their influence in Schumpertian economic theory. Joseph Schumpeter was an Austro-American economist who studied and then taught at the University of Vienna and later at Harvard. A contemporary of Chamberlin, Mason and Bain, Schumpeter developed a theory of competition at a more macro level than his peers. He rejected the idea that, in the long run, competition could be decided by price, position or the internal arrangement of resources and capabilities, and instead focused on the idea of disruptive change. Specifically, he argued that major revolutionary changes in an industry (or economy) are frequently brought about by technological advancement.

These revolutionary changes have an impact on all the competitive forces and disrupt the entire structure of the industry, resulting in some competitors no longer being able to compete due to a lack of necessary resources and capabilities, while others might be able to move from a position of relative weakness into one, conceivably, of market dominance. Until the revolution plays out we simply cannot tell what the outcome will be. Moreover, Schumpeter suggests that once a revolution begins and new innovations appear there will be a snowballing effect as entrepreneurs are attracted to the new offering, which in turn attracts more entrepreneurs, and so on.

Schumpeter also argues that the emergence of a revolution can never be perfectly anticipated, not even by the firm that may in part be responsible for instigating it. Think, for example, of Apple's iPad tablet computer. In its first three years the impact of this product was phenomenal: it undermined sales of traditional computers, smart phones and other computer and entertainment-related technologies; it found a use in a wide range of contexts, from schools and hospitals to the military and commercial airlines; and it sold over 90 million units, despite the initial response to the device being largely negative, with many failing to see a use for it (recall now Penrose's argument about why firms have to diversify). Moreover, within that time period, no competitor came remotely close to competing in terms of either sales or design. This can be seen as an example of a Shumpeterian revolution – redefining the way we live our digital lives.

Schumpeter uses the term *creative destruction* to describe this kind of phenomenon. The innovation is creative in the sense that it establishes new market space and new products or services, but it is also destructive in the way that it disrupts the current industry structure and the balance of its underlying forces. Despite developing these ideas over 50 years ago, it is only in the last 10–15 years that the strategy literature has come to incorporate this logic into a mainstream approach to strategy. This is still very much a developing field and few of the ideas discussed below have yet been subjected to extensive practical application. However, in this chapter we shall do our best to unpack some of the key features and contributions of the value innovation approach by looking at three examples from the literature, beginning with the blue ocean strategy idea.

Blue ocean strategy

W. Chan Kim and Renee Mauborgne (2004) provide us with one of the most widely known contributions to the value innovation approach with their idea of 'blue ocean strategy'. Their central argument, similar to that made by Hamel and Prahalad some years earlier, is that western business has been unable to compete effectively in an increasingly global marketplace and has continually lost out, primarily to Pacific Rim competitors. The reason for this, they argue, is because western management has focused its attention in the wrong areas and on the wrong issues. They argue that western firms are focused far too much on competitors and not enough on customers. By continually focusing their strategies on outperforming and beating competitors they have taken their eye off the bigger prize – customer loyalty. Pacific Rim firms, on the other hand, because they exist in less hostile and more collaborative environments, tend to be more customer-focused and have thus been able to continually innovate and capture larger shares of their respective markets.

Moreover, not only have western firms been too focused on the forces of competition, they have been trying to compete in the least attractive industries – the most established, experiencing low growth, and fiercely contested. Kim and Mauborgne call these industries – or, more correctly, the markets they serve – 'red oceans':

> In red oceans, industry boundaries are defined and accepted, and the competitive rules of the game are well understood. Here, companies try to outperform their rivals in order to grab a greater share of existing demand. As the space gets more and more crowded, prospects for profits and growth are reduced. Products turn into commodities, and increasing competition turns the water bloody.
>
> (Kim and Mauborgne 2004: 77)

As expressed in this colourful description, one of the main problems with red oceans is that there are limited opportunities for growth – the water is overcrowded and in many of them supply far outweighs demand. Yet firms seem to fail to recognize this and continue to invest their resources in them. In a study of new product launches across 108 different companies, Kim and Mauborgne found that 86 per cent of them were either line extensions or new products designed to compete in red oceans. Much of this seemingly irrational behaviour, they suggest, can be explained by the dominance of a logic of rational planning and positioning within the strategy field, underpinned by the economic determinism of IO economics.

In contrast, Kim and Mauborgne advocate the search for 'blue oceans':

> Blue oceans denote all the industries not in existence today – the unknown market space, untainted by competition. In blue oceans, demand is created rather than fought over. There is ample opportunity for growth that is both profitable and rapid. There are two ways to create blue oceans. In a few cases, companies can give rise to completely new industries, as eBay did with the online auction industry. But in most cases, a blue ocean is created from within a red ocean when a company alters the boundaries of an existing industry.
>
> (Kim and Mauborgne 2004: 77–8)

In the language of Schumpeter we might say that blue oceans are those industries and markets that emerge out of innovative revolutions and, in this regard, the idea of a blue ocean is not new. For example, the authors cite Ford Motor Company, which established a blue ocean with its Model T car in the early twentieth century. Moreover, many of today's bloodiest red oceans began life as blue oceans: pharmaceuticals, print media and management consultancy, for example.

In elaborating their main contribution, Kim and Mauborgne identify three key features of a blue ocean:

- While it is certainly not uncommon, blue oceans are not always about technological innovation. Moreover, even in technologically advanced blue oceans it is seldom the technology itself that is the basis of competitive advantage, but rather the value that the technology confers on the customer's use of the product. Thus, the inner workings of a car are less important to most consumers than whether it is safe, reliable and fuel-efficient.
- It is normally incumbents that establish blue oceans. This is not a strategy for start-ups only: 'Blue oceans are right next to you in every industry' (Kim and Mauborgne 2004: 81).
- The main strategic benefit of establishing a blue ocean – recognizing that it will quickly flood with competitors – is the first-mover advantage that it confers. Establishing a blue ocean acts, Kim and Mauborgne suggest, as a barrier to imitation. They even go so far as to suggest that it can confer a 10- to 15-year advantage, which is the time it will take competitors to catch up. This seems like something of a stretch in the contemporary business climate, but the basis of the claim turns first on the familiar economies of experience argument, and second, they argue that blue oceans initiate a kind of self-perpetuating cycle of supply and demand. For example, the more people use eBay, the more people will choose this site to sell their items (as there is a bigger prospective market), and the more goods there are on offer, the more people will choose eBay as their preferred online auction site, and so on.

In short, blue oceans offer uncontested market spaces that are particularly attractive given the propensity of red oceans currently in existence, in which bloody war is played out by existing firms who believe (or are led to believe) that this is the only way of doing business.

The rising imperative of creating blue oceans

If both red and blue oceans have always been present, then why is there now such urgency for pursuing this kind of strategy? Is it not a normal market mechanism? Kim and Mauborgne suggest there is urgency attached to pursuing blue oceans in the contemporary business climate due to two environmental factors. First, they suggest that technological advances and improvements in production processes have allowed suppliers to produce, with alarming frequency, ever-greater quantities of new products and new product variations, so that many markets are becoming flooded with increasingly un-differentiated offerings. The result is competitive convergence as more and more firms compete for the same pool of customers. Second, and relatedly, the situation has been further exacerbated by the forces of globalization. Trade barriers have been dismantled, there is a freer flow of products and services across the globe, and access to market and product information is available 24/7, allowing customers to continually access data on which to make decisions, in real time. This substantial increase in supply is occurring, they suggest, at a time in which there is no apparent comparable increase in demand. The result, they suggest, has been 'accelerated commoditization of products and services, increasing price wars, and shrinking profit margins' (Kim and Mauborgne 2005: 107).

The only sustainable escape from this downward spiral of competitive convergence, they argue, is to pursue a blue ocean. So how does a firm develop a blue ocean strategy? Based on their claim to have studied over 150 blue ocean creations in 30 different industries over a timespan of 120 years, Kim and Mauborgne (2005) feel confident that they have detected certain patterns and practices that lead to the creation of a blue ocean. Below we look at some of those key patterns.

Developing a blue ocean strategy

Creating uncontested market space

The first distinguishing feature of a blue ocean is, of course, pursuit of uncontested market space — a blue ocean from which to escape the violent, bloody waters of a red ocean. The way in which a firm can identify and pursue a blue ocean, Kim and Mauborgne suggest, is by breaking free of the blinders of the dominant logic of value creation and rethinking the notion of value as described earlier in the chapter. This frequently means, as we saw with Virgin Music, a radical reconsideration of the firm's value proposition. Let us take one of Kim and Maurborgne's (1999) examples as a case in point. By the late 1980s the US book retail market had begun to decline. The rise of portable and personal consumer technology meant people were reading fewer and fewer books and increasingly favouring digital and visual media. Booksellers typically followed one or other of two business models: the large discount retailer, competing on price with other large discounters; and the 'local' bookstore, described by Kim and Mauborgne as imposing 'tremendous inefficiencies and inconveniences on consumers. Their staff were generally trained as cashiers and stock clerks; few could help customers find the right book' (p. 89).

Barnes & Noble then broke free from this dominant industry structure and price-based competition and sought to re-imagine the book industry through a new value proposition, one that sought to focus not on the selling of books but on the pleasure of reading. To realize this goal it came up with a wholly new business model. It created vast book superstores that, unlike traditional bookstores, actively encouraged people to stay and browse and maybe even read books on the premises. They did this by providing comfortable seating, in-store coffee shops, and dedicated children's areas with activities and story-telling sessions. The stores were laid out in wide aisles, with soft music playing in the background. Members of staff were carefully recruited from those with a passion for reading — often local college kids — and given a monthly allowance to spend on books and actively encouraged to read in-store during quiet periods. In short, Barnes & Noble sought to recapture the pleasure of reading and of discovering new books as a form of leisure, even opening late to cater to the after-work footfall. Stores became a kind of third place, a space between work and home. The stores also stocked a far wider range of books, up to 150,000 titles compared to the average of just 20,000. In short, they redefined the value proposition and developed a business model that could achieve their goal. Kim and

Mauborgne report that the company saw a 50 per cent increase in sales as a result of this format and it came to define the standard for booksellers throughout the 1990s. That is, of course, until Amazon came along with a different value proposition and so disrupted the industry once again.

By creating new market spaces the firm can also achieve the second key aspect of a blue ocean strategy – making the competition irrelevant. In a sense this is more of an outcome than a part of the strategy, but again we can see how the shift in logic from competition to customers can be a powerful one in breaking free from a red ocean.

Break the value/cost trade-off

Perhaps the most important feature of a blue ocean strategy, Kim and Mauborgne (2004) argue, is the need to break away from the prevailing logic that a firm has to decide between value and cost. Or, to put it another way, to choose a generic strategy of *either* cost leadership *or* differentiation. This prescription, they suggest, has been the root cause of much of the failure of western companies. Instead, pursuit of a blue ocean strategy typically necessities pursuing both low cost and differentiation at the same time. Low cost is a necessary priority for the obvious reason that this is an uncontested and therefore unproven market space. There is no guarantee that it will succeed and consequently the firm needs to exercise caution in its risk-taking. Differentiation is equally necessary, to draw customers away from the established competitors in the red ocean. Even in the example of Barnes & Noble above we can see both a clear point of differentiation and attention to cost. The stores stocked a far greater number of books, which enabled them to buy from suppliers at a more substantial discount than smaller bookstores. The substantial increase in sales again meant that turnover was higher and further discounts could be applied. The business model was also relatively uncomplicated, the key costs being location, staff and stock. All of these are tangible costs and can be carefully managed during growth. There were no upfront costs for propriety technology, patents, and so on. In short, the differentiation was underpinned by a focus on cost management, which then became a virtuous circle.

Creating blue oceans through building complimentary offerings

One of the most effective ways of carving out new market space, Kim and Mauborgne (1999) suggest, is when existing firms seek to combine complimentary products and/or services to create new market offerings. As they note, 'few products and services are used in a vacuum' (p. 89) and by identifying how relationality or complementarity may be achieved, new offerings can open up as a source of 'untapped value' (p. 90). Perhaps the most obvious example here is Apple in the early 2000s, when it brought together its music player, the iPod, with a music delivery system, iTunes, in a move that not only led to its dominance in both industries but served as the catalyst for Apple's revival and future products such as the iPhone and iPad. Again, following the Schumpeterian logic, Apple could not have known how the strategy would unfold but it positioned itself in order to capitalize on the opportunity. Apple released its iPod music player in October 2001 with the promotional line, '1,000 songs in your pocket'. Detractors suggested iPod was an abbreviation for 'idiots price our devices', as the small device retailed at $399, substantially more than comparable devices at the time. Moreover, since it was only compatible with the Mac computer, another niche product at the time, the competition did not deem it a serious product. By early 2003 sales were only averaging 113,000 per quarter. However, by the end of 2003, with the release of its iTunes software for Windows and a vastly improved music catalogue, the value proposition suddenly became much more enticing: a high-end MP3 player that automatically synced with the largest provider of digital music in a way that seemed to 'just work'. Sales rocketed to over 733,000 per quarter by the end of the year and by 2007 iTunes and iPod sales accounted for some 45 per cent of Apple's revenue. Each alone was a good product but when combined they offered far greater value. This, for Kim and Mauborgne, is the essence of the value innovation approach.

Aligning the organization

Finally, Kim and Mauborgne recognize the need for attention to the internal workings of the firm in order to achieve the goal of a blue ocean strategy. It requires, in their view, a whole-system approach – integrating activities, costs and operational practices (Kim and Mauborgne 2004). In other words, this is not merely a vision or desired goal but a commitment to organizational restructuring to align all of the organization's activities with the new business model. Rather than the value chain, Kim and Mauborgne introduce the *strategy canvas* as a diagnostic tool and framework for achieving this.

The strategy canvas

Kim and Mauborgne define the strategy canvas as, first, a diagnostic tool that allows the firm to capture the current competitive forces in the known market space, the red ocean, and second, as providing an 'action framework' for escaping this market space and building new or uncontested market space. In Figure 8.1 we see an example of the strategy canvas for the US wine industry in the late 1990s.

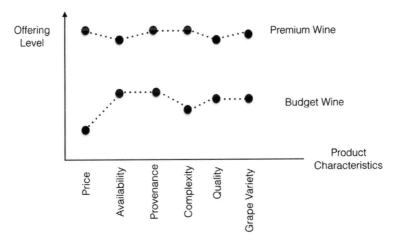

Figure 8.1 The strategy canvas
Source: Adapted from Kim and Mauborgne 2005.

132 *Creating strategy through value innovation*

The strategy canvas depicts the current planes of competition with the horizontal axis expressing the key measure of value within the industry and the vertical the competing business models. By mapping competitive behaviour onto the canvas the firm can see where competitors are converging in terms of their value proposition and where there appears to be uncontested space. In the example of the US wine industry there are clearly two competing business models: high-end premium wines and low-end budget wines. They appear to differ on every measure except availability and provenance. That there are only two competing business models suggests that this industry is marked by two red oceans, with an uncontested space between the premium and budget lines. Having diagnosed the current basis of competition, Kim and Mauborgne introduce the 'Four Actions' framework as a tool for assessing the viability of potential new market space opportunities.

The Four Actions framework

The Four Actions framework poses four key questions that seek to challenge the dominant logic of an industry while opening up opportunities to identify gaps and opportunities that might lead to new market space:

- *Eliminate*. The first issue, or question as Kim and Mauborgne pose it, invites the firm to consider which bases of current competition it needs to eliminate in order to create new market space. In other words, which assumptions no longer have value for the customer. In the example of the wine industry, provenance has long been a key marker of wine quality, but as more wine-making countries have emerged and as the technology and growing methods have become more opaque, the vineyard or chateau has become less important to the consumer of wine.
- *Reduce*. What are the sustaining innovations in this industry that have out-paced consumer need and can therefore be reduced? In other words, in what regards are

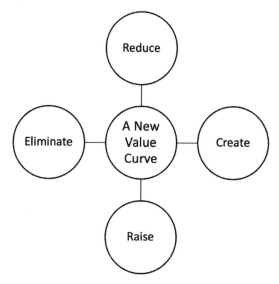

Figure 8.2 The Four Actions framework
Source: Adapted from Kim and Mauborgne 2005.

we over-serving the customer? In this case, it might be suggested that the grape variety and complexity of the wine industry over-serves many customers who are not necessarily connoisseurs but want good-quality wine at a reasonable price.
- *Create.* Where is the untapped value? In the pursuit of competitive convergence and out-performing the competition, what customer needs remain unmet? Referring back to the strategy canvas, the wine industry's focus at the top end means that there could be a large pool of non-consumers or under-served consumers who lack knowledge about wine but want to consume a good-quality product. Thus, accessibility, ease of choice and fun could be created as the new value proposition.
- *Raise.* What aspects of the value proposition are currently being under-served and how can these be raised up? There appears to be a gap in the strategy canvas between budget wine and premium wine. Could a firm create uncontested market space by offering a reasonably priced wine that incorporates the value proposition created above?

The combination of these four questions, the authors suggest, help the firm gain insight into both the weaknesses of the industry as it currently stands and the opportunities that are currently untapped. Collectively, they allow the firm to carve out new market space by creating a new value proposition, or value curve as the authors term it, capitalizing on unmet need while not over-servicing the customer, eliminating waste and maintaining control of cost, a key component of the blue ocean strategy as depicted in Figure 8.3. This, in essence, is the theory and practice of blue ocean strategy.

Although blue ocean strategy has a degree of managerial appeal, it lacks a certain academic rigour. It also lends itself very well to post hoc explanation – you only know you have created a blue ocean after the event, making it difficult to plan for. In this sense, the blue ocean logic is subject to the same tautological critique as the RBV. An alternative perspective on value innovation is offered by Clayton Christensen and his theory of disruptive innovation (1997).

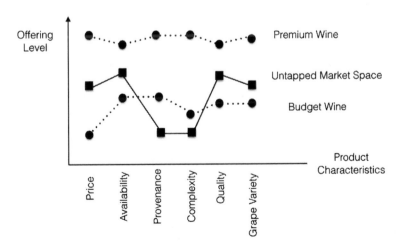

Figure 8.3 The strategy canvas
Source: Adapted from Kim and Mauborgne 2005.

Disruptive innovation

Drawing more explicitly on Schumpeterian economics, Christensen offers a more academically robust approach to value innovation. His point of entry begins with a question – why are large, powerful and incumbent firms so frequently outperformed, even toppled, by small start-ups? Christensen's answer to this question involves what he terms *disruptive innovation*. His argument is that small start-ups and new players simply do not have the capacity to compete with incumbent firms. As a consequence they will tend to adopt alternative strategies in which they seek to serve some small market niche that is not yet being adequately served by the existing industry, thus enabling them to establish a *foothold* in the industry. By serving *non-consumers*, as Christensen calls them, new firms can go largely undetected by the incumbents, who are primarily focused on the more attractive market segments.

Established competitors typically adopt what Christensen calls *sustaining strategies*, that are built on *sustaining innovations*. What he means by this is that new product developments tend to be incremental modifications that are introduced to better address existing needs and wants. Thus we get computers with faster processors and improved graphics, smart phones with better cameras and longer battery life, new cars with improved safety features, more electrical gadgets and greater fuel efficiency, and new cleaning products that soak up even more unwanted stains and spillages. In each case the product does the same thing ... only better (or at least that is what we are led to believe). The trouble is, Christensen argues, we seldom really need these kinds of incremental upgrades – few of us have the need or desire to drive our cars at 120mph, and few of us use even a fraction of the processing power in the components of our latest computer. Thus competition becomes a stagnant race to outperform rivals with modest incremental features and the strategic battle shifts to the arena of marketing, where clever advertising and promotions seek to differentiate these largely undifferentiated offerings. Such an approach, Christensen suggests, is a result of the dominant logic of strategic management – profit maximization, detailed planning, competitor focus, and cautious and conservative risk-taking.

In contrast, small start-ups, bursting with enthusiasm and entrepreneurial zeal and sure to fail if they try to compete head-on with the established players, will often seek to differentiate themselves by focusing on currently ignored or excluded market segments. This frequently involves serving price-sensitive customers or providing some kind of scarce or unique feature that is not currently provided. In this way, the *disruptive innovator*'s strategy is focused on attracting either the low end of the market and those currently priced out or on excluded segments not currently being catered for. By focusing on these ignored groups the firm can get a foothold in the market and slowly acquire the resources, capabilities and experience necessary to compete on a larger scale. Christensen refers to these as *disruptive strategies*. Note, however, that these are not disruptive in the sense that they bring about, overnight, some new technological revolution in the market; rather, it is the *trajectory* of the market that they disrupt by introducing a new plane of competition. Initially Christensen saw disruptive strategies primarily in the form of *low-end disruption*, as depicted in Figure 8.4.

Low-end disruption

The broken line indicates the 'rate of improvement' that the consumer can utilize (Christensen and Raynor 2003: 32). As we can see, this seldom connects with the pace

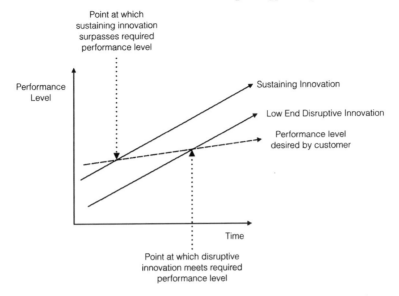

Figure 8.4 The disruptive innovation model
Source: Adapted from Christensen and Raynor 2003.

of technological progress offered by incumbent firms and their sustaining innovations. Indeed, over time the gap grows wider. Therefore, firms continue to over-serve customers simply because they can. Moreover, the customer trajectory plotted and targeted by the incumbent firm represents the high end of the market, those customers that spend the most and are most likely to upgrade on a regular basis. Excluded are those that cannot afford the current offering and are therefore excluded from the market: these are the non-consumers.

Disruptive innovators seek to get a foothold in the market by targeting non-consumers with a lower-level value proposition. The trade-off is that they are typically less expensive, as indicated by the lower line. A good example here is EasyJet when it entered the airline industry. Offering none of the frills of British Airways and other established airlines but instead utilizing a low-cost/low-price strategy by flying into (less accessible) airports with cheaper carrier rates, flying to fewer destinations and offering fewer flights (to maximize ticket sales), and reducing the check-in and in-flight services (to reduce overheads). It used only one model of aircraft and was thus able to achieve significant discounts and, despite common assumptions to the contrary, only acquired new planes as the cost of maintaining older planes was deemed to be too costly. It also adopted a relatively flat organizational hierarchy and employed only a six-month planning cycle. By building a business model around convenience, speed and low price, EasyJet opened up air travel to a vast cohort of UK non-consumers.

Christensen argues that in establishing a new plane of competition catering to non-consumers, the trajectory of the two planes of competition will gradually begin to merge as the benefits of the disruptive innovator's offering slowly become attractive to customers on the higher plane of competition. This then pulls them down to its offering, forcing incumbents to respond. In the case of EasyJet, the attractive prices eventually began to appeal to the lower end of the established market and so the trajectory of the airline industry was disrupted and established competitors were forced to start competing, in some respects on EasyJet's terms – that is, having to offer their own no-frills services alongside their existing provision.

New market disruption

While Christensen's initial model depicted only two dimensions, he would later, with Raynor (2003), add a third dimension and a second form of disruption: what they term 'new market disruption'. Whereas the low-end disruptor competes within the existing market, albeit serving non-consumers, the new market disruptor establishes a whole new plane of competition by competing against non-consumption. This typically reflects a completely new product or service rather than a low-end model of an existing one.

The shackles of incumbency and the innovator's dilemma

The obvious question subsequently arises – how and why do incumbents allow this happen? Why do they not leverage their resources in order to establish a barrier to entry and force these small firms out, as advocated by decades of strategic advice? For Christensen and Raynor (2003), big firms are shackled, or blinded, by a particular logic that delays any ability to respond, often until it is too late. Why? The first reason, the authors suggest, is because of a commitment to 'best' customers, which in the prevailing dominant logic of western business usually means the most profitable customers at the top of the pyramid. This in turn results in a race to outperform rivals with only incremental improvements, with the result that red oceans emerge in which largely undifferentiated products are made to seem different through clever advertising or price-based competition. Disruptive innovations seldom attract high-end customers initially so there is no appetite for pursuing them and therefore they go under the radar.

Second, in pursuit of operational efficiency most firms are orientated towards the perfection of a particular business model and there is significant cost in restructuring for new product categories. Moreover, many firms are too risk-averse to explore disruptive innovations. Also, the dominant logic of most firms is for a business case to be made for exploring a new innovation, these typically hinging on quantitative data. The very nature of a disruptive innovation means that there is seldom hard data with which to make a case. Innovation of this kind tends not to be found in a balance sheet or market report. In essence, the new market equates to a blue ocean and it is difficult to forecast the returns for an uncontested market space that is not currently in existence.

Third, for every successful disruptive innovation there are many more that fail. For an incumbent firm to respond to every new kid on the block would be neither sustainable nor desirable over the long term. Thus, incumbents are shackled by a business model focused on high-end customers and a conservative approach to risk-taking that typically means they will not realize the potential value of a disruptive innovation until it has taken hold. At which point the strategy shifts to one of defensive response. Christensen and Raynor call this 'asymmetric motivation' and it is this that is the core of the innovator's dilemma (2003: 35).

Sources of disruptive innovation

As noted above, disruptive innovations are not the same as technological breakthroughs that reshape an industry overnight. The path to disruption is typically slow (which partly explains why many incumbents fail to spot the danger until it is too late). Moreover, disruption comes in many forms and from many sources. Tidd and Bessant (2009) identify six sources of disruptive innovation:

- **New markets.** For example, the market for text messaging services (SMS) grew out of a pragmatic development in the mobile phone industry. In the early days of mobile phones, the costs of calls were extremely high and many potential customers were priced out of the market (notably the young). At the time, text messaging was seen as only a secondary function among phone manufacturers, but many non-consumers saw messaging as a way of avoiding peak-time calls. In this way they elevated 'texting' into a primary form of communication and a multi-billion dollar industry with profit margins of up to 90 per cent. Of course today this very profitable industry is now being disrupted by free texting services such as iMessage and Facebook.
- **New technologies.** As the world becomes more 'connected', email has posed a continual disruption to more traditional communication industries such as telephony and the postal service, and even travel services, with video conferencing replacing the need to hold face-to-face meetings.
- **New political rules.** The banning of tobacco advertising and later alcohol advertising in many countries forced these industries to come up with more creative forms of marketing communication, one of which was sponsorship. Today sponsorship constitutes one of the highest growth areas in marketing practice and expenditure, disrupting more traditional, and expensive media such as print and TV advertisements.
- **New business models.** As discussed earlier, companies such as Amazon and eBay have disrupted whole industries through their simple business model.
- **New needs and behaviours.** Disruptive innovations can also be driven by consumers. Western society's obsession since the 1980s with health and fitness has led to numerous multi-billion dollar industries including gyms, bottled water, health foods and dieting products and programmes.
- **Unthinkable events.** The attack on the Twin Towers in September 2001 ushered in a new era of security and surveillance, opening the way for what is now one of the fastest-growing industries in the world – private security.

Formulating a disruptive strategy: the innovator's solution

As with blue ocean strategy, one of the main challenges with disruptive innovation is knowing how to develop a practical application for use by managers. Skarzynski and Rufat-Latre (2011), using their survey of previous disruptive innovators, identify what they see as three core competencies that are crucial to achieving this type of strategy:

1 The strategic capability to anticipate and act on market discontinuities and unmet consumer needs. In this regard we can conceive of this as a learning approach to strategy formulation.
2 The strategic capability to link incremental and breakthrough innovations. In this sense we can draw a parallel to the synergy parenting approach in which the cross-fertilization and sharing of objectives and activities across business units is a primary focus.

3   The strategic mindset that both pursues and values the possibilities for innovation. Here, we can take our cue from the emergent perspective and its belief in a more holistic and company-wide approach to strategy.

Leadership and disruptive innovation

As well as building innovation-specific capabilities, Christensen and Raynor (2003) see a crucial role for leadership in fostering and building a disruptive innovation mindset. In this regard, they recount the history of Sony under the leadership of Akio Morita. Between 1950 and 1982, Sony was responsible for no less than 12 different new market disruptive innovations. These included the first battery-powered pocket transistor radio in 1955, the first portable black-and-white television in 1959, the Walkman portable cassette player in 1979, and the 3.5 inch floppy disk drive in 1981. Throughout this period, Morita was heavily involved in all new product development and personally approved each new product launch. He worked primarily with a small group of just five executives and together they searched for new disruptive ideas. Part of the process they employed involved going out into cities and into offices to observe people's everyday lives, and it was through this experience that they came to the conclusion that miniaturizing technology could make it more beneficial in everyday life. Thus, 'pocketability' became a cornerstone of Sony's product development.

In 1981 Moria began to withdraw from the day-to-day management of Sony as he pursued a political career. It was at this point, Christensen and Raynor suggest, that Sony began to lose its innovate touch. The reason? In order to try and replicate their previous success Sony began hiring executive MBAs with marketing backgrounds in the belief that they had the relevant skills and knowledge necessary to continue pursuing innovation. Of course this wasn't the case, for this new cadre of managers bought with them the quantitative, rational management techniques that they had been taught on their MBA courses and these replaced the intuitive practices that Morita had enacted. As soon as you try and formalize innovation and disruption you begin to lose the disruptive edge, the authors suggest.

The role of middle managers

For Christensen and Raynor (2003), key stakeholders in the achievement of a disruptive innovation are those collectively known as mid-level or middle managers. This group, while regularly excluded from the upper echelons of strategic decision-making, at least in the rational model, hold a key role in the dissemination of strategy between those 'on the ground' and senior management. They act as gatekeepers, filtering certain ideas, information and problems up the hierarchy while also judiciously choosing how to communicate orders from above. In this regard, their role as gatekeepers to disruptive innovation is crucial. Typically, innovation takes place lower down the organization where employees work most closely with products, customers, suppliers, etc. Which of their ideas for innovation make it onto the executive agenda for consideration is very much at the discretion of the middle manager. Their effective role as initial arbiters of new ideas is informed by their often lengthy experience as middle managers. More recently, another key stakeholder group has been recognized as crucial to the innovation process – the customer, with whom the firm can co-create value and build new experience-based innovation.

Experience innovation and the co-creation of value

A final approach to value innovation that we shall consider is that of experience innovation and the co-creation of value, associated with C. K. Prahalad and Venkat Ramaswamy. Prahalad, Ramaswamy and colleagues (2004, 2008, 2011) suggest that while a focus on innovation is a productive move forward in the strategy field, previous approaches, including those discussed above, are still too heavily focused on the individual firm. Going forward, these authors see a business world in which there will need to be increasing attention paid to the role of customers and consumers in the development of new products and services, and thus there will be a *co-creation of value*.

In addition, the basis of value differentiation will increasingly be measured not in product/service attributes or features but *experiences*. For example, the internal workings of my computer (the 'spec' as it is often called) will be less of a selling point than the experience this technology can offer me as a consumer to do the things I want to be able to do. The involvement of customers in both delivering and communicating such experience will be crucial. As a simple example of this think of eBay, which depends on the interaction of its customers in an exchange relationship, with its own role being primarily that of facilitator in the exchange. Thus, its strategic goal is to make the shopping experience as safe, enjoyable and efficient as possible so that customers continue to use the site.

That few firms currently think about value in this way, Prahalad suggests, is a result of the dominant logic that underpins both firm-level behaviour and also the wider discourse of strategic management. Reflecting arguments that have made in the marketing field during the same time period (see Vargo and Lusch 2004), Prahalad argues that changing consumer practices and experiences are driving the need for a new dominant logic – thanks to technologies such as the internet and digital communications, consumers are now much more active in the purchase process; comparing offerings, checking review sites, taking a wider interest in the activities of the firms from who they buy products, etc.

This presents the firm with the challenge of ensuring that they remain competitive while being seen to offer perceived value. In the UK for example, supermarkets have had to invest heavily in complex database technology to continually track competitors' prices as savvy shoppers hunt around for the best bargains – price-match guarantees, loyalty schemes and added services are all used to entice the customer to stay with a particular store. This challenge has also opened up an opportunity for more direct communication with individual customers, rather than relying on the more mass communication methods of the past (the store loyalty card has become a key technology in this regard, with firms amassing huge quantities of data on individual shoppers' habits which can then form the basis of targeted offers and communications).

Bringing customers into the value creation process is not new but, as Ramaswamy and Ozcan (2013) argue, the way it has typically operated in the past has been more akin to 'consumer outsourcing', in which activities previously held by the firm are passed on to the consumer, as often as not in order to cut costs and improve efficiency. Think, for example, of services such as 'self-service' kiosks in supermarkets, mass customization programmes such as Dell's ordering process, and online check-in for flights. In each instance, more and more of the labour involved in the exchange relationship is passed on to the customer. Against these efficiency programmes, what Prahalad, Ramaswamy and others argue for is a more embedded and deep-rooted involvement of customers in the innovation process itself. Co-creation and experience-based innovation are at the heart of their argument.

The strategy of co-creation

In a recent interview with Brian Leavy (2013), Ramaswamy reveals that the foundation of the co-creation theory evolved from Prahalad's earlier work on core competencies. Prahalad and Ramaswamy came to identify three important but missing aspects of the logic of core competence:

- customer and consumer communities as a potential source of a competence;
- the idea of competence in relation to not just products but also experiences;
- seeing customers as stakeholders and therefore collaborators in a process of co-creating competences.

(Leavy 2013: 12)

This led Prahalad and Ramaswamy to begin developing the idea of co-creation into a more robust theory for strategic management, which was later published in their 2004 book *The Future of Competition*. In this text they outline a new competitive landscape for the twenty-first century in which the internet and personal technology will come to facilitate the greater involvement of customers in the value creation process. As customers have more and more access to information to shape their decisions, they will no longer accept company promises without challenge. They will look for information on product use, for reviews, for best prices and, increasingly, turn to 'thematic consumer communities' (2004: 4) – consumer groups that coalesce around particular products, brands, activities, hobbies, etc. – for guidance. This access to information means that firms have to reconsider how they interact with customers not as an outside force but as partners:

> Companies can no longer act autonomously, designing products, developing production processes, crafting marketing messages, and controlling sales channels with little or no interference from consumers. Consumers now seek to exercise their influence in every part of the business system. Armed with new tools and dissatisfied with available choices, consumers want to interact with firms and thereby co-create value.
>
> (Prahalad and Ramaswamy 2004: 5)

As an example of the potential power of customers to influence the success of products, Ramswamy (2010) cites Orange, the telecommunications firm, as a useful case study. In relation to the launch of new phone technologies or payment tariffs, Orange has come to realize the power of the online community of bloggers, reviewers and influential technology-based websites that can shape customer reactions to its offering. Adoption rates can vary by as much as 10–16 per cent, Orange has found, depending on the reviews offered by these sites. More specifically, 'when it promotes its Web services, if the first five entries related to their services on search engines are bad reviews from users, there is little likelihood that the product will take off' (Ramaswamy 2010: 22–3). In short, in the crowded and largely undifferentiated world of mobile communications, consumers are turning more and more to fellow customers for advice rather than trusting firms' promotional materials. This has led Orange to develop Lab Orange, a web-based and company-sponsored forum through which Orange offers pre-release beta codes for consumer testing. In a practice that is common in the tech industries, as well as getting valuable feedback from customers, the more strategic belief is that by contributing, in however small a way, to the development of the platform, product or technology, the consumer has a vested interest in it and is therefore more likely to acquire it on final release.

As well as this outside-in approach to co-creation, Orange has also adopted inside-out approaches through employee suggestion programmes. Called 'idClic', it provides an opportunity for any employee to suggest new ideas, modifications, changes in practice and so on for the organization to consider. Akin to the quality circles so popular among Japanese firms in the 1980s, Orange claims to have implemented over 2,300 suggestions from employees, resulting in over 400 million euros in savings and additional revenues (Ramaswamy 2010). A similar scheme is Starbuck's mystarbucks.com site, which offers customers the opportunity to suggest new ideas for drinks, in-store features and the like.

Such examples show the potential power that co-creation programmes can achieve but, as Thomke and von Hippel (2002) observe, the process of achieving this outcome is far from easy or straightforward. They suggest that it requires not only tool kits but new business models. To this end, Ramaswamy advocates the need to build an 'engagement platform' on which experience-based innovation can be built.

Developing engagement platforms

At the heart of the co-creation and experience innovation model is the idea of an engagement platform, by which Ramaswamy means 'an assemblage of persons, interfaces, process and artefacts, designed to amplify and intensify human initiative in creating value together' (Leavy 2013: 13).

Examples of such platforms might include website forums, mobile apps, call centres and physical or virtual meeting spaces. Anywhere, in fact, where customers can engage with the firm in the process of innovation. As a tool for building engagement platforms, Prahalad and Ramaswamy (2004) devised the DART model, which stands for Dialogue, Access and choice, Risk assessment and Transparency, and constitutes the foundation of the experience innovation approach:

- Dialogue. This refers to the need for interactivity and engagement with customers, rather than assuming we know what they want. The use of social networking sites as a means of both observing consumer-to-consumer communication and accessing customers has become a common practice in this regard.
- Access and choice. Customers are being increasingly selective in the way they use the products and services they acquire. If we take music as an example, the success of Spotify and other digital download sites speaks to customers' increasing desire to be more in control of their music consumption – buying the individual songs they want and editing and combining them into personal playlists, rather than being forced to buy whole albums with little or no control over the listening experience.
- Risk assessment. In part thanks to the internet, customers are taking greater interest in the risks and responsibilities of various offerings, from food to healthcare. We check health websites before and after a visit to the doctor to confirm the diagnosis was 'correct'. We trawl through the review sites before committing to buying the latest television, camera or mobile phone. We check travel advice sites before booking a hotel to ensure it has received positive reviews. This active process of risk assessment, one in which we seemingly trust other consumers more than the service provider, poses a challenge to companies that are now having to think about the ways they can

influence and shape the reception of their product or service. For example, TripAdvisor now offers hoteliers, restaurateurs and others the chance to respond to customer feedback – to both demonstrate regret at failed service and challenge 'unreasonable' critique.

- Transparency. All of the above means that there is now greater transparency in relation to both what a company does and the experience it offers its customers. This is a markedly new situation as, historically, there has been a knowledge asymmetry between company and customer: 'Firms can no longer assume opaqueness of prices, costs, and profit margins. And as information about products, technologies, and business systems becomes more accessible, creating new levels of transparency becomes increasingly desirable' (Prahalad and Ramaswamy 2004: 7). For example, delivery tracking software invested in by couriers such as FedEx and UPS now allow customers to track the movements of their package through the distribution system and even track, in real time, the movement of the vehicle on which it is to be delivered.

Integrating the building blocks of transparency, risk assessment, access and dialogue, the authors argue, should enable firms to better engage customers as collaborators which can result in achieving a sustainable competitive advantage based on experience innovation.

Building a co-creation architecture

The ability to create and maintain an experience innovation-based strategy through the practice of co-creation requires a 'full philosophy of doing business that requires not just new ways of operating but also deep change in a company's outlook and culture' (Leavy 2013: 17). In this regard, the role of leadership becomes akin to that described in the discussion of the emergent perspective – facilitating learning, experimentation and processes of adaptive change. By adopting such practices, the firm can break from the traditional assumptions of value creation that Prahald and Ramaswamy see as a major failing of many firms. Table 8.2 outlines the two competing logics.

The experience innovation approach constitutes, in many respects, a radical change in perspective in the context of strategic management. As Clegg et al. (2010) rightly observe,

Table 8.2 Assumption of experience-based value

Traditional assumptions of value creation	New assumptions of experience-based value
Value is exchanged between the firm and a customer.	Value is created at the point of exchange.
Value is created by the firm.	Value is co-created by the consumer and the firm.
Value is embedded in products and services (therefore innovation is about products and services).	Value is embedded in experiences: products and services are carriers.
Value chain represents the value creation process.	Experience fulfilment webs are not sequential and linear value chains.
Innovation is about technologies, products and process.	Innovation is about experiences; technologies/products/processes are critical but not the goal.
Customers have a 'buy' or 'not buy' choice and managers are there to persuade them.	Customers make the key decision and the associated trade-offs.

Source: Prahalad 2004.

the history of strategy has for the most part been a history of building defensible position against competitors based on hard-to-detect, carefully hidden resources, capabilities and positions. This approach advocates a much more open system in which strategy, technology and products effectively have to be shared, not just with customers but ultimately with the competition. After all, it would be naive to think that competitors do not sign up for the beta or developer builds of competitors' products or technologies.

Chapter summary

In this section we have introduced some of the more recent thinking in the mainstream strategy literature, which we labelled the 'value innovation' approach. The main argument underpinning this approach is that there can be no universal answer to the problem of strategy: the dominant tools, techniques and frameworks of the past have continually failed to produce sustainable competitive advantage. If anything, they seem to have held back 'big business' while allowing smaller competitors to emerge, often undetected, to build up a position of dominance, with incumbent firms too slow to realize or react. Finding blue oceans, capitalizing on disruptive innovations or engaging in the co-creation of value with customers has broken down many of the previously established competitive barriers. Facilitated by technology, most notably the internet, and the wider forces of globalization, we are now experiencing a much more turbulent and complex business environment, one in which the old rules of the game seem no longer to apply. But does that mean we should reject all previous solutions to the strategy problem? In our concluding discussion we will tackle this question and argue for a more integrated understanding of the strategy literature, one which might, in turn, lead to a more holistic view of strategy that takes the best from each approach to produce a more meaningful and robust understanding. We will finish with some final reflections on our opening question – what is strategy?

Concluding discussion

So what is strategy?

In this book we have examined a range of distinctive approaches to the practice and process of creating strategy: we have conceived of it as a formal deliberate planning process and a pattern of emergent behaviour; we have considered it as a way of managing a multi-business firm and making important resource allocation decisions; we have considered strategy as a process of industry analysis and positioning and as a route to achieving competitive advantage through pursuit of a strategic intent and the creation of core competencies; and finally, through a focus on innovation, value and customers we have explored strategy as a disruptive force. Each approach has its own solution to the problem of achieving sustainable competitive advantage and each offers its own answer to the question 'what is strategy?'.

If we accept that there is more than one way to do strategy, the notion of choice becomes central to our concerns. Which is the 'best' approach to developing a strategy is a common question. However, to take such a reductionist position is probably to miss the point. The fact than none of the ideas, frameworks and theories we have explored has proved able to provide a sustainable solution to the problem of strategy but each has stood the test of time in the sense that it is still used presents something of a paradox to the would-be strategist. As a result, maybe we should be thinking less about either/or decisions and instead about how these competing logics might actually work together, thus creating a more holistic and integrated approach to strategy.

Towards a holistic theory of strategy?

Drawing on the work of Barney (1986), let us first look at the way in which the work of the outside-in, inside-out, and value innovation theorists combines through considering in more detail the theoretical frames on which they are built and how these play out 'in practice'. We noted in Chapter 8 that, from a Schumpeterian perspective, new markets emerge through revolutions in technology, changing consumer demand, or some other unanticipated force. These revolutions can be usefully conceived of as a starting point for a new round of strategy-making activity. The new markets and industries that emerge out of Schumpeterian revolutions cannot be perfectly anticipated or planned for and they usually happen at such a gradual pace that they are not always immediately detectable, even to the firm that may be at the heart of that revolution. However, once the revolution is in full flow the underlying forces of the industry begin to change, as do the requirements necessary for any firm that wishes to compete within it.

After a Schumpeterian revolution has unfolded, firms are faced with the strategic challenge of how to respond, and here the theories of IO economics and Chamberlinian economics become more important: should the firm respond to the revolution by identifying the new underlying forces that are shaping the industry, looking for the weak spots and seeking to exploit them through finding a position of best fit and only then configuring the organization to achieving this strategy (a Porterian outside-in approach)? Or should the firm seek to identify the necessary competencies and capabilities required to compete successfully on this new plane of competition, in the belief that what goes on inside the organization is more important than the external environment (as advocated by Hamel and Prahalad and the inside-out approach)? The firm's answer to this question will largely be informed by the deeper dominant logic, or perspective, that drives it: whether it subscribes to a rational, deliberate, formal planned approach, or whether it adopts a more pragmatic, emergent and learning approach – with the outside-in approach more closely associated with the rational logic and the inside-out approach more inclined toward an emergent logic.

Outside-in or inside-out: does it matter?

In light of a Schumpeterian revolution we might ask if it really matters whether a firm chooses a broadly inside-out or a broadly outside-in response. After all, doesn't every firm need to consider both the internal and external environment when constructing its strategies? By this stage in the book I would hope that you do think it matters and, hopefully, you are able to articulate why. If you have followed the logic of the book then you will know that the decision between inside-out and outside-in is a fundamental choice – even if not always a conscious one (in the sense that firms do not 'pick' an approach but rather the approach constitutes a post hoc theoretical frame for explaining real-world practice) – that will shape subsequent strategy-making. From our academic study we know that these two approaches are underpinned by quite distinct economic theories and that the logic that drives them will lead the strategist in quite contrary directions (even if the final goal is the same).

For example, an outside-in approach, drawing on the strategic tools of industry analysis, generic strategies and the value chain would likely lead to the adoption of plans and ploys that specifically address the perceived threats and opportunities in the external environment. Thus, we would see strategic manoeuvres that focus on raising industry barriers to entry, gaining favourable supplier and buyer relations, and seeking and communicating explicit points of differentiation. By contrast, pursuit of an inside-out strategy reduces these kinds of concern to a secondary status. Instead, attention is focused on the distinctive 'know how' (Leavy and McKiernan 2009: 143) of the firm and its perceived strengths, which can be leveraged to compete in different markets. Strategy here will focus more on building core competencies, developing cross-organizational structures that can foster learning, collaboration and innovation, and on adaptive responses to emergent threats and opportunities.

Outside-in or inside-out: where does it matter?

We have identified above that it does appear to matter whether an outside-in or an inside-out approach to strategy is followed, at least in the sense that the decision shapes the strategic decision-making agenda in terms of what is and what is not deemed to be of strategic importance. However, it seems it also has wider strategic significance. For example, at times of strategic change or renewal, the pursuit (conscious or otherwise) of one or other of these two approaches will likely determine both the terms of reference for the renewal strategy (the adoption of top-down data-driven modelling vs. creative scenario planning, for example) and the options than can be put on the table, and by extension, those left off, excluded or thrown in the garbage can. Second, it also matters in the context of corporate-level strategy. If you recall, we introduced a number of different parenting approaches and subsequent relations between the corporate centre and the individual business units. A corporation underpinned by an outside-in logic is more likely to engage in portfolio parenting approaches. The logic being that, if each business unit is subject to its own industry forces and is concerned primarily with finding a position of best fit within that industry, there is little need to worry about the interconnectedness of each business unit, other than for pragmatic or tactical reasons. The test for diversification and acquisition will be one of industry attractiveness, not 'fit' with the current portfolio. In contrast, an inside-out logic would suggest a synergy-parenting approach due to the need to foster closer relationships between business units, with each having its place in the portfolio because it permits the distinctive know-how of the firm to be utilized in a new context or market. The test for diversification and acquisition here will be less about innate attractiveness or profit potential and more about building or enhancing core competencies. The seemingly illogical and unrelated diversified form of Canon or Honda makes sense when underpinned by this deeper organizational logic.

In summary then, despite their seeming uniqueness – at least in the way in which they are presented (and let us not forget that most of these strategy academics are also strategy consultants looking to sell their own distinctive package of solutions) – these different strategy approaches are in fact far more closely connected than at first appears. For this reason, we might be able to develop, from this literature, a more holistic view of strategy, in which Schumpeterian revolutions force a strategic change for the organization that will be informed by a preference (conscious or otherwise) for positioning- or competency-based strategies. This preference will shape both business-level and corporate-level strategy, as well as the strategic decision-making processes in the firm.

In conclusion, we might therefore argue that the strategy question has not really changed all that much from its original inception to the present day. Indeed, from everything we have discussed it seems as though strategy has always been about mediating between the forces of the internal environment and those of the external environment. All that has changed has been the terminology to explain the dynamics of this relationship and the preferencing of one environment over the other at various points in time.

Case 1
IKEA: daring to be different

Introduction

IKEA, the furniture store from Sweden, began life in 1943 when its 17-year-old founder, Ingvar Kamprad, used money given to him by his father to begin a small business selling pens, pencils and even seeds in his local area. Over the following eight years Kamprad built this small enterprise into a household goods and furniture mail order business and gave it the name IKEA, which combined the initials of his name with those of Elmtaryd, the farm he grew up on, and his hometown of Agunnaryd to create the now iconic yellow and blue (the colours of the Swedish flag) branded furniture retailer (Lief 2008).

Today IKEA has some 345 company-owned stores in 42 countries around the world (fortune.com). It employs over 131,000 employees and in 2014 revenues closed at 29.2 billion Euros (ikea.com). At the heart of IKEA's success is a value proposition that has barely changed since its earliest days. Put simply it aims to provide good design and functionality at a low price. It does this through combining a low-cost value chain with a clearly defined point of differentiation. But what is perhaps most interesting about IKEA is the way that its current business model emerged out of a series of unanticipated and serendipitous events over the years. In short, IKEA's business did not develop from the outset through clearly defined goals, plans and positions but rather emerged as a pattern of adaptive responses to unanticipated events. The unique combination of Kamprad's vision and the organizational culture he built enabled IKEA to capitalize on these 'lucky breaks' to build a global brand and a unique business model that we see present in every IKEA store across the globe.

The emergence of the IKEA business model

IKEA's business model today is built on a set of mutually reinforcing practices that allow it to achieve a hybrid strategy of achieving low cost while simultaneously sustaining a clear point of differentiation. The key features of this model are the retail stores themselves, the 'flat-pack' furniture range, in-house design and close collaboration with suppliers. However, what is remarkable is that each of these core foundations emerged out of quite unexpected circumstances. Let us look at each in turn.

In-house design and supplier relations

Kamprad has always held firm to his belief in offering low-priced furniture and while such a strategy is commonplace and not particularly remarkable today, the environment in which Kamprad founded IKEA was a markedly different one. In post-World War II

Swedish society, furniture was seen as a high-priced luxury item. Typically handcrafted and handed down through the generations, furniture was designed to last and was therefore an infrequent purchase. However, in the late 1940s and early 1950s a new generation of young householders was in need of furnishings but could seldom afford the high prices. An ageing population also meant that parents retained furniture for a longer period of time. Kamprad saw a gap in the market, a blue ocean if you will, of non-consumers priced out of what is a market for essential goods. In the early days, Kamprad offered high-quality furniture at much lower prices than his rivals, relying on higher-volume sales to offset the lower margins. The response from the competition, Lief (2008) notes, was swift and aggressive. Unhappy at being undercut by a new competitor, one unwilling to play by the rules of the game, they organized a boycott of IKEA's suppliers, threatening to withdraw their own custom if they continued to supply IKEA. Fearful of losing big orders the suppliers capitulated, and this left IKEA exposed with no future stock.

At this point Kamprad faced a choice: raise his prices in line with competitors or face being forced out of the market. Kamprad, holding true to his belief in low-priced furniture, made another rather bold decision. He decided instead to hire designers of his own and begin designing new products for IKEA that would then be outsourced to neighbouring countries for manufacture. In this way Kamprad was able to avoid rather than confront the competition. IKEA quickly established suppler relations with firms in Denmark and then Poland, where low labour costs meant that he could drive his prices down even further while also offering a unique product range that none of his competitors could source. Had Kamprad's hand not been forced then the unique and distinctly IKEA-designed furniture that we see today may never have been. Likewise, by being forced into outsourcing arrangements long before such a practice was commonplace, IKEA was able to establish strong supplier relationships and exclusive contracts that ensured a regular and consistent supply of materials and products for its stores. Today, IKEA is the world's third largest consumer of wood (ikea.com).

The IKEA store concept

Another key component of the IKEA business model is its famous store design. Briefly, the key aspects of the store design comprise an out-of town location close to main roads giving customers easy access. Each store consists of a large entranceway, often with a small crèche where young children can be looked after while parents shop. The stores are then laid out as a series of show rooms full of both the large furniture items and the many accessories that IKEA stocks. The order of the rooms is always the same: living room, bedrooms, kitchen, bathroom and children's rooms. Customers cannot take any short cuts to specific areas but are required to walk through each room until they arrive at the one they are interested in. Provided with pen, paper and tape measure, customers are required to note down the items they want as they walk through the show rooms. After the show rooms there is often a restaurant where customers can take a break and experience some of the now famous IKEA meatballs or other delicacies from the Småland area of Sweden, where Kamprad (and IKEA) come from. Once rested, customers then move on to the accessories areas with their kitchen items, lamps, rugs, etc. These then lead into the warehouse where customers can collect the large items they have spotted along the way – thankfully, everything is flat-packed. Then comes the checkout and possibly another small café.

So what is remarkable about this store design? First, there is the location itself, which facilitates ease of travel but also ensures lower rents for IKEA compared to premium-priced centre-of-town units. Indeed, IKEA was an early pioneer of the out-of-town retail park concept. Forcing customers to travel one route through the stores prevents a trip to IKEA ever being a quick affair but helps stimulate additional purchases while young children, the bane of many a shopping trip, are happily ensconced in the crèche. The use of show rooms not only provides a visual prompt but also helps customers see how rooms might fit together. Given that IKEA's target market is the young and less affluent, often furnishing a new home, IKEA provides a one-stop shop for everything they might need. Having customers collect their own furniture also significantly reduces staff costs, and IKEA does not employ sales staff in the traditional sense. The simple café and restaurant services offer very cheap food but have become something of an institution in their own right and with high margins contribute some $2 billion per year in revenue alone.

So refined and slick is the operation that we might think it was ever thus, but the retail store concept emerged from a lesson learnt from failure and a disaster. When Kamprad opened the first IKEA store in his hometown of Almhult in 1958, it was an instant success. This led to gradual expansion and the building, in 1965, of a new flagship store in Kungens Kurva, Stockholm. Some 18,000 people waited in line on opening day, starting a trend that continues to this day, sometimes with disastrous consequences: when IKEA opened a store in Edmonton, London, in 2005, so immense was the queue that the store had to be closed to prevent a dangerous crush through the doors. The overwhelming popularity took Kamprad by surprise: the store had too few staff, too few checkouts, and was not big enough to accommodate such a large footfall. The result was customer backlash, with complaints about queues and delays while staff had to collect items from the warehouse. Some customers took to simply leaving without paying (Duke 2011b). Out of desperation the store manager decided to open up the warehouse to customers so that they could collect their furniture themselves, thus reducing the waiting time and the tension. Indeed, 'it was this spontaneous reaction rather than conscious decision that launched the start of the innovative "self-service" IKEA model' (Duke 2011b: 8).

IKEA continued to refine the store design through the 1960s and then in 1970 disaster struck – the Kungens Kurva store burnt down. Kamprad decided to rebuild and make it the biggest and best store yet. Hans Ax, the store manager, was tasked with leading the redesign and it was then that the show-room concept emerged (previously it had been a more traditional furniture warehouse). It was the first store to offer a crèche, a streamlined warehouse collection system, and a restaurant. Ax also set new opening hours so as to open longer and later to catch people on their way home from work. Had the store not burnt down and had Ax not been the man to reinvent it (using his previous store experience as tacit knowledge), who knows what IKEA stores would look like today. It was another example of how the unexpected and the unplanned led to what would become a core component of the IKEA business model. Central to the store design was the self-service warehouse, but this then led to another problem – how would customers transport potentially large furniture items home? To achieve this, another unplanned opportunity presented itself.

The innovation of flat-packed furniture

As mentioned already, the prevailing business model in the furniture industry in Sweden in the 1950s and 1960s was built round expensive handcrafted furniture that came ready built. This often resulted in long shipping times and high delivery costs. In the early years, IKEA conformed to this model as it was acting as a retailer only. However, once it began designing its own furniture it began exploring alternatives modes of packaging and delivery. Keen to keep costs and prices down, IKEA did not offer a delivery service and instead customers had to collect their own furniture. So the story goes, one day Gillis Lundgrem, IKEA's fourth employee, was struggling to put a piece of furniture in a customer's car. In order to make it fit, he removed the legs and gave the customer instructions on how to 're-assemble' it. In this one move, Lundgren 'invented the flat-pack approach to furniture' (Lief 2008: 3). Lundgrem's experience quickly reached the ears of Kamprad, who saw the potential of 'flat-pack' – and the rest, as they say, is history. Flat-pack also helped facilitate the in-store warehousing system and significantly reduced shipping costs from the manufacturing plants to the stores.

Product range

The final component of the IKEA business model is the product range on offer. In a sense this is the culmination of all of the other building blocks of the company's business model. Having been forced out of the traditional sector and deciding to undertake in-house design meant that IKEA could be more creative and inventive in its offering, in the face of a rather conservative and formal competitive environment. The pursuit of low cost meant that IKEA could also use lower-cost materials and offer a narrower range, thus concentrating design and purchases around a limited number of core collections. The discovery of flat-pack was not only beneficial to the customer but also created substantial savings in storage and distribution. Being freed up in this way led to one of IKEA's key sources of competitive advantage – the innovative but fun design of its products, right down to the quirky names they were given. But even here we can see how patterns of behaviour led to this end, as opposed to a clearly defined plan. Let us take, for example, the naming of the products. Most furniture retailers use numerical codes to identify different pieces. However, as retold by I.-B. Bayley, Kamprad's cousin and key architecture of the famous IKEA catalogue, 'In the first catalogues, there were few names, but then Ingvar decided to give names to everything – he found numbers difficult' (Duke 2011b: 5). Thus, whereas IKEA began by following the industry norm – using numerical codes – the simple fact that Kamprad had a terrible memory for numbers (he was later diagnosed with dyslexia) led to the naming of products such as the now iconic Billy Bookcase, still its most popular product – according to IKEA, one is sold somewhere in the world every ten seconds. To the native English speaker, the names of IKEA products seem a little kooky and strange but in fact there is a rationale behind them: beds are named after Norwegian places of interest; sofas take the name of Swedish towns; kitchen tables are named after Finnish geographic points of interest, chairs are male first names, glasses and cups are given adjectives, and so on (ikea.com).

The importance of culture: some lessons learnt

As well as its emergent business model, IKEA's success is also rooted in its concern with culture. Indeed, the importance of culture is at the heart of the IKEA business model: both the culture of Sweden (and in particular Kamprad's own region) and the culture of the organization itself are key to IKEA. Today, IKEA is frequently lauded for its strong corporate culture, setting numerous benchmarks of good practice that others have tried to emulate. However, it was not always so. In the 1950s and 1960s Kamprad adopted a more formal managerial style and fostered quite a rigid conservative culture. He dressed in suits, seldom engaged with employees and displayed his wealth with ostentatious purchases such as luxury cars. However, in the early 1970s a transformation took place (Duke 2011b). Kamprad dropped the suits in favour of casual clothes of the kind now worn by all employees. He replaced his Porsche with a more ordinary car and started to engage more with employees. Kamprad began to embody the values of IKEA and this gave birth to today's IKEA culture. Employees still wear informal dress, address one another with first names and informal salutations, are referred to as co-workers rather than employees and even the most senior managers are required to spend one week a year working in the stores. IKEA also operates numerous forms of employee participation scheme, all with an underlying cost-cutting goal. For example, in 2000 it launched an internal 'air hunt competition'. Air, in the form of excess packaging, increases costs as it increases the size of packaging. With the offer of a two-week holiday for the winner, IKEA set the challenge of creating a way of reducing packaging for a specific item. The winner came up with a better method of packing and shipping tea lights, which IEKA sells millions of each year (Kowitt 2015). Rather than pack them loosely in bags, the invention was a stackable tray that could be vacuum-sealed, much like the method used to ship that other Nordic export, fish sticks!

Such playful schemes reflect what Kling and Goteman (2003) identify as a set of core values that permeate and drive all aspects of the organization: cost-cutting, innovation, informality and simplicity. The structure is also relatively flat with just four levels of hierarchy separating the CEO from the store co-worker. In 1967, Kamprad outlined his values in his 'corporate bible', *Testament of a Furniture Dealer*, a book given to every new employee. New employees often also undergo the ritual of having to join the furniture assembly team early in their employment. While this constitutes a 'rite of passage', it also serves as an opportunity to break the ice and build relationships. Moreover, it offers IKEA a crucial business insight. The relative ease, or not, with which these flat-pack novices can assemble the furniture is fed back into the design process. In the past IKEA has sometimes been accused of making self-assembly too complex, creating what are internally known as 'husband killer' products (Kowitt 2015). The continual feedback from new employees helps to refine the design process, simplify assembly instructions and thus reduce the burden on the customer.

The values that IKEA promote also reflect the wider Scandinavian culture that IKEA is proud to celebrate: from product names to the location of its head office and product design down to the food served in its restaurants and cafes, all celebrates Scandinavian culture. So fundamental has Swedish culture been to the IKEA business model that it has sought to make this a part of its value proposition in all the international markets it has entered, Kamprad's aim being to 'bring a little bit of Sweden to the world' (Lief 2008: 1). Such a noble enterprise has met with huge success, albeit with a few bumps along the way. While IKEA's international growth strategy has always been geared towards cautious, steady, organic growth, it would be fair to say that this has not always been a smooth process. For example, it had to rethink and redesign many of its products when it entered the American market in the 1980s. Put simply, the products were not big enough for the American market – beds were too narrow and too short, glasses were too small – many choosing instead to buy vases as drinking vessels – and serving plates were mistaken for dinner plates. Moreover, the American market also presented IKEA with new demographics that it had not previously targeted during its European expansion. In particular, it initially failed to attract the large Hispanic population. As a result, 'designers visited the homes of Hispanic staff. They discovered that US Hispanics did not like the subdued palettes of IKEA furnishings, preferring bright colours with warmer hues. They also liked large dining tables and sofas that seated more than two people' (Duke 2011a: 7). This early experience in the US market provided two key lessons that IKEA would use going forward. First, the experience of understanding potential customers through visiting their homes has led to an increase in market research, especially in markets far removed from the Scandinavian base. This has even involved having anthropologists live with volunteer customers to study how they use furniture. The aim is not to create market-specific offerings (remember IKEA's business model is about high volume and lows cost) but rather to consider how their products might be used differently. Thus, studies of Japanese customers found that few sat on the sofas but rather sat on the floor and used them as back rests. Such observations have fed their way into the store designs, with items displayed differently according to customer taste and cultural practice. The second lesson learnt was to better understand the culture and society of new markets. Thus, IKEA spent six years researching South Korean culture and society prior to opening its first store there in December 2014 (Kowitt 2015). In this regard, akin to its wider strategic development over time, we can see how IKEA's international growth has also being a product of learning, of adaptive response to emergent events, and of a willingness to modify its business model to suit the needs of the market.

Case questions

1 IKEA's strategy seems to have emerged in response to a number of unexpected challenges. Explain how IKEA was able to rise to and overcome these challenges. What insights into IKEA's approach to strategy does this reveal?
2 What is IKEA's position in its competitive environment?
3 What trade-offs has IKEA made in order to sustain this position?
4 Identify three major strategic issues that IKEA faces. Describe them all, say why they are strategically important, and offer some recommendations for how it might address each of them.

Case 2
Fast fashion at Zara

Introduction

Zara is the flagship brand of the Spanish retail giant Inditex, shipping over 450 million items of clothing per year. In 2014 it achieved sales of $12.6 billion. Founded by Amancio Ortega when he opened his first clothing store in the Galicia town of Arteixo in 1975, today Zara operates over 2,000 stores in some 88 countries. While Spain remains its key market, in 2013 China overtook France to become Zara's second largest market (Berfield and Baigorri 2013).

At the heart of Zara's success is a business model built on the ability to design, manufacture, ship and sell a vast array of fashion items at a speed that few, if any, of its competitors can match. Underpinning this business model are two key principles that Ortega has never diverted from – give customers what they want, and get it to them faster than anyone else (Walt 2013). Most fashion retailers offer four to eight collections per year, often with anything up to a 40-week lead time (Caro 2011), placing at least 80 per cent of orders in advance of release (Berfield and Baigorri 2013). Zara manages to produce something approaching 100 collections per year (Magretta 2012) with lead times as little as two weeks. So how does it manage such an achievement?

In this case study we will explore some of the key aspects of Zara's strategy with a particular emphasis on the key activities of the value chain as a way of identifying how its various activities are aligned to create value and synergy in the pursuit of a clearly defined value proposition – the latest fashions at reasonable prices – through a strategy know colloquially as 'fast fashion'.

Unpicking Zara's business model

Design

Whereas most fashion retailers employ big-name designers to develop their premier collections, often at great cost and significant lead time, Zara has a large team of in-house designers that produce most of the collections within its range. While having a large team speeds up the design process Zara goes further than this by not committing to starting from scratch with each new collection. Rather, Zara has a large team of fashion scouts whose primary role is to observe and report back on emerging fashion trends in the fashion hotspots across the globe. Shunning fashion shows, scouts tend to frequent nightclubs bars, restaurants and the preferred hang-out spots of celebrities and the fashionable. These scouts then report back on the designs, trends and themes they observe. These observation are then developed into imitative designs by the team of in-house designers who work at a frantic pace, often creating as many as three of four separate designs per day (Walt 2013).

It is not just the scouts that are on the look-out for new ideas. Walt (2013) recounts how Ortega, travelling to work one day, pulls up alongside a motorcyclists at traffic lights and notices the rider's jacket. Ortega picks up his cellphone: 'His eyes fixed on the biker, describes the jacket's stitching, its shape and color, and signed off with a single instruction: "Hácedla!" Make it!'

To achieve its fast fashion, designers at Zara also work very closely with store managers and employers who feed back on which collections are selling well and also their own observations on customer fashions and trends. Indeed, its store employees are a crucial part of the Zara business model. Store managers and employees are invited to offer feedback, criticism and suggestions on new collections and use a sophisticated technology for keeping track of stock. Store employees walk the store with handheld devices that record numbers of items sold, inventory levels and so on. This information is then sent back to HQ in real time so that future shipments can be modified accordingly. Unlike many of its competitors, Zara does not ship all items to all stores but instead uses the store information to target particular lines, colours, sizes, etc. The result is that less than 10 per cent of its stock is typically returned unsold, a figure less than half the average (Berfield and Baigorri 2013).

Operations management

One of the key features of Zara's business model is its tight control of the manufacturing process. Some 50 per cent of its garments are manufactured on site in Spain or in one of the 11 company-owned factories in nearby Portugal and Morocco. It also relies on an army of local sub-contractors to undertake various aspects of the manufacturing process, including over 500 local sewing firms in the Galicia region alone (Caro 2011).

Zara's primary facility and corporate headquarters, known as 'the Cube', is, as Walt (2013) describes it, 'part sci-fi machine, part old-fashioned retailer'. To encourage close collaboration and speed up the communication process between departments, designers literally sit alongside design cutters and sewing teams that quickly construct prototypes that can then be modified before being sent to the manufacturing floor. Even Ortega, the world's third richest man in 2013, never had a separate office, preferring instead to sit at a desk at the end of one of the work stations (Walt 2013).

Zara only outsources production to third-party manufacturers for its basic ranges that do not tend to change much. For its new and short-run fashion collections it uses company-owned facilities. Because it employs a short cycle run it has also adopted the methods of just-in-time production – which it learnt through a collaborative project with Toyota in the 1990s (Caro 2011) – to ensure the timely arrival of materials and fabrics of sufficient quantity for that production run only. This also means it has a much lower stockpiled inventory than many of its competitors.

Logistics

To ensure the timely arrival of collections to the stores, Zara maintains its own logistics hub built close by the Cube. The five million-square-foot distribution centre has been built to maximize value and speed. Zara has even built an underground rail system consisting of some 124 miles of track connecting the factories to the logistics hub to ensure the timely arrival of garments (Berfield and Baigorri 2013). The distribution centre itself consists of a labyrinth of conveyor belts five stories high that transport items from section to section as they prepare for shipping. Once packed, items are loaded onto Zara's own fleet of trucks for either store delivery or the airport for long-distance shipping. So efficient has its logistics processes become that garments can go from the factory floor to its logistics hub to European stores in just 24 hours and in no more than 48 hours to Asian and Latin American stores (Magretta 2012).

In order to further speed up the process, all garments are priced and placed on hangers prior to being shipped, meaning they can be placed straight on the rails when they arrive at the stores. This saves time on the lengthy process of 'merchandising' that most clothing retailers have to undertake when new stock arrives. As Magretta (2012) notes, it increases shipping costs but this is an acceptable trade-off for the speed and efficiency it offers. The result is a two-week turnaround from initial design to manufacture to shipping to the item appearing in store for sale (Zillman 2014).

Zara stores

As Magretta (2012) describes them, Zara retail stores tend to be large units in areas of high footfall in more prestigious shopping locations with higher-spending consumers. The store designs are simple, spacious and well laid out, avoiding the mass of rails and random display of goods that typify more low-end competitors but with more range and styles on visible display than higher-end competitors. Due to its batch production system and its emphasis on a regular turnover of stock, Zara invests little in advertising and instead relies on the learnt behaviour of its customers who know to buy as soon as they see things for fear they will not be available in a few days time. This has created something of a buzz around the stores and the anticipation of new collections, with some loyal customers knowing exactly when new stock will arrive, so predictable and reliable is the value chain underpinning it.

Again, Zara makes a trade-off here, investing in more expensive retail locations but offsetting that cost against a relatively low marketing budget by relying on word of mouth. The small batch offerings also mean that Zara seldom has to discount in order to shift stock and the impulse purchase behaviour of its customers also encourages a regular flow of sales throughout the year rather than a reliance on critical periods and seasonal sales.

In order to foster strong working relationships between store workers and designers, store employees are incentivised through programmes such as store-level reward programmes, above-average pay and clearly defined career progression, with responsibility for individual product ranges distributed among employees rather than in the hands of a single manager: a practice Ortega believes essential to develop loyal and enthusiastic employees (Caro 2011). This division of labour and specialization also allows individual members of staff to develop a deep understanding of just one area of the store, thus allowing them to better understand consumer needs – which is crucial for the next production run.

Future challenges: the dangers of speed

Crucial to Zara's business model is the tight control it retains from its Spanish headquarters. However, as the brand grows internationally it will increasingly feel the challenge to its centralized distribution system (sales have grown by 50 per cent since 2000). Operating a hub-and-spoke system, all items, even those manufactured by third parties, are first shipped to the main distribution centre in Spain before going out to the stores. The logistics (both in terms of costs and timeframes) of managing this activity will become more and more challenging as growth continues. In particular, with rapid expansion in China and Asia the goal of achieving its 48-hour turn around will be sorely tested.

Another challenge to Zara will be competition. Its success with its fast fashion value proposition has attracted the attention of other fashion retailers and many are now seeking to replicate this business model. Caro (2011) notes that both H&M and Fast Retailing have sought to create similar value propositions as they target Zara's key markets.

Zara has also made certain blunders that some have put down to the speed at which it puts out new collections, leaving little time for market testing or more considered quality control. In 2007, for example, customers complained about a new handbag embossed with green swastikas. While the bag itself had been designed in-house, the third-party Indian supplier who had been contracted to manufacture the bag had added the swastikas as an additional design feature. In Indian culture the shape of the swastika is a sign of good fortune but it has very different connotations in western Europe. More recently, in 2014 the consumer blog site +972 raised concerns about a new children's collection that 'looked a whole lot like the striped garments and yellow stars that Jews were forced to wear during the Holocaust' (Zillman 2014). Such avoidable PR blunders, while not resulting in any significant damage to the brand, do raise concerns about the dangers of fast fashion.

A further challenge, given Zara's speed of expansion, has been the need to manage its corporate image with respect to its suppliers and some of its sub-contracted manufacturers, relying as it does on low-cost labour in some of the poorest regions of the world. According to Caro (2011), Zara now depends on 1,800 production facilities across Africa, Asia, Europe and the Americas. In response to criticisms about its use of low-cost labour, Zara has sought to invest heavily in its corporate social responsibility programmes to improve working standards and wages with some of its suppliers.

Finally, questions have arisen as to whether Zara can continue its rapid expansion during the current period of austerity in many of its key markets, such as Spain and Portugal. While there is little evidence that growth is slowing, in large part due to its expansion elsewhere, there is certainly a need to balance international growth with the core tenets of its basic value proposition.

In sum, what we can see above is the practical application of a value chain that is geared towards a clearly defined value proposition – fast fashion – and a number of trade-offs that ensure that Zara can maintain its business model over the long term. However, even the most well oiled machine is prone to occasional breakdowns and the dangers of speed have more than once damaged Zara's reputation.

Case questions

1. Use the value chain to identify the key components of Zara's strategy.
2. What are the risks and opportunities attached to this configuration or primary and support activities?
3. How does Zara's value chain help it defend against its competitors?
4. Identify three major strategic issues that Zara faces. Describe them all, say why they are strategically important, and offer some recommendations for how Zara might address each of them.

Case 3
Innovation and change at Nike

Introduction

Founded in 1964 and a dominant player in the sports apparel industry for over 30 years, the Nike brand, with its iconic swoosh logo, has become as familiar as those other stalwarts of American customer culture, Apple, Coca Cola and Wal-Mart. With revenues of $27.4 billion in 2014, Nike appears to be going from strength to strength. At the heart of Nike's success has been a historical record of innovation in everything from shoe design – including its patented 'Air' technology in 1987 – to sports clothing and equipment to high street fashion. This has been matched by a peerless marketing capability, with famous campaigns including the Emmy award-winning 'move' campaign in 2002, its regular use of sponsored endorsers such as Andre Agassi, Tiger Woods and Michael Jordan, and perhaps most famous of all, its long-running 'Just do it' campaign, first launched in 1988.

Never one to rest on past success, Nike's latest innovation in sports apparel is the Flyknit Racer, an extremely light running shoe that is manufactured using a knit-threaded process rather than the standard use of multiple fabric layers. The result is a shoe that has far greater elasticity, allowing itself to model around the runner's foot more like a sock than a traditional shoe. The shoe is also more environmentally friendly, minimizing waste in the production process.

As well as sticking close to its core business, Nike has also begun to diversify into a number of unrelated areas where again innovation is core to its strategy. In this case study we will explore Nike's approach to innovation by considering its move into digital platforms and wearable technologies, posing questions regarding the strategic logic of such a move and identifying the core principles of Nike's approach to innovation.

Nike's move into digital platforms

Joga.com

One of Nike's first moves into the digital realm took place during the 2006 football World Cup when it partnered with Google to set up the Joga.com social networking site. While the site linked through to Nike stores and contained adverts for its products as well as offering links to some of its key footballing endorsers, it was primarily user-focused and user-built. The site invited individuals to film their own soccer stunts and skills and upload them to the site. Visitors to the site could then rate and comment on the videos. Available in 140 countries and in 14 different languages, the website proved hugely successful. With over 1 million hits the site proved strategically important in raising Nike's presence in the field of football, where it had traditionally lagged being competitors such as Adidas (a move reinforced by the large number of World Cup players choosing Nike boots). It also showed Nike the potential power of digital technology and user-created content.

Nike ID

Drawing on its success with Joga.com, Nike then sought to redesign its other user-created online innovation, Nike ID. First set up in 1999, Nike ID allows customers to design their own Nike footwear. By getting customers involved in the design process Nike sought not only to offer a more customizable experience but also to learn from customers about emerging fashions based on their selections. To relaunch the service, Nike held a competition inviting a number of well-known designers to design a completely new shoe for Nike. Visitors to the site were then encouraged to comment on the designs and vote for a winner.

As Ramaswamy (2008) has noted, the strategic value to Nike of such engagement platforms has been to help in develop a better understanding of its customers and to build relationships with them on a previously unprecedented scale. Whereas historically the purchase of sports apparel had typically been made through a third-party retailer, with Nike relying on traditional mass media marketing to entice purchases, the internet provided a forum for Nike to connect directly with its customer. The realization of the true power of this platform came when Nike sought to connect its online presence with its innovation in wearable technology.

Wearable technology

Nike+ and the FuelBand

Launched in 2006, Nike+ was a collaboration between Nike and Apple to develop a platform that runners could use to keep track of their activity levels. Built into the design of certain Nike running shoes, a sensor would track key information that could then be transmitted to an Apple iPod where a purpose-built app would process and record the information. This in turn could then be uploaded to the Nike+ website where runners could track their activity levels over time and also share their stats with fellow runners. The site also provided forums for discussion about running tips, preferred apparel and so on. As both Nike's competence with tracking monitors and Apple's handheld technologies improved, in 2012 Nike released the FuelBand, a watch-like device worn on the wrist that not only tracked activity but also vital statistics such as heart rate, blood pressure, calories burnt and so on. Linking the FuelBand to an Apple iPhone could then permit wireless transmission of data, making it even easier to record and track performance levels.

Critical to the success of both was the Nike+ website, which functioned as an engagement platform that allowed the company to engage directly with customers and gather deep levels of information about them. However, Nike+ was always about more than just user data. It became a community forum that facilitated not only business-to-consumer dialogue but also runner-to-runner. By offering a forum for runners to connect with one another the Nike+ platform has been able to help foster dialogue between runners as they share their information and also offer tips, news of running events, injury-prevention strategies – even compete with one another by setting shared goals.

By partnering with Apple, a company fast emerging during that time as a market leader in MP3 players and then smart phones, the Nike+ site became a natural home for large numbers of runners. Through its personal and web-based technologies Nike was able to provide runners with access to both their personal information, other runners, and even Nike-employed running experts with whom they could consult and who could provide training programmes and so on. In an age increasing defined by consumer-to-consumer communication and brand community, Nike was able to facilitate this activity for runners. Moreover, the ease of use of the technology reduced the risk of runners losing their data due to the frequency with which they would use the service, i.e. every time they ran. Through wireless technology and by collaborating with Apple and making the service extremely simple and user-friendly, it encouraged high rates of return. As Ramaswamy notes: 'This input provides Nike with a goldmine of ideas for potential innovations' (Ramaswamy 2008: 12).

Through the establishment of this engagement platform and by fostering forms of co-creation Nike was able to draw ideas for new innovations, products and services from the community but to do so in an open and transparent way. In addition, for a company renowned for its marketing creativity it constituted a powerful marketing tool: as of 10 April 2015, the Nike+ community has clocked up over 85,300,123,733 steps burning some 12,827,604,378 calories.

So successful has the combined Nike+ platform and FuelBand been that Nike has found itself, as is so often the way, attracting the attention of numerous competitors and in 2015 a number of large technology firms will be releasing their own wearable technologies – these include Apple with its Apple Watch and HealthKit software, Google and its Android Wear range, and new offerings from recent start-ups such as Jawbone and Fitbit.

Riding the wave of success through its focus on innovation and engaging the customer through co-creation initiatives, it might be surprising to learn that Nike has now substantially scaled back its future development in this area. While it will retain its Nike+ website and software it will no longer design new wearable technology. Having only recently got into the business and seemingly being very successful at it, this would seem a strange strategy to adopt: surely it should capitalize on its position by investing more heavily in the area? To understand the strategic rationale here we need to look beyond products and services to the deeper dominant logic of innovation at Nike.

Nike's approach to innovation

Mark Parker, current CEO of Nike, following the announcement that Nike had been nominated the 2013 'World's Most Innovative Company' by Fortune magazine, outlined Nike's strategy by stating: 'Business models are not meant to be static. In the world we live in today, you have to adapt and change. One of my fears is being this big, slow, constipated, bureaucratic company that's happy with its success. That will wind up being your death in the end' (Carr 2013). Thus, Nike's original move into digital media and wearable technology constituted a break from its core business in the early 2000s and, having made headway in those markets, Parker feels the time is right to move on again.

When Parker took over in 2006 he quickly moved to establish a shift in strategy at Nike, and at its 2007 investors conference he outlined a new value proposition that saw Nike move away from being primarily a sportswear brand to becoming an 'enabler of customized, personal experiences' (nike.com). This new position was encapsulated in a new corporate theme, 'The Consumer Decides', one of the 11 maxims that make up Nike's core philosophy. Number one on that list is: 'It is in our nature to innovate.' In a recent Fast Company profile of the company, based on interviews with top Nike executives, current and former designers, engineers, and long-time collaborators, Austin Carr (2013) outlines the four distinct rules that guide Nike's approach to innovation:

1 *To disrupt, you must go all-in.* A common feature of many disruptive innovators is the need to 'bet the company' on a single idea or innovation that, in most instances is yet unproven. Whether it be the original Model T Ford or eBay or EasyJet, the common feature of each is the high level of risk that each founder was willing to take against an unknown and untested value proposition. Thus, Carr notes for Nike, the innovation is not in the FlyKnit as a specific design but in the willingness to consider a whole new way of imagining and manufacturing shoes.

2 *Anticipate a product's evolution.* Borrowing from the example of his friend and mentor Steve Jobs, Parker is a great believer in looking beyond current market conditions and sustaining innovations to consider how new innovations may evolve, not into a quick profit but into a longer-term shift in consumer behaviour. Much in the same way that the iPod led to the development of the iPhone and iPad, Parker sees a similar trajectory for the FlyKnit technology or its online community presence. As Carr notes, Parker would have been excused for initially dismissing the original Flyknit prototype, which resembled more a ballerina's slipper than a running shoe, but he was able to see the potential of the innovation. 195 iterations later, it seems he may have been right. Today, Nike is experimenting with new ways of using FlyKinit in other apparel and has begun building communities around other sporting activities.

3 *Rule your partners.* Recognizing the need to establish collaborative arrangements with best-in-class partners in a range of different industries is something Nike has long practiced. However, the proactive role Nike has taken in managing its partners is perhaps a key component of its success. In the case of the FuelBand, for example, Nike worked closely with a range of partners including Astro Studios, Whipsaw and Synapse to develop both the technology and the aesthetic design of the band but in each instance only worked with one partner at a time revealing only what it needed to. Thus Nike was the only firm in the wider network that was involved in all aspects of the development. This enabled it to maintain overall control while also ensuring a degree of secrecy.

4 *Feed company culture.* Crucial to Nike's success has been its attention to building a strong, open and collaborative organizational culture. Much of this is based on celebrating and respecting the company's history, as Carr recalls walking round Nike headquarters: 'Nike's campus is full of odd talismans, a living museum of itself, a container of legends and oral histories. The waffle iron that cofounder Bill Bowerman ruined making rubber soles in the 1970s? It's enshrined on campus like the Liberty Bell. In fact, with so many bits of lore around, anything can be mistaken as symbolic.' In addition, Nike manages to maintain a relatively low turnover of staff with a benefits package that includes above average remuneration and a clearly defined career progression. As Nike's head of corporate education, Nelson Farris describes it, Nike's encourages employees to decide what they want their career trajectory to be and then 'when you see something that would help you get there, ask us for it.' Perhaps Mark Parker best exemplifies this belief having worked his way up from his original role, in 1979, as a shoe designer to its present CEO. More than this though, employees seem to

exhibit a certain evangelism around the brand and the organization, with many succumbing to the trend for having a Nike swoosh tattooed on their leg: 'Workers quote the company's maxims like the Ten Commandments. More than a dozen tell me, independently and unprompted, "Be a sponge" and "If you have a body, you're an athlete." "We can almost finish each other's sentences," Parker says. "But not in a drinking-the-Kool-Aid, cultlike way."'

(Carr, 2013)

Nike: where next?

Known historically as a product-centric business Nike has proven its ability to adapt and respond to a changing environment by diversifying into new and seemingly unrelated areas of activities. However, underlying these strategic moves has been an approach to innovation and a business model that is centred more on adaptability and creativity than product or market-focused categories. So successful has Nike become that it now engages in 200 million-plus interactions with its customers every day (Cendrowski 2012). Having established itself in online social media and wearable technology and with so much customer data to hand, the burning question is where next for the world's most innovative company?

Case questions

1 Why did Nike go into wearable technology? What can explain this seemingly unrelated diversification strategy?
2 Use the DART model to explore Nike's digital platform strategy. What strategic lessons can we learn from Nike's approach to the co-creation of value?
3 What are Nike's core competencies and where should Nike leverage them next?
4 Identify three major strategic issues that Nike faces. Describe them all, say why they are strategically important, and offer some recommendations for how Nike might address each of them.

Case 4
Apple Inc. in 2014

Introduction

In its quarterly conference call for the period July–September 2014, held on Monday, 20 October 2014, Apple reported revenues of $42.12 billion (against expectations of $39.85 billion) and a quarterly net profit of $8.5 billion. In the same quarter the previous year Apple made $37.5 billion in revenue and a net profit of $7.5 billion (www.macworld.co.uk). During the quarter, Apple sold 39.272 million iPhones and 12.316 million iPads. Mac sales were up 5 per cent to a total of 5.520 million. This is against a global decline in PC sales overall and, by revenue, Apple made more from Macs than from its iPad products for the first time ($6,626 billion and $5.316 billion respectively). On the day of the earnings call, Apple shares closed at $99.76 per share.

At the time of writing, Apple is the world's most valuable company, measured by market capitalization. On 25 November 2014 Apple achieved a record market cap of over $700 billion on shares of $120 (following a 7:1 split). The company's market capitalization has doubled since Tim Cook was named CEO in August 2011 and its stock has risen by nearly 60 per cent in the 12 months to November 2014 and by over 24 per cent just since the company's October 2014 media event (www.macworld.co.uk). Its cash reserves are estimated to be $180 billion, which is more than three times those held by the US federal government. For a company that was just 90 days away from going into administration in 1997, this transformation is remarkable. So how did they do it?

History

Apple: the early years

Apple was founded by Steve Jobs and Steve Wozniak, a pair of 20-something college dropouts, on 1 April (April Fool's Day) 1976. They began by building computer circuit boards – which they named Apple I. Right from the outset Jobs had the ambition of bringing to market an easy-to-use computer, and it is that *ease of use* that has become the dominant logic guiding Apple ever since. In April 1978 they launched the Apple II, a relatively simple computer that consumers could use straight out of the box. The Apple II sparked a computing revolution and Apple quickly became a market leader.

In 1981 IBM entered the market, launching the 'personal computer' (PC) using Microsoft's DOS operating system and a processor from Intel. This was a much more 'open' platform than Apple's, which allowed other manufacturers to clone it. As a result IBM became the standard in what was now called the PC market. In 1984 Apple introduced the Macintosh – marking another breakthrough in ease of use, industrial design and technical elegance. But the machine had a lower specification (spec) and higher retail price than the IBM and Apple lost market share. In 1985, the Apple board removed Jobs from operational duties and he resigned.

The Sculley years (1985–1993)

John Sculley, formerly CEO of Pepsi, had been brought into Apple by Jobs. Sculley's strategy as CEO was to make Apple a market leader in the education and desktop publishing markets – a focused, differentiation strategy. Ease of use, quality software and a proprietary strategy (building both hardware and software) meant that Apple's products were well received and commanded premium prices. Top-of-the-line Macs were selling for $10,000 in the early 1990s. However, IBM still remained the market leader due to its corporate appeal and lower prices. In response, Sculley decided to move Apple into the mainstream in order to compete directly with IBM – in essence shifting strategic position away from Apple's core offering. Sculley even forged an alliance with IBM to co-create a new operating system. Under Sculley, Apple sought to drive down costs by outsourcing manufacturing. None of these changes in strategy worked and in 1993 Sculley was replaced by Michael Spindler.

The Spindler and Amelio years (1993–1997)

Spindler tried to reinvigorate Apple's core markets – education and desktop publishing. He also made the decision to license out the Mac operating system to enable Mac clones. In 1995 Apple and IBM parted company having each spent $500 million on a new OS that neither company wanted to switch to. In the first quarter of 1996, Apple reported a loss of $69 million and Spindler was replaced by Gilbert Amelio.

Amelio sought to push Apple into new high-margin segments which included servers, internet access devices and PDAs. In 1997 Apple acquired NeXT (the company Steve Jobs set up on leaving Apple) in order to develop a new OS. Amelio also led the company through three separate reorganizations and several deep payroll cuts. Despite the austerity measures, Apple lost $1.6 billion during his two-year tenure and he was forced out in 1997. Steve Jobs returned as interim CEO, or iCEO, in 1997.

Steve Jobs and the Apple turnaround

Jobs returned as interim CEO on a salary of $1 per year, which remained his salary to the day he stepped down as CEO (needless to say this was complemented with extensive stock options and other payments, including the provision of a private jet).

Steve Jobs moved fast to shake things up on his return:

- He ended the Mac OS licencing programme.
- He consolidated the product range from 15 lines to just three.
- He cancelled the proposed new OS plans.
- He axed 70 per cent of new products in development.

Apple refocused on Jobs' original vision of easy-to-use machines encompassing leading-edge design and a tightly integrated user experience at a premium price. Jobs proceeded

164 Case 4: Apple

to simplify Apple's product mix in terms of two lines of desktop computer and two lines of portable computer, one category of each for the professional and consumer markets. Jobs also focused attention on the value chain. He restructured the organization and outsourced manufacturing to carefully selected Taiwanese contractors; the distribution system was revamped in order to reduce stock levels. Due to its small product line-up, the company was able to develop exclusive relationships with its suppliers.

Key milestones

- In 1997 Apple launched a retail website
- In 1998 Apple launched the iMac – a new format desktop with no floppy-disk drive and no tower but a machine housed within the monitor itself. Within 3 years the iMac had sold 6 million units.
- This was followed in 1999 by the iBook – a new standard in laptop computing.
- In 2001 Apple launched the first iPod – marking its entry into the consumer electronics market.
- In 2003 Apple launched iTunes – arguably one of its most important innovations and another game-changer
- In 2007 Apple launched the iPhone
- In January 2007, Apple Computer changed its name to Apple Inc. signifying a shift away from its computer vendor roots.
- In 2010 it launched the iPad to much scepticism but massive commercial success
- In 2014 Apple announced the 2015 launch of a new category of product, the Apple Watch

Core business activity and competitive environment

Key product and service portfolio

In 2014, Apple's portfolio of activities spanned a range of hardware, software and service offerings, including:

- Computer hardware (including iPad and Macs);
- Phone hardware (iPhone);
- Music hardware (iPods);
- Software, internet services, networking (iWork, iLife, OS X, iOS, iCloud, Safari, QuickTime);
- Peripherals (trackpads, keyboards, ear buds, cases, etc.);
- Retail services (Apple Store, web store, App stores).

Given this range of activities we might be tempted to think of Apple as a classic diversified corporation and treat each of its different activity areas as competing in separate industries. However, to do so would be to miss key aspects of Apple's strategy. Steve Jobs, in a keynote speech in 2010, described Apple as being a 'mobile devices company' rather than a PC company (reflecting that even in their PC provision, most sales are of notebooks).

Conceiving of Apple as a mobile devices company necessarily expands the competitive environment in which it does business, away from purely the PC industry to one that includes competitors such as Google, Yahoo, Amazon and Microsoft. It is also a reflection of an increasing trend in the tech industry towards a preference for platform strategies, in which hardware, software and services are brought together to offer a single, differentiated value proposition. As consumers becoming increasingly 'locked in' to a particular platform – iOS/OS X or Android or Windows – this becomes a high barrier to switching as few of the services are cross-platform and there are thus significant costs for consumers choosing to move from one platform to another. Moreover, the synchronization and interoperability within platforms is often seen as a crucial component of the value proposition. An added benefit of the platform strategy, when done well, is the perceived 'halo effect', in which enjoyment of one product in the portfolio leads to a preference for that platform when making purchases in other categories.

Looking at the competitive terrain in these terms has significant implications for how we might define the industry in which Apple competes, its key rivals and also the possible threat of substitution.

Apple's value proposition

Apple is widely known for its high-quality products for which it charges a significant price premium. However, Apple also has one of the leanest value chains in the tech industry. This allows it to realize incredible margins. For example, in 2010 Apple sold just 17 million iPhone handsets compared to over 400 million sold by Nokia, Samsung and LG. And yet Apple received 39 per cent of the industry profit from these 17 million. The 400 million sold by its competitors returned only 32 per cent of the industry profit (O'Reilly 2010).

Much of the explanation for these staggering margins rests with Apple's impressive inventory management system, developed under the then COO, and now CEO, Tim Cook. Building good relationships with suppliers and developing sophisticated real-time inventory tracking systems, Apple was able to turn over its inventory in a matter of days, compared with the weeks, and sometimes months, that its competitors found themselves holding stock.

But how sustainable is Apple's business model in the long term? As components become increasingly standardized, many traditional PC makers have cut spending on research and development in order to focus on retail and marketing. Moreover, faster and faster strategies of imitation are blurring the boundaries between company offerings for many consumers, with price becoming a key driver in the purchase decision. Moreover, as the recent decline in iPod, iTunes and iPad sales shows, Apple may also be reaching saturation point in some of its key markets.

Apple's resource base

On its website, Apple describes its business thus:

> Apple designs Macs, the best personal computers in the world, along with OS X, iLife, iWork and professional software. Apple leads the digital music revolution with its iPods and iTunes online store. Apple has reinvented the mobile phone with its revolutionary iPhone and App Store, and is defining the future of mobile media and computing devices with iPad.
>
> (www.apple.com)

This stated mission clearly seeks to position Apple as an innovator and leader in its field. Steve Jobs has publically stated that 'Apple's DNA has always been to try to democratize technology', a worthy intent we might think. This democratization seems to be based on a series of capabilities that have driven product design and innovation at Apple, as seen, for example, in Apple's original, and on-going, desire to make technology simple in both design and use. From the beginning, Apple products were conceived of as being interactive in the sense that people would be able to integrate them into their workflows with minimal change or disruption. Even the packaging of products and the style and utility of the cabling reflects this competence. This ease of use has been achievable through the synergies created by an integrated approach to design in which hardware and software are built together and in unison. This is surprisingly rare in the consumer tech industry where, frequently, design teams and business units work in isolation from one another.

We might also suggest that Apple's proprietary and closed ecosystem is also core to its strategy. That Apple does not licence out its operating systems, unlike Google and Windows, means that it has a much higher degree of control over the design process and can develop tighter integration between hardware, software and services. Such an approach has allowed Apple to build a number of core products that have then been leveraged into many end-user markets. Examples of core products might include iOS, OS X, the iPod and the Mac. Such core products have then been leveraged to roll out a continual stream of innovation. For example, the first iPod led to iTunes, which in turn led to a broader suite of iPods, then Apple TV, then the iPhone and iOS, then the App store, then the iPad. All of this is underpinned by the same set of core competencies and these core products have manifested themselves in multiple generations of product lines. The 'halo effect' of newer Apple products, starting with the iPod, have also driven sales of Mac computers – due to shared focus on design, ease of use and interoperability.

While Apple has tended not to engage in extensive diversification we can certainly see a narrow focus on growth through acquisition, where the acquired firm can complement or be integrated into existing activities. Typically this means small start-ups that possess a proprietary technology that Apple wants to develop, as seen in its 2010 acquisition of Siri, a mobile assistant app. It is not averse, however, to making high-profile acquisitions, however, as witnessed in 2014 when it bought Beats Music for an estimated $2.6 billion.

Culture as a key resource

Apple is a famously secretive and closed-off firm that does not willingly share many of its working practices. Steve Jobs has described aspects of Apple's culture in the following ways:

- 'Apple has a long tradition of very long hours, relatively modest pay and the relentless pursuit of perfection coupled with great secrecy and punishment for those that leak information.'
- 'Apple recruits the very best in class and seeks to retain them through the working environment rather than benefits.'

While few current or former employees have offered much more insight into the internal workings of Apple, we can gain some additional purchase on its culture from the limited information available. First, Apple has always adopted a 'start-up mentality' and rebellious character – Steve Jobs famously flew the skull and crossbones above the Apple campus to remind employees of this. Relatedly, Apple claims to be the 'antibusiness school' business in that it rejects pretty much all mainstream orthodox management practice – from leadership style, to industry/sector practice, to marketing, and more. However, this culture has become increasingly difficult to maintain in recent years as the organization continues to grow rapidly, both in employee numbers and customer base.

Along with the rebel spirit, Apple has a tradition of long working hours in relentless pursuit of perfection, with employees expected to be available weekends and evenings and to dedicate themselves to the company. Tim Cook is reported to regularly be on the email by 4.30 a.m. every morning. Despite its market value, Apple's employees are only paid the industry average. They are not pampered, nor do they enjoy unique privileges. Rather, Apple seeks to position the working environment as the key draw for prospective employees. This has fostered a culture based on innovation and a desire to be 'part of Apple'. This in turn reinforces Apple's sense of superiority against its competitors.

Apple is not necessarily an enjoyable firm to work for – at least not in the same way that it might be to work for Google, which tries to encourage its employees to have fun. Rather, as Adam Lashinsky observes: 'Apple is known for being tough and perfectionist. If any product release does not meet expectations, Apple can be a "brutal and unforgiving place, where accountability is strictly enforced"' (Lashinsky 2012: 53). Against this view, Jobs prefers to see the positive: '[W]e have wonderful arguments!' he says. This accountability is a reflection of the higher levels of relative autonomy and freedom project teams are given:

> If you want to hire great people and having them stay working for you, you have to let them make a lot of decisions and you have to be run by ideas. Not hierarchy. The best ideas have to win. Otherwise good people don't stay.
> (Interview with Walt Mossberg at the All Things Digital conference, 2010. Available at www.youtube.com/watch?v=f60dheI4ARg)

To facilitate this devolved responsibility, Apple also maintains a relatively flat organizational structure. Although Apple does not have an official organization chart, one interpretation of its structure is that the organization radiates around the CEO, with just nine senior vice presidents and a further five vice presidents overseeing the main functions. In terms of this structure, the CEO is only two levels away from any key part of the company; and financial management is centralized, with the only executive responsible for costs and expenses being the chief financial officer. Jobs aimed for simplicity in the company structure as an enabler of the ability to be agile and successfully engage in its 'deep collaboration' model. Jobs described this structure as one based on teamwork and trust. However, despite the advantages of flexibility and focus, the tight, CEO-centric organization structure built around Jobs' leadership has raised concerns regarding whether it will remain as successful under a different CEO.

Another key feature of the company's culture is secrecy. Apple has always tried to maintain tight control over information leaks, so much so that the launch of a new product is the first time many employees hear about it. Such secrecy limits our understanding of what takes place at Apple but also creates a lot of buzz around new product launches. The company is known for its professional and entertaining press conferences, often watched by millions on Apple devices. Typically a dreary affair attended by a few tech journalists, Apple keynotes are hotly anticipated, debated and dissected. However, as Apple has grown and come to rely on an increasing number of partners to manufacture its products, this veil of secrecy has been progressively harder to maintain, with many new products and innovations correctly predicted ahead of time.

Innovation at Apple

Right from its inception Apple had been a company committed to building innovative products using the latest technologies. As such, innovation has become embedded in the culture and dominant logic of the company. However, it is important to note that Apple has seldom come up with a genuinely new product. There were MP3 players before the iPod, tablets before the iPad, and smart phones before the iPhone. However, what seemingly distinguishes Apple is its ability to take an existing technology or product category and create a new market space or new plane of competition with its offering. Apple does not claim to invent new products; instead it likes to say that it creates 'whole new categories of products', much like Henry Ford could claim when introducing the Model T car.

What frequently accompanies Apple's new launches is scepticism and negative reaction: the iPod was seen as an over-priced, niche product only available to Mac users and dubbed 'idiots price our devices'; the iPhone was criticized for its limited capabilities; and the iPad was derided for being nothing more than an over-sized iPhone. In each instance Apple's products went on to be hugely popular and category-defining. In each instance, then, the market seemed unable to appreciate the *value* of the innovation that Apple was proposing. To help address this problem, Apple launched its own retail stores in 2008. Launched at a time when many were heralding the end of the high street in favour of online shopping, the Apple Store has been one of Apple's most innovative services. Compared to rivals who sold their technology products through third parties, often in generic department stores or tech warehouse stores, Apple's retail concept offered a high level of personal service and 'hands-on' experience that was largely unknown at the time and has been much applauded and copied since. Built on the same values and competencies as its products, the stores provided a way of demonstrating the value proposition to a mass of consumers that might otherwise not consider purchasing Apple products due to their high price. In short, the stores sold the value of the products.

Apple is also famous for its restraint, typically launching new products on only an annual, or sometimes longer, refresh cycle. In a tech industry moving as fast as it currently does, this is both surprisingly and extremely uncommon. Steve Jobs was keen to point out that the innovations that his company produced were not invented overnight. Rather, Jobs described it as a pretty slow process:

> Things happen fairly slowly, you know. They do. These waves of technology, you can see them way before they happen, and you just have to choose wisely which ones you are going to surf. If you choose unwisely, then you can waste a lot of energy, but if you choose wisely, it actually unfolds fairly slowly.
>
> (Cited in Heracleous and Papachroni 2012: 12)

By way of example, Apple only released the iPad in 2010 but had been 'playing with the idea' for ten years. Likewise, its much anticipated Apple Watch, due for release in 2015, has been in design for more than five years. Such time frames are highly revealing of the innovation process at Apple compared to many of its competitors, who appear much keener to be first to market and meet with varying degrees of success.

Apple's innovation strategy had always been customer-centric, in the sense that new products are developed around the perceived needs of customers, and yet the company has famously declared it does not carry out market research (a publically disputed claim), believing that customers do not know what they want. Jobs once remarked:

> it's not about convincing people that they want something they don't. We figure out what we want. And I think we're pretty good at having the right discipline to think through whether a lot of other people are going to want it, too. That's what we get paid to do. So you can't go out and ask people, you know, what's the next big thing. There's a great quote by Henry Ford. He said, 'If I'd have asked my customers what they wanted, they would have told me 'A faster horse!'
>
> (Cited in Qumer 2011: 6)

Apple's slow and steady approach to innovation means that it never focuses on more than a few products at any one time. Indeed, its industrial design team is uncommonly small and consists of a core group of fewer than 20 people. While it is extremely secretive about its research and design process, with few Apple employees having access to key areas of its industrial design unit, what we do know is that Apple spends huge amounts on R&D. In its more recent earnings call it claimed R&D spending was $6 billion for 2014, and that is up from $4.5 billion in 2013.

Apple is nearly unique among contemporary technology companies in doing all its own design in-house, at its Cupertino campus. Many other companies have outsourced most or all of their product design function, relying on outsourced design manufacturers (ODMs) to develop the products that, with minor adaptations, will fit into their product lines. Apple, however, believes that having all the experts in one place – the mechanical, electrical, software and industrial engineers, as well as the product designers – leads to a more holistic perspective on product development; and that a critical mass of talent makes existing products better and opens the door to entirely new products (Heracleous and Papachroni 2011: 12).

By retaining all R&D internally, Apple has been able to develop what its employees call 'deep collaboration', 'cross pollination' or 'concurrent engineering' – this refers to products not being developed in discrete stages but by 'all departments at once – design, hardware, software – in endless rounds of interdisciplinary design reviews' (Heracleous and Papachroni 2011: 11). Many would point to this as key to Apple achieving the ease of use on which it has built its value proposition.

In order to try and document key aspects of Apple's strategy and business model, Jobs created the Apple University in 2008, hiring Joel Podolny, then dean of the Yale School of Management, to lead a team of business professors to create a series of case studies on critical points in Apple's history. According to Adam Lashinsky (2012), these cases described strategic issues such as Apple's retail strategy and its iPhone supply chain strategy; and how Apple executives took decisions at these points. The cases are not only used as a learning tool but also seek to inculcate Apple's values and DNA into its future executives. While these may prove valuable in a post-Jobs era, will Apple really be able to maintain its innovative streak without what many sees as its key asset, Jobs himself?

Case questions

1 What industry does Apple compete in?
2 What is the basis of Apple's competitive advantage in this competitive environment?

3 Using Hamel and Prahalad's 'three tests', identify and describe Apple's core competencies. How sustainable are these core competencies in the long term?
4 Does Apple meet the criteria necessary to be considered a disruptive innovator?
5 Identify three major strategic issues that Apple faces. Describe them all, say why they are strategically important, and offer some recommendations for how Apple might address each of them.

References

Abdallah, C. and Langley, A. (2014) 'The double edge of ambiguity in strategic planning', *Journal of Management Studies*, 51(2): 235–264.
Abernathy, W. and Wayne, K. (1974) 'Limits of the learning curve', *Harvard Business Review*, 52(5): 109–120.
Ackoff, R. L. (1970) *A Concept of Corporate Planning*. New York: Wiley Interscience.
Aktouf, O., Chennoufi, M. and Holford, W. (2011) 'The strategic management framework: a methodological and epistemological examination' in Huggins, R. and Izushi, H. (eds) *Competition, Competitive Advantage, and Clusters: The Ideas of Michael Porter*. Oxford: Oxford University Press.
Allard-Poesi, F. (2010) 'A Foucauldian perspective on strategic practice: strategy as the art of (un)folding' in Golsorkhi, D., Rouleau, L., Seidl, D. and Vaara, E. (eds) *Cambridge Handbook of Strategy as Practice*. Cambridge: Cambridge University Press.
Alvesson, M. and Willmott, H. (1996) *Making Sense of Management: A Critical Introduction*. London: Sage.
Andersen, T. and Nielsen, B. (2009) 'Adaptive strategy making: the effects of emergent and intended strategy modes', *European Management Journal*, 6: 94–106.
Ansoff, H. I. (1965) *Corporate Strategy* (revised edition 1987). London: Penguin.
Aoki, M. (1990) 'Toward an economic model of the Japanese firm', *Journal of Economic Literature*, 28(1): 1–27.
Argyres, N. and McGahan, A. (2002) 'An interview with Michael Porter', *Academy of Management Executive*, 16(2): 43–52.
Astley, W. and Fombrun, C. (1983) 'Collective strategy: social ecology of organizational environments', *The Academy of Management Review*, 8(4): 576–587.
Augier, M. and Teece, D. (2008), 'Strategy as evolution with design: the foundations of dynamic capabilities and the role of managers in the economic system', *Organization Studies*, 29(8–9): 1187–1208.
Bachmann, J. (2002) 'Competitive strategy: it's OK to be different', *Academy of Management Executive*, 16(2): 61–65.
Bain, J. (1956) *Barriers to New Competition*. Cambridge, MA: Harvard University Press.
Barnes, D. (ed.) (2000) *Understanding Business Processes*. London: Routledge.
Barney, J. (1986) 'Types of competition and the theory of strategy: toward an integrative framework', *Academy of Management Review*, 11(4): 791–800.
Barney, J. (1991) 'Firm resources and sustained competitive advantage', *Journal of Management*, 17(1): 99–120.
Barney, J. and Clark, D. (2006) *Resource-Based Theory: Creating and Sustaining Competitive Advantage*. Oxford: Oxford University Press.
Barney, J., Wright, M. and Ketchen, D. (2001) 'The resource-based view of the firm: ten years after 1991', *Journal of Management*, 27(6): 625–41.

References

Bartlett, C. and Ghoshal, S. (1991) 'Global strategy management: impact on the new frontiers of strategy research', *Strategic Management Journal*, 12(Special Issue, Summer): 5–16.

Bass, B. (1990) 'From transactional to transformational leadership: learning to share the vision', *Organizational Dynamics*, 18(3): 19–31.

Berfield, S. and Baigorri (2013) 'Zara's Fast-fashion Edge', www.bloomberg.com.

Besanko, D., Danove, D. and Shanley, M. (1996) *The Economics of Strategy*. New York: John Wiley.

Blackmur, D. (1997) 'Determinants of organisational size: BHP and vertical integration', *Journal of the Australian and New Zealand Academy of Management (JANZAM)*, 3(1): 15–29.

Bodwell, W. and Chermack, T. (2010) 'Organizational ambidexterity: integrating deliberate and emergent strategy with scenario planning', *Technological Forecasting & Social Change*, 77: 193–202.

Bose, P. (2004) *Alexander the Great's Art of Strategy*. London: Profile Books.

Bovel, D. and Martha, J. (2000) 'From supply chain to value net', *Journal of Business Strategy*, 21(4): 24–28.

Bowman, C. (2008) 'Generic strategies: a substitute for thinking?', *360° The Ashridge Journal*, Spring: 6–11.

Brandenburger, A. and Nalebuff, B. (1996) 'The right game: use game theory to shape strategy', *Harvard Business Review*, 73(4): 57–71.

Brusoni, S., Jacobides, M. A. and Prencipe, A. (2009) 'Strategic dynamics in industry architectures and the challenge of knowledge integration', *European Management Review*, 6(4): 209–216.

Cabantous, L. and Gond, J.-P. (2011) 'Rational decision making as performative praxis: explaining rationality's eternel retour', *Organization Science*, 22(3): 573–586.

Cabantous, L., Gond, J.-P. and Johnson-Cramer, M. (2010) 'Decision theory as practice: crafting rationality in organizations', *Organization Studies*, 31(11): 1531–1566.

Campbell, A. and Nash, L. (1992) 'A Sense of Mission: Defining Directions for the Large Corporation'. Reading, MA: Addisson-Wesley.

Canato, A. and Giangreco, A. (2011) 'Gurus or wizards? A review of the role of management consultants', *European Management Review*, 8: 231–244.

Caro, F. (2011) 'Zara: Staying Fast and Fresh', UCLA Anderson School of Management case study, ECCH ref. 612–006–1.

Carr, A. (2013) 'Death to Core Competency: Lessons from Nike, Apple, Netflix', www.fastcompany.com.

Carter, C. (2013) 'The age of strategy: strategy, organizations and society', *Business History*, 55(7): 1047–1057.

Carter, C., Clegg, S. and Kornberger, M. (2008) *A Very Short, Fairly Interesting and Reasonably Cheap Book About Studying Strategy*. London: Sage.

Carter, C., Clegg, S. and Kornberger, M. (2010) 'Re-framing strategy: power, politics and accounting', *Accounting, Auditing & Accountability Journal*, 23(5): 573–594.

Cendrowski, S. (2012) 'Nike's new marketing mojo', *Fortune*, 27 Feb.: 57–61.

Chaffee, E. (1985) 'Three models of strategy', *Academy of Management Review*, 10(1): 89–98.

Chamberlin, E. H. (1933) *The Theory of Monopolistic Competition*. Cambridge, MA: Harvard University Press.

Chandler, A. (1962/1990) *Strategy and Structure: Chapters in the History of the American Industrial Enterprise*. Cambridge, MA: MIT Press.

Chandler, A. (2009) 'History and management practice and thought: an autobiography', *Journal of Management History*, 15(3): 236–260

Chia, R. (2004) 'Strategy-as-practice: reflections on the research agenda', *European Management Review*, 1(1): 21–32.

Chia, R. and MacKay, B. (2007) 'Post-processual challenges for the emerging strategy-as-practice perspective', *Human Relations*, 60(1): 217–242.

Chia, R. and Rasche, A. (2010) 'Epistemological Alternatives for Researching Strategy as Practice: Building and Dwelling Worldviews' in Golsorkhi, D., Rouleau, L., Seidl, D. and Vaara, E. (eds) *Cambridge Handbook of Strategy as Practice*. Cambridge: Cambridge University Press.

Christensen, C. (1997) *The Innovator's Dilemma*. Boston, MA: Harvard University Press.
Christensen, C. and Overdorf, M. (2000) 'Meeting the challenge of disruptive change', *Harvard Business Review*, 78(2): 66–76.
Christensen, C. and Raynor, M. (2003) *The Innovator's Solution: Creating and Sustaining Successful Growth*. Cambridge, MA: Harvard Business School Press.
Clark, T. (2004) 'Strategy viewed from a management fashion perspective', *European Management Review*, 1: 105–111.
Clegg, S., Carter, C. and Kornberger, M. (2004) 'Get up, I feel like being a strategy machine', *European Management Review*, 1(1): 21–28.
Clegg, S., Carter, C., Kornberger, M. and Schweitzer, J. (2010) *Strategy: Theory and Practice*. London: Sage.
Clegg, S., Jarvis, W. and Pitsis, T. (2013) 'Making strategy matter: social theory, knowledge interests and business education', *Business History*, 55(7): 1247–1264.
Coase, R. (1937) 'The nature of the firm', *Economica*, 4(16): 386–405.
Cohen, M., March, J. and Olsen, J. (1972) 'A garbage can model of organizational choice', *Administrative Science Quarterly*, 17(1): 1–25.
Collins, J. and Porras, J. (1991) 'Organizational vision and visionary organizations', *California Management Review*, 34(1): 30–52.
Collis, D. and Montgomery, C. (1995). 'Competing on resources: strategy in the 1990s', *Harvard Business Review*, 73(4): 118–128.
Colvin, G. (2012) 'Why Dreaming Pays Off Big' in Harnish, V. (ed.) *The Greatest Business Decisions of All Time*. Des Moines, IA: Fortune Books.
Cox, M., Daspit, J., McLaughlin, E. and Jones, R. (2012) 'Strategic management: is it an academic discipline?', *Journal of Business Strategies*, 29(1): 25–42.
Cummings, S. (1993) 'Brief case: the first strategists', *Long Range Planning*, 26(3): 133–135.
Cummings, S. (1995), 'Drawing on the essence of strategic leadership', *Business Horizons*, Jan./Feb.: 22–27.
Cummings, S. (2007) 'Shifting foundations: redrawing strategic management's military heritage', *Critical Perspectives on International Business*, 3(1): 41–62.
Cummings, S. and Davies, J. (1994) 'Mission, vision, fusion', *Long Range Planning*, 27(6): 147–150.
Cummings, S. and Daellenbach, U. (2009) 'A guide to the future of strategy? The history of long range planning', *Long Range Planning*, 42(2): 234–263.
Cyert, R. and March, J. (1956) 'Organizational factors in the theory of oligopoly', *Quarterly Journal of Economics*, 70(1): 44–64.
Davidson, K. (2009) 'Ethical concerns at the bottom of the pyramid: Where CSR meets BOP', *Journal of International Business Ethics*, 2(1): 22–33.
Davies, H. and Ellis, P. (2000) 'Porter's "competitive advantage of nations": time for the final judgement?', *Journal of Management Studies*, 37(8): 1189–1213.
Davies, P. (2003) 'Military Strategy' in Jenkins, M. and Ambrosini, V. (eds) *Strategic Management: A Multi-Perspective Approach*. Basingstoke: Palgrave Macmillan.
Dawson, S. (1986) *Analysing Organisations*. London: Macmillan.
Deal, T. and Kennedy, A. (1982) *Corporate Cultures*. Reading, MA: Addison-Wesley.
Dessler, G. (1976) *Organisation and Management: A Contingency Approach*. Englewood Cliffs, NJ: Prentice Hall.
Devadas, R. and Argote, L. (2006) 'Organizational learning and forgetting: the effects of turnover and structure', *European Management Journal*, 3(2): 77–85.
De Wit, R. and Meyer, R. (2010) *Strategy: Process, Content, Context*. London: International Thomson Business Press.
Dowries, L. and Nunes, P. (2013) 'Big-Bang Disruption', *Harvard Business Review*, March.
Duke, L. (2011a) 'IKEA: A Furniture Dealer', INSEAD case study, ECCH ref. 311-217-1.
Duke, L. (2011b) 'How IKEA's Strategy Was Formed', INSEAD case study, ECCH ref. 311-218-1.

References

Eisenhardt, K. and Zbaracki, M. (1992) 'Strategic decision making', *Strategic Management Journal*, 13(Special Issue): 17–37.

Eschen, E. and Bresser, R. (2005) 'Closing resource gaps: toward a resource-based theory of advantageous mergers and acquisitions', *European Management Journal*, 5: 167–178.

Espeland, W. and Hirsch, P. (1990) 'Ownership changes, accounting practices and the redefinition of the corporation', *Accounting, Organizations and Society*, 15(1–2): 77–96.

Fayol, H. (1949) *General and Industrial Management*. London: Pitman.

Freedman, L. (2013) *Strategy: A History*. Oxford: Oxford University Press.

Fuller, M. (1996) 'Strategic planning in an era of total competition', *Strategy & Leadership*, 24(3): 22–27.

Gaddis, P. (1997) 'Strategy under attack', *Long Range Planning*, 30(1): 38–45.

Gavetti, G. and Levinthal, D. (2004) 'The strategy field from the perspective of management science', *Management Science*, 50(1): 1309–1318.

Ghemawat, P. (1985) 'Building strategy on the experience curve', *Harvard Business Review*, March/April.

Ghemawat, P. (2002) 'Competition and business strategy in historical perspective', *The Business History Review*, 76(1): 37–74.

Giraudeau, M. (2008) 'The drafts of strategy: opening up plans and their uses', *Long Range Planning*, 41(3): 291–308.

Golsorkhi, D., Rouleau, L., Seidl, D. and Vaara, E. (2010) 'Introduction: What is Strategy as Practice?' in Golsorkhi, D., Rouleau, L., Seidl, D. and Vaara, E. (eds) *Cambridge Handbook of Strategy as Practice*. Cambridge: Cambridge University Press.

Goold, M., Campbell, A. and Alexander, M. (1998) 'Corporate strategy and parenting theory', *Long Range Planning*, 31(2): 308–314.

Grant, R. (1991) 'Porter's "competitive advantage of nations": an assessment', *Strategic Management Journal*, 12(7): 535–548.

Hagel, J. and Brown, J. (2005) *The Only Sustainable Edge*. Boston, MA: Harvard Business School Press.

Hagel, J., Seely Brown, J. and Davison, L. (2008) 'Shaping strategy in a world of constant disruption', *Harvard Business Review*, October: 81–89.

Halberstam, D. (1987) *The Reckoning*. London: Bantam.

Hambrick, D. C. and Chen, M.-J. (2008) 'New academic fields as admittance-seeking social movements: the case of strategic management', *Academy of Management Review*, 33(1): 32–54.

Hamel, G. (2007) *The Future of Management*. Cambridge, MA: Harvard Business School Press.

Hamel, G. and Prahalad, C. K. (1985) 'Do you really have global strategy?', *Harvard Business Review*, July/Aug.: 139–148.

Hamel, G. and Prahalad, C. K. (1989) 'Strategic intent', *Harvard Business Review*, May/June: 63–76.

Hamel, G. and Prahalad, C. K. (1993) 'Strategy as stretch and leverage', *Harvard Business Review*, March/April: 75–84.

Hamel, G. and Prahalad, C. K. (1994) *Competing for the Future*. Boston, MA: Harvard Business School Press.

Harjula, L. (2007) 'Tensions between venture capitalists' and business-social entrepreneurs' goals', *Greener Management International*, 51(Summer): 79–87.

Harvey, M., Kiessling, T. and Moeller, M. (2010) 'A view of entrepreneurship and innovation from the economist "for all seasons": Joseph S. Schumpeter', *Journal of Management History*, 16 (4): 527–531.

Haspeslagh, P. (1982) 'Portfolio planning: uses and limits', *Harvard Business Review*, 60(1): 58–73.

Hatchuel, A., Starkey, K., Tempest, S. and Le Masson, P. (2010) 'Strategy as Innovative Design: An Emerging Perspective' in Baum, J. and Lampel, J. (eds) *The Globalization of Strategy Research*. Bingley: Emerald.

Hayes, R. (1985) 'Strategic planning: forward in reverse?' *Harvard Business Review*, Nov/Dec: 111–119.

Hedley, B. (1977) 'Strategy and the "business portfolio"', *Long Range Planning*, 10(1): 9–15.

Heracleous, L. and Papachroni, A. (2012) 'Strategic Leadership and Innovation at Apple Inc', case study. Coventry: Warwick Business School.

Hickson, D. J., Butler, R. J., Cray, D., Mallory, G. R. and Wilson, D. C. (1986) *Top Decisions: Strategic Decision Making in Organizations*. San Francisco, CA: Jossey-Bass.

Hill, T. and Westbrook, R. (1997) 'SWOT analysis: it's time for a product recall', *Long Range Planning*, 30(1): 46–52.

Hitt, M., Tihanyi, L., Miller, T. and Connelly, B. (2006) 'International diversification: antecedents, outcomes, and moderators', *Journal of Management*, 32(6): 831–867.

Ho, S. and Choi, A. (1997) 'Achieving marketing success through Sun Tze's Art of Warfare,' *Marketing Intelligence and Planning*, 15(1): 38–47.

Hodgkinson, G. and Healey, M. (2008) 'Toward a (pragmatic) science of strategic intervention: design propositions for scenario planning', *Organization Studies*, 29(3): 435–457.

Hodgson, A., Li, G. and Weston, R. H. (1998) 'Manufacturing strategies and next century enterprises', *International Journal of Business Performance Management*, 1(1): 90–109.

Hofer, C. W. and Schendel, D. E. (1978) *Strategy Formulation: Analytical Concepts*. St Paul, MN: West Publishing.

Hollander, S. (1987) *Classical Economics*. Oxford: Blackwell.

Hopwood, A. (1974) *Accounting and Human Behaviour*. London: Accountancy Age Books.

Hoskin, K., Macve, R. and Stone, J. (1997) 'The Historical Genesis of Modern Business and Military Strategy: 1850–1950', paper submitted to the Interdisciplinary Perspectives on Accounting Conference, Manchester, 7–9 July.

Hoskin, K., Macve, R. and Stone, J. (2006) 'Accounting and Strategy: Towards Understanding the Historical Genesis of Modern Business and Military Strategy' in Bhimani, A. (ed.) *Contemporary Issues in Management Accounting*. Oxford: Oxford University Press.

Hoskisson, R., Hitt, M., Wan, W. and Yiu, D. (1999) 'Theory and research in strategic management: swings of a pendulum', *Journal of Management*, 25(3): 417–456.

Huff, A. (2001) 'The continuing relevance of strategy', *Human Relations*, 54(1): 123–130.

Ireland, R., Hoskisson, R. and Hitt, M. (2011) *The Management of Strategy*. Mason, OH: South-Western Cengage.

Itami, H. (1987) *Mobilizing Invisible Assets*. Boston, MA: Harvard University Press.

Jarzabkowski, P. (2004) 'Strategy as practice: recursiveness, adaptation and practices-in-use', *Organization Studies*, 25(4): 529–560.

Jeacle, I. and Parker, L. (2013) 'The "problem" of the office: scientific management, governmentality and the strategy of efficiency', *Business History*, 55(7): 1074–1099.

Johnson, G. (1992) 'Managing strategic change: strategy, culture and action', *Long Range Planning*, 25(1): 28–36.

Johnson, G., Scholes, K. and Whittington, R. (2009) *Fundamentals of Strategy*. Harlow: Prentice Hall.

Jordi, L. (2010) 'Rethinking the firm's mission and purpose', *European Management Journal*, 7(4): 195–204.

Kalantari, B. (2010) 'Herbert A. Simon on making decisions: enduring insights and bounded rationality', *Journal of Management History*, 16(4): 509–521.

Kaplan, D. (2013a) 'How Intel Got Consumers to Love Chips' in Harnish, V. (ed.) *The Greatest Business Decisions of All Time*. Des Moines: Fortune Books.

Kaplan, D. (2013b) 'Jack's Cathedral' in Harnish, V. (ed.) *The Greatest Business Decisions of All Time*. Des Moines: Fortune Books.

Karnani, A. (2006) 'Misfortune at the Bottom of the Pyramid', Ross School of Business Working Paper Series, Working Paper no. 1035.

Keller Johnson, L. (2003) 'Value innovation: a balanced approach to strategy', *Balanced Scorecard Report*, Nov./Dec.: 10–13.

Khanna, T. and Palepu, K. (1999) 'Policy shocks, market intermediaries and corproarte strategy: the evolution of business groups in Chile and India', *Journal of Economics and Management Strategy*, 8(2): 271–310.

Kiechel, W. (2010) *Lords of Strategy: The Secret Intellectual History of the New Corporate World*. Cambridge, MA: Harvard Business Review Press.

Kim, W. and Mauborgne, R. (1997) 'Value innovation: the strategic logic of high growth', *Harvard Business Review*, Jan./Feb.

Kim, W. and Mauborgne, R. (1999) 'New market space: a systematic approach to value innovation can help companies break free from the competitive pack', *Harvard Business Review*, Jan./Feb.

Kim, W. and Mauborgne, R. (2004) 'Blue ocean strategy', *Harvard Business Strategy*, October: 76–84.

Kim, W. and Mauborgne, R. (2005) 'Blue ocean strategy: from theory to practice', *California Management Review*, 47(3): 105–121.

Kim, W. and Mauborgne, R. (2009) 'How strategy shapes structure', *Harvard Business Review*: September.

Kipping, M. (1999) 'American management consulting companies in western Europe, 1920 to 1990: products, reputation, and relationships', *The Business History Review*, 73(2): 190–220.

Kling, K. and Goteman, I. (2003) 'IKEA CEO Anders Dahlvig on international growth and IKEA's unique corporate culture and brand identity', *Academy of Management Executive*, 17(1): 31–37.

Knights, D. and Morgan, G. (1991) 'Corporate strategy, organizations, and subjectivity: a critique', *Organization Studies*, 12(2): 251–273.

Knights, D. and Mueller, F. (2004) 'Strategy as a "project": overcoming dualisms in the strategy debate', *European Management Review*, 1(1): 55–61.

Kolk, A., Rivera-Santos, M. and Rufin, C. (2013) 'Reviewing a decade of research on the "base/bottom of the pyramid" (BOP) concept', *Business & Society*, 53(3): 338–377.

Kor, Y. and Mahoney, J. (2004) 'Edith Penrose's (1959) contributions to the resource-based view of strategic management', *Journal of Management Studies*, 41(1): 183–191.

Kornberger, M. (2012) 'Governing the city: from planning to urban strategy', *Theory, Culture & Society*, 29(2): 84–106.

Kornberger, M. (2013) 'Clausewitz: on strategy', *Business History*, 55(7): 1058–1073.

Kowitt, B. (2015) 'It's IKEA's world', *Fortune*, 15 March.

Krause, D. (1996) *Sun Tzu: The Art of War for Executives*. London: Nicholas Brealey Publishing.

Küpers, W., Mantere, S. and Statler, M. (2013) 'Strategy as storytelling: a phenomenological collaboration', *Journal of Management Inquiry*, 22(1): 83–100.

Lampel, J. and Baum, J. (2010) 'The Globalization of Strategy Research: Permanent Pluralism or Prelude to a New Synthesis?' in Baum, J. and Lampel, J. (eds) *The Globalization of Strategy Research*. Bingley: Emerald.

Langley, A. (1988) 'The roles of formal strategic planning', *Long Range Planning*, 21(3): 40–50.

Lashinsky, A. (2012) *Inside Apple: The Secrets Behind the Past and Future Success of Steve Jobs's Iconic Brand*. London: John Murray.

Learned, E., Christensen, C., Andrews, K. and Guth, W. (1965) *Business Policy: Text and Cases*. Homewood, IL: Irwin.

Leavy, B. (2012) 'Collaborative innovation as the new imperative: design thinking, value co-creation and the power of "pull"', *Strategy & Leadership*, 40(2): 25–34.

Leavy, B. (2013) 'Interview with Venkat Ramaswamy: a ten-year perspective on how the value co-creation revolution is transforming competition', *Strategy & Leadership*, 41(6): 11–17.

Leavy, B. and McKiernan, P. (2009) *Strategic Leadership: Governance and Renewal*. Basingstoke: Palgrave Macmillan.

Levy, D., Alvesson, M. and Willmott, H. (2003) 'Critical Approaches to Strategic Management' in Alvesson, M. and Willmott, H. (eds) *Studying Management Critically*. London: Sage.

Liedtka, J. (2005) 'In defence of strategy as design', *California Management Review*, 42(3): 8–30.

Lief, C. (2008) 'IKEA: Past, Present, and Future', International Institute for Management Development, Lausanne.

Lilley, S. (2009) 'Strategic Management' in Linstead, S., Fulop, L. and Lilley, S. (eds) *Management and Organization: A Critical Text* (2nd edition). London: Palgrave Macmillan.

Lindblom, C. E. (1990) 'The science of "muddling through"' in Pugh, D. S. (ed.) *Organization Theory, Selected Readings*, Harmondsworth: Penguin; originally published 1959 in *Public Administration Review*, 19(2): 79–88.

Linstead, S. and Grafton-Small, R. (1992) 'On reading organizational culture', *Organization Studies*, 13(3): 331–355.

Ma, H. (2003) 'To win without fighting: an integrative framework', *Management Decision*, 41(1): 72–84.

MacKay, B. and McKiernan, P. (2004) 'Exploring strategy context with foresight', *European Management Review*, 1(1): 69–77.

Macve, R., Hoskin, K. and Stone, J. (2006) 'Accounting and Strategy: Towards Understanding the Historical Genesis of Modern Business and Military Strategy' in Bhimani, A. (ed.) *Contemporary Issues in Management Accounting*. Oxford: Oxford University Press Oxford.

Magretta, J. (2012) *Understanding Michael Porter: The Essential Guide to Competition and Strategy*. Boston, MA: Harvard University Press.

Mantere, S. and Sillince, J. (2007) 'Strategic Intent as a Rhetorical Device', *Scandinavian Journal of Management*, 23: 406–423.

Markides, C. (1999) 'In search of strategy', *Sloan Management Review*, 40(3): 6–7.

Mason, E. (1949) 'The current state of the monopoly problem in the US', *Harvard Law Review*, 29(1): 61–74.

Mason, R. (2007) 'The external environment's effect on management strategy', *Management Decision*, 45(1): 10–28.

McKenna, C. (2012) 'Strategy Followed Structure: Management Consulting and the Creation of a Market for "Strategy", 1950–2000' in Kahl, S., Silverman, B. and Cusumano, M. (eds) *Advances in Strategic Management, Volume 29: History and Strategy*. Bingley: Emerald Group Publishing Limited.

McKiernan, P. (1997) 'Strategy past; strategy futures', *Long Range Planning*, 30(5): 790–798.

McKinlay, A. and Wilson, J. (2012) '"All they lose is the scream": Foucault, Ford and mass production', *Management & Organizational History*, 7(1): 45–60.

McKinlay, A., Carter, C., Pezet, E. and Clegg, S. (2010), 'Using Foucault to make strategy', *Accounting, Auditing & Accountability Journal*, 23(8): 1012–1031.

McSweeney, B. (2002) 'Hofstede's model of national cultural differences and their consequences: a triumph of faith: a failure of analysis', *Human Relations*, 55(1): 89–118.

Meyer, A. (1991) 'What is strategy's distinctive competence?', *Journal of Management*, 17(4): 821–833.

Miller, A. and Dess, G. (1993) 'Assessing Porter's (1980) model in terms of its generalizability, accuracy and simplicity', *Journal of Management Studies*, 30(4): 553–585.

Minkes, A. L. (1987) *The Entrepreneurial Manager: Decisions, Goals and Business Ideas*. Harmondsworth: Penguin.

Mintzberg, H. (1987a) 'The strategy concept I: five Ps for strategy', *California Management Review*, 30(1): 11–24.

Mintzberg, H. (1987b) 'The strategy concept II: another look at why organizations need strategies', *California Management Review*, 30(1): 25–32.

Mintzberg, H. (1987c) 'Crafting strategy', *Harvard Business Review*, July/Aug.: 66–75.

Mintzberg, H. (1990) 'The Design School: reconsidering the basic premises of strategic management', *Strategic Management Journal*, 11(3): 171–195.

Mintzberg, H. (1994) 'Rethinking strategic planning, part 1: pitfalls and fallacies', *Long Range Planning*, 27(3): 12–21.

Mintzberg, H. and Waters, J. (1985) 'Of strategies, deliberate and emergent', *Strategic Management Journal*, 6(3): 257–272.

Mintzberg, H., Ahlstrand, B. and Lampel, J. (2009) *Strategy Safari*. London: Prentice Hall.

Morck, R., Shleifer, A. and Vishny, R. (1990) 'Do managerial objectives drive bad acquisitions?', *The Journal of Finance*, 65(1): 31–48.

Morrison, A. and Wensley, R. (1991) 'Boxing up or boxed in? A short history of the Boston Consulting Group share/growth matrix', *Journal of Marketing Management*, 7(2): 105–129.
Mueller, D. (1969) 'A theory of conglomerate mergers', *Quarterly Journal of Economics*, 83(4): 643–659.
Munir, K., Ansari, S. and Gregg, T. (2010) 'Beyond the Hype: Taking Business Strategy to the Bottom of the Pyramid' in Baum, J. and Lampel, J. (eds) *The Globalization of Strategy Research*. Bingley: Emerald.
Murray, W. and Grimsley, M. (1994) *The Making of Strategy: Rulers, States, and War*. Cambridge: Cambridge University Press.
Mutch, A. (2006) 'Organization theory and military metaphor: time for a reappraisal?', *Organization*, 13(6): 751–769.
Narayanan, V. and Fahey, L. (1982) 'The micro-politics of strategy formulation', *Academy of Management Review*, 7(1): 25–34.
Newbert, S. (2007) 'Empirical research on the resource-based view of the firm: an assessment and suggestions for future research', *Strategic Management Journal*, 28(2): 121–146.
Ocasio, W. and Joseph, J. (2008) 'Rise and fall – or transformation? The evolution of strategic planning at the General Electric Company, 1940–2000', *Long Range Planning*, 41(3): 248–272.
Ogilvy, J. (1998) 'Learning Scenario Planning: An Introduction to Scenario Thinking', a four-day simulation course, 1–5 February, presented by Australian Business Network and Global Business Networks, Sydney.
O'Reilly, R. (2010) 'Apple's Segmentation Strategy and the Folly of Conventional Wisdom', radar.oreilly.com.
O'Shaughnessy, N. (1996) 'Michael Porter's competitive advantage revisited', *Management Decision*, 34(6): 12–20.
Oster, S. (1994) *Modern Competitive Analysis*. New York: Oxford University Press.
Paroutis, S. and Pettigrew, A. (2007) 'Strategizing in the multi-business firm: strategy teams at multiple levels and over time', *Human Relations*, 60(1): 99–135.
Pascale, R. (1996) 'The Honda effect', *California Management Review*, 38(4): 80–91.
Pearson, G. (1999) *Strategy in Action*. London: Prentice Hall.
Pech, R. and Durden, G. (2003) 'Manoeuvre warfare: a new military paradigm for business decision making', *Management Decision*, 41(2): 168–179.
Penrose, E. (1959/2009) *The Theory of the Growth of the Firm* (4th edition). Oxford: Oxford University Press.
Peters, T. and Waterman, R. (1982/84) *In Search of Excellence*. New York: Harper and Row.
Pfeffer, J. (1981) *Power in Organizations*. London: Pitman.
Pheng, L. and Sirpal, R. (1995) 'Western generic business and corporate strategies', *Marketing Intelligence and Planning*, 13(6): 34–40.
Pina e Cunha, M., Rego, A. and Clegg, S. (2011) 'Beyond addiction: hierarchy and other ways of getting strategy done', *European Management Journal*, 29(6): 491–503.
Porter, M. (1980) *Competitive Strategy: Techniques for Analysing Industries and Competitors*. New York: Free Press.
Porter, M. (1981) 'The contribution of industrial organization to strategic management', *Academy of Management Review*, 6(4): 609–620.
Porter, M. (1985) *Competitive Advantage: Creating and Sustaining Superior Performance*. New York: Free Press.
Porter, M. (1987) 'From competitive advantage to corporate strategy', *Harvard Business Review*, 65(3): 43–43.
Porter, M. (1990) 'The competitive advantage of nations', *Harvard Business Review*, 68(2): 73–93.
Porter, M. (1991) 'Towards a dynamic theory of strategy', *Strategic Management Journal*, 12(4): 95–117.
Porter, M. (2008) 'The five competitive forces that shape strategy', *Harvard Business Review*, 86(1): 78–84.

Prahalad, C. K. (2002) 'Strategies for the bottom of the economic pyramid: India as a source of innovation', *Reflections*, 3(4): 6–17.
Prahalad, C. K. (2004) 'The blinders of dominant logic', *Long Range Planning*, 37(2): 171–179.
Prahalad, C. K. and Hamel, G. (1990) 'The core competence of the corporation', *Harvard Business Review*, 68(3): 79–91.
Prahalad, C. K. and Hamel, G. (1994) 'Strategy as a field of study: why search for a new paradigm?', *Strategic Management Journal*, 15(5): 5–16.
Prahalad, C. K. and Lieberthal, K. (1998) 'The end of corporate imperialism', *Harvard Business Review*, 76(4): 68–79.
Prahalad, C. K. and Hammond, A. (2002) 'Serving the world's poor, profitably', *Harvard Business Review*, 80(9): 48–57.
Prahalad, C. K. and Hart, S. (2002) 'The fortune at the bottom of the pyramid', *Strategy+Business*, 26(1): 54–67.
Prahalad, C. K. and Ramaswamy, V. (2011) 'Co-creating unique value with customers', *Strategy and Leadership*, 32(3): 4–9.
Pryor, M. and Taneja, S. (2010) 'Henri Fayol, practitioner and theoretician: revered and reviled', *Journal of Management History*, 16(4): 489–503.
Quinn, J. B. (1978) 'Strategic change: "Logical incrementalism"', *Sloan Management Review*, 20(1): 1–21.
Quinn, J. B. (1980) *Strategies for Change: Logical Incrementalism*. Homewood, IL: Irwin.
Qumer, S. (2011) 'Innovation at Apple', case study. Pradesh: BS Center for Management Research.
Ramaswamy, V. (2008) 'Co-creating value through customers' experiences: the Nike case', *Strategy & Leadership*, 36(5): 9–14.
Ramaswamy, V. (2010) 'Competing through co-creation: innovation at two companies', *Strategy & Leadership*, 38(2): 22–29.
Ramaswamy, V. and Ozcan, K. (2013) 'Strategy and co-creation thinking', *Strategy & Leadership*, 41(6): 5–10.
Ravenscraft, D. and Scherer, F. (1987) *Mergers, Sell-Offs and Economic Efficiency*. Washington, DC: The Brookings Institution.
Robinson, J. (1933) *The Economics of Imperfect Competition*. London: Macmillan.
Roll, R. (1986) 'The hubris hypothesis of corporate takeovers', *Journal of Business*, 59(2): 197–216.
Rumelt, R. (1991) 'How much does industry matter?', *Strategic Management Journal*, 1(2): 167–185.
Rumelt, R. (2011) *Good Strategy/Bad Strategy: The Difference and Why it Matters*. London: Profile Books.
Schachter, H. (2010) 'The role played by Frederick Taylor in the rise of the academic management fields', *Journal of Management History*, 16(4): 437–448.
Schoemaker, P. (1995), 'Scenario planning: a tool for strategic thinking', *Sloan Management Review*, 36(2): 25–36.
Schwartz, P. (1996) *The Art of the Long View*. NSW: Australian Business Network (originally published in 1991, New York: Currency/Doubleday).
Segil, L. (1998) 'Strategic alliances for the twenty-first century', *Strategy and Leadership*, 26(12–16).
Simon, H. (1960) *Administrative Behavior*. New York: Macmillan.
Skarzynski, P. and Rufat-Latre, J. (2011) 'Lessons to jumpstart disruptive innovation', *Strategy & Leadership*, 39(1): 5–10.
Sloan, A. (1963) *My Years with General Motors*. New York: Random House.
Smith, A. (1776/1976) *An Inquiry into the Nature and Causes of the Wealth of Nations*. New York: The Modern Library.
Snowdon, B. and Stonehouse, G. (2006) 'Competitiveness in a globalized world: Michael Porter on the microeconomic foundations of the competitiveness of nations, regions, and firms', *Journal of International Business Studies*, 37(2): 163–175.

Spee, A. and Jarzabkowski, P. (2011) 'Strategic planning as communicative process', *Organization Studies*, 32(9): 1217–1245.

Spender, J.-C. and Kraaijenbrink, J. (2011) 'Why Competitive Strategy Succeeds – and With Whom' in Huggins, R. and Izushi, H. (eds) *Competition, Competitive Advantage, and Clusters: The Ideas of Michael Porter*. Oxford: Oxford University Press.

Stacey, R. (1990) 'Strategy as order emerging from chaos', *Long Range Planning*, 26(1): 10–17.

Stalk, G., Evans, P. and Schulman, L. (1992) 'Competing on capabilities: the new rules of corporate strategy', *Harvard Business Review*, 70(2): 57–69.

Stern, C. and Deimler, M. (2006) *The Boston Consulting Group on Strategy: Classic Concepts and New Perspectives*. Oxford: Wiley.

Stonehouse, G. and Snowdon, B. (2007) 'Competitive advantage revisited: Michael Porter on strategy and competitiveness', *Journal of Management Inquiry*, 36(3): 256–273.

Sturdy, A. (2011) 'Consultancy's consequences? A critical assessment of management consultancy's impact on management', *British Journal of Management*, 22(3): 517–530.

Takeuchi, H., Osono, E. and Shimizu, N. (2008) 'The contradictions that drive Toyota's success', *Harvard Business Review*, 86(6): 96–104.

Talbot, P. (2003) 'Management organisational history: a military lesson?', *Journal of European Industrial Training*, 27(7): 330–340.

Taylor, A. (2013) 'The Single Greatest Decision of All Time? Henry Ford Doubles his Workers' Wages' in Harnish, V. (ed.) *The Greatest Business Decisions of All Time*. Des Moines, IA: Fortune Books.

Taylor, F. W. (1916) *The Principles of Scientific Management* (revised edition 1967). New York: Norton.

Teece, D. (2009) *Dynamic Capabilities and Strategic Management*. Oxford: Oxford University Press.

Teece, D., Pisano, G. and Shuen, A. (1997) 'Dynamic capabilities and strategic management', *Strategic Management Journal*, 18(7): 509–533.

Thomas, P., Wilson, J. and Leeds, O. (2013) 'Constructing the history of strategic management: a critical analysis of the academic discourse', *Business History*, 55(7): 1119–1142.

Thomke, S., and von Hippel, E. (2002) 'Customers as innovators: a new way to create value', *Harvard Business Review*, 80(4): 74–81.

Tidd, J. and Bessant, J. (2009) *Managing Innovation: Integrating Technological, Market and Organizational Change*. Chichester: Wiley.

Tsoukas, H. (2010) 'Practice, Strategy Making and Intentionality: A Heideggerian Onto-epistemology for Strategy as Practice' in Golsorkhi, D., Rouleau, L., Seidl, D. and Vaara, E. (eds) *Cambridge Handbook of Strategy as Practice*. Cambridge: Cambridge University Press.

Tung, R. (1994) 'Strategic management thought in East Asia', *Organizational Dynamics*, 22(4): 55–65.

van Driel, H. and Dolfsma, W. (2009) 'Path dependence, initial conditions, and routines in organizations: The Toyota production system re-examined', *Journal of Organizational Change Management*, 22(1): 49–72.

Vargo, S. and Lusch, R. (2004) 'Evolving to a new dominant logic for marketing', *Journal of Marketing*, 68(1): 1–17.

Volberda, H. (2004) 'Crisis in strategy: fragmentation, integration or synthesis', *European Management Review*, 1(1): 35–42.

Von Krogh, G. and Roos, J. (1996) *Managing Knowledge*. London: Sage.

Wack, P. (1985a) 'Scenarios: shooting up the rapids', *Harvard Business Review*, 63(6): 139–150.

Walt, V. (2013) 'Meet Amancio Ortega: The Third-richest Man in the World', www.fortune.com.

Waterman, R., Peters, T. and Phillips, J. (1980) 'Structure is not organization', *Business Horizons*, 23(3): 14–26.

Watson, T. (2003) 'Strategists and strategy-making: strategic exchange and the shaping of individual lives and organizational futures', *Journal of Management Studies*, 40(5): 1305–1323.

Weihrich, H. (1982) 'The TOWS matrix: a tool for situational analysis', *Long Range Planning*, 15(2): 54–66.

Wernerfelt, B. (1984) 'A resource-based view of the firm', *Strategic Management Journal*, 5(2): 171–180.
Wernerfelt, B. (1995) 'The resource-based view of the firm: ten years after', *Strategic Management Journal*, 16(3): 171–174.
Whitley, R. (1990) 'Eastern Asian enterprise structures and the comparative analysis of forms of business organization', *Organization Studies*, 11(1): 47–74.
Whittington, R. and Cailluet, L. (2008) 'The crafts of strategy: introduction to Special Issue', *Long Range Planning*, 41(3): 241–247.
Whittington, R. (1996) 'Strategy as practice', *Long Range Planning*, 29(5): 731–735.
Whittington, R. (2001) *What is Strategy and Does it Matter?* London: Cengage.
Whittington, R. (2004) 'Strategy after modernism: recovering practice', *European Management Review*, 1(1): 62–68.
Whittington, R. (2006) 'Completing the practice turn in strategy research', *Organization Studies*, 27(5): 613–634.
Whittington, R., Cailluet, L. and Yakis-Douglas, B. (2011) 'Opening strategy: evolution of a precarious profession', *British Journal of Management*, 22(3): 531–544.
Williamson, O. E. (1975) *Markets and Hierarchies*. New York: Free Press.
Wilson, D. and Jarzabkowski, P. (2004) 'Thinking and acting strategically: new challenges for interrogating strategy', *European Management Review*, 1(1): 14–20.
Wilson, I. and Ralston, W. (2006) *Scenario Planning Handbook: Developing Strategies in Uncertain Times*. Belmont: South-Western Educational.
Winsor, R. (1996) 'Military perspectives of organizations', *Journal of Organizational Change Management*, 9(4): 34–42.
Wren, D. (2001) 'Henri Fayol as strategist: a nineteenth century corporate turnaround', *Management Decision*, 39(6): 475–487.
Wright, P., Paroutis, S. and Blettner, P. (2013) 'How useful are the strategic tools we teach in business schools?', *Journal of Management Studies*, 50(1): 92–114.
Yetton, P., Craig, J., Davis, J. and Hilmer, F. (1992) 'Are diamonds a country's best friend? A critique of Porter's theory of national competition as applied to Canada, New Zealand and Australia', *Australian Journal of Management*, 17(1): 89–120.
Zillman, C. (2014) 'Why Zara Can't Seem to Stop Selling Anti-Semitic Clothing', www.fortune.com.

Index

(italics indicate tables/figures)

+972 blog 157
3M 43, 45, 124
5Ps (Mintzberg) 6–8
15% rule 124
1960s 58
1970s 21–3, 48, 53
1980s 23
1990s 24–5
2000s 25

Abernathy, William 64, 70
Acer 77
acquisitions 57–58
adaptive responses 147
Adidas 158
advertising 2, 137, 155, 157
advisory role 59
Agassi, Andre 157
agriculture 95
Aineias the Tactiturn 13
airline industry 82, 122; no frills companies 135
Aktouf, Omar 98
alcohol 137
Alexander the Great 14
Alexander the Great's Art of Strategy (Bose) 14
Alvesson, Mats 2, 10, 29
Amazon 81, 91, 118, 122, 129, 137, 165
AMD 78
Amelio, Gilbert 163
America (USA) 8, 16, 20, 24, 70, 94, 151–2
analysis 81
Ancient Greece 13, 15
Andersen, Torben 42, 46
Android Wear 159
Ansoff, Igor 14, 19–20
Aoki, Masahiko 108
Apple Corporation 7, 79, 81, 84, 86, 111–12, 118, 122, 124, 130, 157–9; case study 162–70; employee culture 166–7
Apple Watch 159, 164, 168
Arab-Israeli War 48

Arteixo 153
Asian Tiger economies 70, 72, 98, 106, 112
Astley, Graham 118
Astro Studios 160
Asus 79
ATI 78
audits 50
Augier, Mie 104
automobile industry 56, 90, 95–6, 110, 114
Ax, Hans 149

Bain, Joe 126
balanced portfolio 67
Barnes & Noble 129–30
Barney, Jay 24, 101, 103–4, 105, 144
Bartlett, Christopher 24, 72
battlefield metaphors 14–15
Bayley, I. B. 150
Beats Music 166
Berkshire Hathaway Group 60
Bessant, John 136
best practice 23
Betamax 84
Bierce, Ambrose 35
biotech industry 96
Black Friday sales 91
blue ocean strategy 120, 122, 125, 126–31, 137
Blu-Ray 84
Bodwell, Wendy 52
Book of Five Rings (Musashi) 14
booksellers 129–30
Borch, Fred 55
Bose, Partha 14
Boston Box 2, 64, 70
Boston Consulting Group 21, 60–67
Boston Safe Deposit Company 62
bounded rationality 40
Bowerman, Bill 160
Boxing Day sales 91
brand loyalty 79
Brandenburger, Adam 118

Branson, Richard 32, 59
Brazil 8, 25
BRIC countries 8, 25
British Airways 135
Brusoni, Stefano 90
Buffett, Warren 60
building mode 42
Burberry 85
Business Policy: Texts and Cases (Learned) 32
business schools 17, 21

Campbell, Andrew 32
canals 16
Canon 107, 111–12, 114, *115*, 146
car industry *see* automobile industry
Carnegie, Andrew 17–18
Carnegie Foundation 18
Carnegie Mellon University 18
Caro, Felipe 156
Carr, Austin 160
Carter, Chris 15, 35, 48, 52, 96
Carter, Dennis 78
cash cows (growth/share matrix) 65–7
Caterpillar 107
celebrity endorsement 157
Cellar-Kefauver Amendment 57
CEOs 55, 97; as strategy architects 27–9, 36, 46, 119
Chamberlin, Edward 101, 125, 145
Chandler, Alfred 3, 4–5, 6, 15, 16–17, 19–20, 54, 87
chemical manufacture 54, 96
Chen, Ming-Jer 22
Chermack, Thomas 52
Chia, Robert 3–4, 42
Chicago 95
Child, John 22
Chile 56
China 8, 25, 116
Choi, Amy 14
Christensen, Clayton 25, 120, 125, 133–8
Christmas 38
Clark, Delwyn 103, 105
Clarkson, John 62
Clegg, Stewart 29, 35, 38, 84, 104, 142
clusters, strategic 96–7
Coca Cola 85–6, 112, 157
co-creation 139–42
Cohen, Michael 45
collaboration 108, 116, 119
collective strategy 118
Collins, Jim 32
Collis, David 100
colonizing tendencies 10
Colvin, Geoffrey 124
Commentry, Fourchambault & Decazeville 29
Compaq 77

competencies *see* core competencies
competition 2, 24, 86, 132, 134
competitive advantage 8, 120; of nations 23, 94, 98–9
Competitive Advantage (Porter) 23, 73, 87
The Competitive Advantage of Nations (Porter) 23, 98–9
Competitive Strategy (Porter) 23, 73, 87
conduct 73–4
confectionary 38
confidentiality 160
consultancy 61, 127
consumer communities 140
consumers 78; and non-consumers 135
Cook, Tim 162, 165, 167
co-opetition 117–18
core competencies 60, 107, 110–15
core products 111
corporate culture 150
Corporate Strategy (Ansoff) 19
cost leadership 83–4, 91
crafting metaphor 43–4
creative destruction 126
Critical Management Studies 10
culture, reflecting and understanding 151–2
Cummings, Stephen 13, 15, 31
customers 78; and co-creation 139–42; lower-spending 125; strategic focus on 120
Cyert, Richard 40

Daewoo 112
DART model 141
databases 139
Davies, John 31
Davies, P. 13
De Wit, Bob 34
Deal, Terrence 24
decentralization 20
decision theory 20
decision-making 33–4, 59; garbage-can model 45
delegation 16
Dell 63, 77, 79, 122, 139
demand, local 95
design 148, 153–4, 156, 169
Detroit 95
dialogue 141
differentiation 83, 84–5, 130
direction setting 34, 59
diversification 53–8, 60
division of labour 16, 155
dogs (growth/share matrix) 65–7, 70–71
Dolfsma, Wilfred 44
Doz, Yves 22
Drew, Richard 124
Du Pont 49, 53–4, 56
DVD 84

dwelling mode 42, *42*
dynamic capabilities 104

EasyJet 84, 122, 135, 160
eBay 124, 128, 137, 138, 160
efficiency, and diversification 56
Electronic Arts 14
electronics 110
email 136
emergent approach 39–40, 42, 45–6
empire-building 57
employees 29, 109; benefits packages 160–61; and decision-making processes 46–7; empowerment schemes 46; loyalty 161, 166–7; participation schemes 140, 151, 154
'enemies' 14
engineering 96
entertainment industry 95
entrepreneurship 24
environment: complexity of 120; external to the organization 5, 7, 21, 23, 106
Espeland, Wendy 67, 71
ethnography 3
experience curve model 21, 62–3, *62*
experience innovation approach 121, 138–9
experimentation 124
Exploring Corporate Strategy (Johnson et al.) 5
explosive manufacturing 53
external audits 50

Facebook 136
The Fall and Rise of Strategic Planning (Mintzberg) 37
family-run businesses 8
Farris, Nelson 160
fashion 85, 96, 153–6
fast fashion 153, 156
fast food industry 95
Fast Retailing 156
fate 8
Fayol, Henri 29
Federal Express 14, 110
Fitbit 159
fitness industry 137
five forces (Porter) 2, 51, 72–3, 76, 76, 80–83, 94, 98
flat-packs 149–50
Flyknit Racer 157, 160
focus 85–6
Fombrun, Charles 118
football 157
Ford, Henry 72, 168
Ford Foundation 18
Ford Motors 19, 64, 84, 113, 116, 127, 160
forecasting 48
formality 151
formalization 37, 38

formulation, separate from implementation 20, 37–8
Fortune 500 55, 69
Fortune magazine 72, 159
Four Actions framework 131–3
Freedman, Lawrence 4
Fry, Art 43, 45
FuelBand 158–9, 160
Fuller, Mark 36
furniture 147–50
The Future of Competition (Prahalad and Ramaswamy) 140

games consoles 79
garbage-can model 45
Gateway Inc 77
Gavetti, Giovanni 3, 20
Gay, Edwin 18
GE/McKinsey matrix 21, 69
gender bias 10
General and Industrial Administration (Fayol) 29
General Electric 14, 28, 39, 55, 69, 117
General Instrument 62
General Motors 19–20, 64, 84, 113, 116; diversification 58
Germany 23, 54, 96
Ghemawat, Pankaj 18, 64, 70
Ghoshal, Sumantra 24, 72
Global Business Networks 49
globalization 24, 38, 95, 100, 106, 116, 143
goals 4, 30, 107
Google 81, 118, 123–4, 157, 159, 165, 167
Goold, Michael 59
Grove, Andy 78
growth maximization hypothesis 58
growth/gain matrix 69
growth/share matrix 21, 64–7, *67*

H&M 156
halo effect 166
Hambrick, Donald 22
Hamel, Gary 24, 47, 100, 102, 105–15, 118–19, 123
Hammond, Allen 125
hardware 7
Harjula, Liisa 125
Hart, Stuart 125
Harvard Business Review 125
Harvard Business School 18, 23, 40, 55, 74
Harvard University 96
Haspeslagh, Philippe 69, 70
Hatchuel, Armand 46
Haupt, Herman 16–17
Hayes, Robert 70
Healey, Mark 51
HealthKit 159
Henderson, Bruce 62

Hewlett Packard 77
hierarchies 47, 108
Hill, Terry 33
Hirsch, Paul 67, 71
history 12–26
History of the Peloponnesian War (Thucydides) 13
H-mode 108
Ho, Samuel 14
Hodgkinson, Gerard 51
Hofer, Charles 22, 23
holistic view 121, 144
Honda 14, 60, 107, 110, 113, 146
Hong Kong 72
horizontal structures 108
Hoskin, Keith 16
Hoskisson, Robert 20
How to Survive under Siege (Aineias) 13
human engineering 16
human resource management 13, 89
hybrid strategies 86

IBM 7, 49, 77, 162–3
idClic 140
IKEA 85, 117, 122; case study 147–52; corporate structure 151; store design 148
imitation 111, 128
implementation 27, 31; separate from formulation 29, 37–8
inbound logistics 89
incrementalism 40–41
India 8, 25, 56
Inditex 153
Indonesia 8
industrial organization economics (IO) 73, 74, 97, 98, 101–2, 122, 125
industry analysis 75, 76–9, 80, 100
infrastructure 89
innovation 56, 120–43, 159–60; disruptive 121, 133–8, *134*
inside-out view 101
Intel 78, 112, 118
International Studies of Organization and Management 22
iPad 79, 126, 130, 160, 164
iPhone 86, 130, 158, 160, 164, 168
iPod 130, 158, 160, 164, 165, 168
Iran-Iraq War 49
Italy 95
iTunes 130, 164, 165

Japan 18, 23, 44, 46, 60, 70, 72, 91, 94–8, 106, 112–13; after World War II 96–7, 108–9
Jawbone 159
J-mode 108
Jobs, Steve 2, 160, 162–4, 166, 168
Joga.com 157–8
Johnson, Gerry 5, 6, 60

Jordan, Michael 157
Joss 8
just-in-time production 124, 154

Kahn, Herman 48
Kamprad, Ingvar 147–50
Kanto region 96
Kaplan, David 78
Kennedy, Allan 24
Khanna, Tarun 56
Kia 112
Kiechel, Walter 62, 64, 72, 85, 90
Kim, W. Chan 25, 120–33
Kipping, Matthias 61
Knight, William 124
Komatsu 107
Korean War 44
Kornberger, Martin 12
Krause, Donald 14

language 12, 14–15
Lashinksy, Adam 167, 169
lead times 153
leadership 13, 24, 46, 107–8, 118
Learned, Edmund 21, 32
learning approach 39–40, 42, 45–6, 118
learning curve 62–63
Leavy, Brian 2, 51, 57, 63, 116–17, 120
legal restrictions 137
Lenovo 77
leverage 107, 113–14, 166
Levinthal, Daniel 3, 20
Levy, David 6
LG 86, 111
Lieberthal, Kenneth 125
Lief, Colleen 148
life science research 96
Lilley, S. 34
limiting factors 102
Lindblom, Charles 40–41
Little, Arthur D. 62
local conditions 43, 95
logic, dominant 121
logistics 89
luxury goods 96

M form (multidivisional) 54–5
Ma, Hao 14
MacBook Air 118
Machiavelli, Niccolò 14
MacKay, Brad 3–4
Magretta, Joan 82, 93, 155
Mahan, Alfred 16
manufacturing, outsourcing 116–17, 154, 164
March, James 40
market entry 116, 136
market failure 56

market research 152, 169
market share 65, 75
marketing 2, 61, 89, 91, 139
Markides, Constantinos 5
masking tape 124
Mason, Edward 73, 126
Mauborgne, Renee 25, 120–33
Mazda 109
MBA 21, 24
MBF (multi-business firm) 53, 55
MBFs (multi-business firms), and corporate parenting 59–60
McCarthyism 101
McDonald's 14, 93
McGraw University 37
McKenna, Christopher 61
McKiernan, Peter 2, 15, 47, 51, 57, 63, 116–17, 120
McKinlay, Alan 38
McKinsey & Company 21, 55, 60, 68
McNamara, Robert 19
Mead Paper Company 64
merchandising 155
mergers 57–8, 67
Mexico 8
Meyer, Ron 34
M-form (multidivisional) 16, 19
Microsoft 7, 31, 78, 112, 116, 118, 162, 165
military strategy 4, 12–20; language drawn from 14–15, 107
MINT countries 9
Mintzberg, Henry 5–8, 21–2, 24, 27–8, 52, 118; critique of Porter 97–8; emergent approach 41–2, 45–6; three fallacies of strategic planning 37–9
mission statements 31–2
MIT 96
Montgomery, Cynthia 100
Morita, Akio 137–8
motorcycle industry 95
Motorola 14
MP3 players 130, 168
'muddling through' 40–41
Mueller, Dennis 58
multidivisional form *see* M form (multidivisional)
Musashi, Myamoto 14
Mutch, Alistair 15
My Years with General Motors (Sloan) 19

Nalebuff, Barry 118
Nash, Laura 32
national competitiveness 95–6, 97
neo-liberalism 23
network-level strategy 115–18
new markets, and diversification 56–7
NeXT 163

next practices 123–4
N-form 19
Nielsen, Bo Bernhard 42, 46
Nigeria 9
Nike 116, 157–61; core philosophy 160–61; Nike+ 158–9
Nokia 86
non-consumers 135
Nvidia 78, 116

objectives 4, 30
observation 3
oil, stockpiling 49
oil crisis 21, 48–9, 53
On War (von Clausewitz) 14
OPEC 21, 48
operations 89
optics 96
Orange 140
Ortega, Amancio 153
O'Shaughnessy, Nicholas 98
Osono, Emi 47
outbound logistics 89
outsourcing 92, 116–17
overstocking 44
own label products 85
Ozcan, Kerimcan 139

Pacific Rim 60, 106, 112, 126–7
packaging 166
Packard Bell 77
Palepu, Krishna 56
parent, corporate 59–60
parental developer 60–61
Parker, Mark 159, 160
partnerships 160
passivity 106
PC industry 7, 75, 77–8, 81, 85, 112, 116, 162–70
Pearson, Gordon 71
Pennsylvania Rail Road (PRR) 17
Penrose, Edith 24, 56, 101–2, 125
Pepsi 112
performance 73–4
perspective 7–8
PESTEL exercises 50
Peters, Tom 24, 86, 116
Pettigrew, Andrew 22
pharmaceutical industry 77, 127
Pheng, Low Sui 14
philosophy 13, 32
PIMS database 21
Pittsburg University 22
planning 6, 23, 34–5, 42; cycles 135; fallacies of 37–9; separate from implementation 108
platform strategy 123, 165
Podolny, Joel 169

policy, separate from operations 20
Porras, Jerry 32
Porter, Michael 2, 7, 23–4, 51, 57, 71–83, 85–9, 96–9, 112, 122; *see also* five forces (Porter)
portfolio management 23, 55, 67–71, 72
portfolio parent 60
positioning 7, 106
Post-it notes 43, 45, 124
Prahalad, C. K. 7, 24–5, 100, 102, 105–15, 118–21, 123, 125, 138–9
predetermination 37
pressure 96
price sensitivity 83
primary activities 88–9
The Prince (Machiavelli) 14
printers 107, 112
procurement 89
product launches 127
product life cycles 23, 63, 65
product placement 2
production, costs 63; as dominant role of business 68; systems 44, 110
Profit Impact Market Share (PIMS) 55
profit margins 88
profit maximization 28–9, 82
proximity 96
prudence 28

qualitative methodology 20, 98
quality assurance 89
quality circles 46
quantitative methodology 2, 21, 33, 98
question marks (growth/share matrix) 65–7
Quinn, James Brian 14, 41
quotas 116

railroad building, influence of military strategy 16–17
Ralston, Bill 49
Ramaswamy, Venkat 121, 138–41, 158–9
RAND Corporation 48
Rasche, Andreas 42
rationality 8, 20, 27–8, 98; bounded 40
Ravenscraft, David 57
Raynor, Michael 135–8
Reagan, Ronald 23, 94
recruitment 109
recycling competencies 113–14
red oceans 127, 129, 130
reduction 132
research and development (R&D) 91–2, 106, 112, 169
resource allocation 2, 5, 59
resource mobility 74
resource-based view (RBV) 25, 100–105, 123, 133

resources 4; leveraging 113–14; non-tangible 101–2
restructuring 54
retail displays 152
retail parks 149
risk assessment 141–2
risk reduction 57, 136
risk taking 124
rivalry 79, 81
Roll, Richard 58
Roman legions 14
Rufat-Latre, Jorge 137
Rumelt, Richard 5, 15, 100
running 158–9
Russia 8, 25
Ryanair 63

Samsung 84, 86, 110, 112, 117, 124
Sanyo Electric Corporation 14
satisficing behaviour 40
SBU (strategic business unit) 55, 111
scenario planning 47–52
Schendel, Dan 20, 22, 23
Scherer, Frederic 57
Schoemaker, Paul 49–50
Scholes, Kevan 5
Schumpter, Joseph 25, 120, 126, 130, 145
scientific credentials 18
Scott, Thomas C. 17
scriptwriters 50
Sculley, John 163
secrecy 160
Securities and Exchange Commission (SEC) 61
security industry 137
self-service shopping 149
Selznick, Peter 3
service 89
services 102
Sharp 113
Shell 21, 31, 48–9
Shimizu, Norihiko 47
short-termism 8
showrooms 149
Silicon Valley 95
Silver, Spencer 43, 45
Simon, Herbert 40
Singapore 72, 106
Sirpal, Rajeshwar 14
situational analysis *see* SWOT
size, problems of 54
Skarzynski, Peter 137
Sloan, Alfred 19–20
small businesses 95
smartphones 79, 122, 124
Smith, Adam 16, 28
Smith, Fred 14
social media 123, 136

software 7
Sony 14, 77, 110, 137–8
South Korea 8, 72, 84, 106, 112, 113, 116
specialization 108
Spindler, Michael 163
sponsorship 137, 157
sportswear 157–61
Spotify 141
Springfield Armoury 16
SRI Limited 49
staff *see* employees
stakeholders 5
Stalk, George 67
Starbucks 31, 122, 140
start-ups 133
stockpiling 49
strategic business units (SBUs) 68–70, 75
strategic clusters 96–7
strategic fit 91
strategic intent 107
Strategic Management Journal 22
Strategic Management Society 23
strategic positioning 73
strategy: art, science or humanity? 2–3; business-level 30; corporate-level 30, 53; definition 1–11, 144; functional-level 30; history of 12–26; holistic view 144; not a fixed term 9; origin of word 4, 13; term only common in business after World War II 4
Strategy and Structure (Chandler) 4, 19–20
strategy architecture 114–15
strategy canvas 131–3,
strategy process 107
stretch 108–110
structure-conduct-performance (SCP) 73–4
substitutes 79, 81
subsystems 41
Sun Tzu 13, 14
Sun Tzu: The Art of War for Executives (Krause) 14
supermarkets 85, 139
suppliers 77–8
support activities 89
surveillance industry 137
SWOT 2, 23, 31–3, 51–2
Synapse 160
synergy parent 60
systems analysis 20

tablets 79, 126
Taiwan 72, 106
Takeuchi, Hirotaka 47
Talbot, Philip 19
targets 107
Taylor, Frederick Winslow 18, 29, 61
techniques 30, 43

technological changes 84, 126, 136
Teece, David 87, 104–5
Testament of a Furniture Dealer (Kamprad) 151
Texas Instruments 63
text messages (SMS) 136
Thayer, Sylvanus 16
The Art of War (Sun Tzu) 13
The Theory of the Growth of the Firm (Penrose) 56
thinking the unthinkable 48
Thomke, Stefan 140
The Three Kingdoms 14
Thucydides 13
Tidd, Joe 136
time frames 109
tobacco 137
tools 30, 43
top-down control 8
Toyota 44, 47, 85, 110, 113, 116, 124, 154
Toyota Production System 44
trade barriers 116, 128
training 109
tram companies 58
Transaction Cost Economics 56
transparency 142
transport networks 95
Tsoukas, Hari 43
Tung, Rosalie 14
Turkey 9
Twin Towers attacks (9/11) 137
Tyler, Daniel 16

UK businesses 70
Ultrabooks 118
umbrella strategies 45–7
uncertainty, harnessing 47
universities 17
University of Pennsylvania 17

value chain 87–93, *88*
value creation *121*
value innovation approach 121–43
value networks 93
value proposition 87, 165
van Driel, Hugo 44
Vanderbilt University 18
VHS 84
Vietnam War 21, 53
Virgin 32, 60–61, 123, 129; diversification strategy 57
Virgin Atlantic 59
vision 31–2
Volvo 110
von Clausewitz, Carl 14
von Hippel, Eric 140
VRIN framework 103

Wack, Pierre 35, 48–9
Walkman 137
Wall Street 13
Wal-Mart 84, 157
Walt, Vivienne 154
Waterman, Robert 24, 54, 86, 116
Waters, James 42
Watson, Tony 58
Wayne, Kenneth 64
The Wealth of Nations (Smith) 16, 28
Welch, Jack 14, 39, 69
Wernerfelt, Birger 24, 101–3, 105
West Point Military Academy 16–17
Westbrook, Roy 33
Western Railroad 16
Wharton, Joseph 17
Whipsaw 160
Whistler, George W. 16
Whittington, Richard 5, 19, 35, 44, 58
Willmott, Hugh 2, 10, 29
Wilson, Ian 49

Windows operating system 7, 165
wine industry 131, 132
Winsor, Robert 14–15
Woods, Tiger 157
World Cup (football) 157–8
World War I 53
World War II 18–19, 35, 48, 95
Wozniak, Steve 162
written reports 16

Xenophon 13
Xerox 107, *115*

Yahoo 165
Yale University 40
Yamaha 107
Yetton, Philip 96

Zakon, Alan 64
Zara 153–6
zero-sum games 79